HOSTAGES OF
CIVILISATION

HOSTAGES OF CIVILISATION

THE SOCIAL SOURCES OF NATIONAL SOCIALIST ANTI-SEMITISM

By

EVA G. REICHMANN

Dr. Phil. (Heidelberg), Ph.D. (London)

GREENWOOD PRESS, PUBLISHERS
WESTPORT, CONNECTICUT

PREFACE

THE HISTORY OF GERMAN JEWRY after extending over a thousand years has come to an end. It has not ended in the gradual decline and slow exhaustion of its ethnic and spiritual strength as had been repeatedly predicted, but in a political catastrophe of unequalled horror. A great and flourishing community has been wiped out by " atrocities at which the heart of humanity trembles—unatonable, unforgettable ".*

No account of the events leading up to this catastrophe will be given in this study, nor any description of the horrors by which it was accompanied, or its practical consequences. Rather will an attempt be made to discover the causes of the catastrophe, particularly by examining the nature of German anti-Semitism in its interaction with other relevant social factors, and the part it played in bringing about the final outcome.

The place occupied by German Jewry among the Jewish communities of the world was such that its annihilation raises questions of profound importance for all of them. German Jewry stood, as it were, for the idea of Emancipation in its purest form, for the idea, that is, that Jews can successfully live as an integral part of the Gentile world. Its downfall, therefore, could not fail to raise grave doubts as to the validity of this idea in any shape, and has led some people to speak of " the Failure of Emancipation ". The question how far this defeatist attitude is justified by the events in Nazi Germany will form the starting-point and one of the principal subjects of this study. The exact point which the author has set out to elucidate on the basis of the most reliable evidence is *whether a particular Jewish community was expelled and destroyed because the Gentiles amongst whom it lived decided for any serious reasons that life with the Jews had become unbearable for them.* The nature and implications of this enquiry will be set forth in greater detail in the Introduction.

The enquiry will naturally begin with a discussion of the problem of anti-Semitism. By analysing the character of group tensions in general, and of anti-Semitism as a special case

* Thomas Mann, " The End ", in *Free World*, New York, March 1945, p. 18.

5

of group tension in particular, we shall learn to distinguish between the objective and the subjective reasons for anti-Semitism. Objective reasons will be seen to exist where a group antagonism arises from the more or less legitimate demand of a group to maintain its coherence and homogeneity in the face of another group seeking to intrude into its realm. Subjective reasons will be found to consist primarily in personal grievances or ambitions of a large number of individuals who deliberately seek to satisfy them by turning the contact between the groups into hostile collision.

This distinction will serve to show how questionable is the causal connection which by many is naïvely held to exist between anti-Semitism and the Jewish way of life. By applying it to the successive phases of German anti-Semitism we shall see how small a part in the development of this evil was played by the objective or " genuine " Jewish question.

If by this means we shall make it clear that modern German anti-Semitism was only to a comparatively small extent accounted for by the way of life of the Jews, the question will naturally arise, what else did account for it. This question will be approached from two sides. First, the epoch during which the emancipation of the West European Jews took place, viz. the 19th and 20th centuries, will be examined with a view to discovering how far it was particularly favourable to the generation of those subjective or " sham " reasons for anti-Semitism on the existence of which the spread of anti-Semitism increasingly depended. Secondly, the scene of the catastrophe of German Jewry, viz. Germany, will be submitted to a similar investigation, in the course of which special attention will be paid to the morbid character of German national consciousness.

Both investigations will tend to show that conditions in Europe in this period favoured the growth of a spirit of collective aggressiveness which in Germany found an obvious scapegoat in the Jewish group, in spite of the fact that this group was offering less and less provocation for " genuine " antagonism. A short review of conditions in Germany after the first World War will explain how a series of crises, culminating in mass unemployment, largely shattered the curbs imposed by civilisation on primitive human urges, which thereupon imperiously sought an outlet. It will then be shown that National Socialism gave the desperate and inarticulate masses

6

exactly the lead for which they were waiting, and why it chose anti-Semitism and not some other channel as an outlet for their destructive passions. From this it will become clear that Nazi anti-Semitism had hardly any connection with the Jewish question proper, and that the part played by anti-Semitism in inducing the German public to accept the Nazi doctrine was of a secondary nature.

A last chapter will summarise the conclusions arrived at in the course of the study. As far as these conclusions concern the relation between Jews and Gentiles anywhere they will contain a note both of encouragement and of warning. And without countering the more general arguments for the defeatism with regard to Emancipation, they will at least contest the propriety of basing this idea on the lessons of National Socialist anti-Semitism.

E. G. R.

LONDON, *March* 1949

ACKNOWLEDGMENTS

THE PRESENT BOOK was written in the course of studies at the London School of Economics and Political Science, where I had the privilege of working under the guidance of Professor Morris Ginsberg. I am deeply indebted to him for his never-failing advice and many valuable suggestions.

I have been enabled to write the book by the generous help of the Research Institute on Peace and Post-War Problems of the American Jewish Committee. This Committee has established a great reputation for approaching Jewish problems on the basis of scholarly detachment. It has never been satisfied with proclamations and protestations, but has applied scientific methods to the examination of the Jewish question in all its aspects. I should like to express my sincere thanks to the Committee and to Dr. Max Gottschalk, director of its Foreign Affairs Department, for their active interest in my attempt to establish the real significance of the anti-Semitic outburst in Central Europe as contrasted to popular interpretations.

I further wish to thank The Nathan and Adolphe Haendler Charity, London, who were kind enough to place a sum at my disposal for the conclusion of my research.

Miss Kathleen Wood Legh, M.A., Cambridge, and Mr. Maurice Simon, M.A., London, very kindly assisted me in editing the book.

Acknowledgments are gratefully made to the following publishers and authors for permission to quote :

George Allen & Unwin, Ltd., London, from Benedetto Croce, *History of Europe in the 19th Century*; from Friedrich Wilhelm Förster, *Europe and the German Question*; from Ortega y Gasset, *The Revolt of the Masses*; from Joseph A. Schumpeter, *Capitalism, Socialism and Democracy*; from Georges Sorel, *Reflections on Violence.*

Ernest Benn, London, from Le Bon, *The Crowd: A Study of the Popular Mind*; from W. Trotter, *Instincts of the Herd in Peace and War*; and to Ernest Benn, Ltd., as present proprietors of Fisher Unwin copyrights, from Pietro Gorgolini, *Fascist Movement in Italian Life*; from L. T. Hobhouse, *Democracy and Reaction*, and *World in Conflict.*

Jonathan Cape, Ltd., London, from H. G. Baynes, *Germany Possessed.*

Columbia University in the City of New York. The Columbia

Studies in History, Economics, and Public Law, New York, from Mildred S. Wertheimer, *The Pan-German League, 1890–1914*.

Constable & Co., London, from Graham Wallas, *Human Nature in Politics*.

Friends of Europe Publications, London, from Wilhelm Kusserow, *The Creed of the Nordic Race*; from Wilhelm Rödiger, *The Teaching of History*; from L. G. Tirala, *Race, Mind and Soul*; from Prof. Dr. Ziegler, *The New Spirit of Military Education*.

Victor Gollancz, Ltd., London, from Franz Neumann, *Behemoth*; from Hugo Valentin, *Antisemitism*.

William Heinemann, Ltd., London, from J. Huizinga, *In the Shadow of To-morrow*.

Hogarth Press, Ltd., London, from Sigmund Freud, *Civilization, War and Death*; *Group Psychology and the Analysis of the Ego*; *Moses and Monotheism*.

Hurst & Blackett, Ltd., London, from Adolf Hitler, *Mein Kampf*, translated by James Murphy.

John Lane The Bodley Head, Ltd., London, from Houston Stewart Chamberlain, *The Foundations of the 19th Century*.

Mrs. Frieda Lawrence and Messrs. William Heinemann from D. H. Lawrence, *Stories, Essays and Poems*.

Longmans Green & Co., Ltd., London, from Morris Ginsberg, *Reason and Unreason in Society*; from G. P. Gooch, *Germany and the French Revolution*.

McGraw-Hill Publishing Co., Ltd., London, from H. D. Lasswell, *World Politics and Personal Insecurity*.

Macmillan and Co., Ltd., London, from the *Encyclopedia of the Social Sciences*, article, " Antisemitism ", by Benjamin Ginzburg.

Methuen & Co., Ltd., London, from Morris Ginsberg, *The Psychology of Society*.

The Ronald Press Company, New York, from Raymond Leslie Buell *et al.*, *New Governments in Europe*.

Routledge & Kegan Paul, Ltd., London, from Erich Fromm, *The Fear of Freedom*; from Milton Steinberg, *The Making of the Modern Jew*; from Jan D. Suttie, *The Origins of Love and Hate*.

Oxford University Press, London, from Norman H. Baynes, *The Speeches of Adolf Hitler, April 1922–August 1939*; from Morris Ginsberg, *Sociology* (The Home University Library); from A. J. Toynbee, *A Study of History*. (For the latter acknowledgment is also due to the Royal Institute of International Affairs, London.)

Martin Secker & Warburg, Ltd., London, from Thorstein Veblen, *Imperial Germany and the Industrial Revolution*.

10

Social Research, New York, from vol. vii, Carl Mayer, *Judaism Reconsidered*.

University Press Cambridge, Cambridge, from William McDougall, *The Group Mind*.

The University of Chicago Press, Chicago, Ill., from the *American Journal of Sociology* ; Bertrand Russell, " The Intellectual in the Modern World " ; Edward Scribner Ames, " Morale and Religion " ; Paul J. Tillich, " Protestantism in the Present World Situation " ; Louis Wirth, " Urbanism as a Way of Life ".

CONTENTS

Emancipation shifted the Jewish problem from the legal to
the social field—at the time of their emancipation the Jews
differed widely from their fellow citizens—assimilation,
Jewish-Gentile integration and counteracting forces—the
Jews continued to form separate groups of diminishing coherence—the degree of coherence depends on (1) the length
of time during which the process of integration has been going
on, (2) the attitude of the Gentile environment, (3) the effect
of Jewish migration

The co-existence of groups creates a social problem arising
from the dislike of the stranger and the demand for group
homogeneity—this social problem is the kernel of the " objective " or " genuine " Jewish problem—different principles
of group homogeneity—religion, nationality, State, class—
lack of homogeneity in modern society and effect on the Jews
—capacity of absorption and point of saturation

The actual Jewish question includes much more than this
objective kernel—it is considerably intensified by certain
subjective leanings of individuals, such as the need of self-
assertion and aggressiveness—these are called " subjective "
or " sham " causes of anti-Semitism—origin of aggressiveness, its displacement and rationalisation—group antagonism
as its favourite outlet

The situation of the Jewish group makes it a particularly suitable object of aggression—the Jews are late-comers, weak,
ubiquitous, recognisable—they are considered overbearing
and prominent in extremist movements—the socio-economic
position of the Jews is equally precarious—owing to their
pre-emancipatory concentration in money-lending and petty
trade, and certain inevitable trends of social advance, the
bulk of the Jews remained in middlemen occupations of all
kinds—traditional preferences and anti-Jewish prejudice in
the environment accounted for the conservation of a fairly
strict group character even where the Jews went over to
manufacture, industry, and the liberal professions—Jews are

II. THE EPOCH   65

—in the political sphere the lowering of standards found
expression in the dominance of economic considerations

The decline of civilisation had fateful effects on the Jews,
who depend for their existence in a Gentile world on a
civilised state of society

Digression on the political doctrine of Marxism as an example
of the manner in which, and the extent to which, it is possible
to uphold " difficult " ideals like humanitarianism, education,
and international solidarity among the working masses

Jewish emancipation in the Western world took place in a
period of rapid increase in population—causes and figures—
the structure of society changed—disproportionate increase of
the lower middle-class—the psychological condition of the
lower middle-class made it prone to accept anti-Semitism

The change of character of national representation—the
" thinkers and poets " as spokesmen of the whole German
people—gradual democratisation—this consists not only in
an extension of the franchise, but also in the will of the enfranchised to make use of their rights—modern anti-Semitism
as a problem of mass democracy—democracy is an exacting
political system—disappointment with democracy among
(1) the propertied class, (2) the working class, (3) the
intellectuals

If during a crisis the masses make full use of their political
rights, democracy may be endangered—it shares this danger
with other political ideologies—the masses accept only the
primitive, " easy " ideological elements—an ideological
element is felt as the more " easy ", the fewer demands it
makes on reason and morality and the more immediately
it appeals to the instincts

At the time of the last tolerably free election to the Reichstag,
in March 1933, both conditions of " total " democratisation
were fulfilled—the masses had been enfranchised without any
limitation, and they were anxious to use their powers—this
election completed, for the time being, the change of character of the national representation in Germany—the voice
of Germany was no longer that of the intellectual and
artistic *élite*, nor even of the professional politicians, but of
the disappointed and frustrated masses

III. THE SCENE

Germany's central position in Europe—her lack of natural
frontiers—her delayed unification—conflict between divergent
trends of development—Germany's belated economic development resulting from her remoteness from the Atlantic

IV. THE CATASTROPHE

INTRODUCTION

FAILURE OF EMANCIPATION ?

It is the privilege—often a melancholy one—of those who live through stirring events to retain vivid impressions of them such as cannot be derived from a mere description. But the closeness of view has also its disadvantage, since it prevents the average student from observing the events with that detachment and freedom from emotional bias which would enable him to draw from them the right conclusions. In the case of the catastrophe of the German Jews, which forms the starting-point of this study, this inevitable warping of the judgment has led many to accept a view of the Jewish situation which may be summed up in the expression: " Emancipation has proved a failure ". They arrive at this view by the following reasoning.

The German Jews, they say, formed the one Jewish community which was to a high degree integrated with its social environment without losing its character as a Jewish community. The German Jews were more Jewish and more numerous than, *e.g.*, those of Italy or France. They were more closely bound to their country than the Jews in Eastern Europe and had lived longer in it than those of the United States and the majority of the Jews in Great Britain. The German Jews formed thus the classic example of that Jewish way of life which enables Jews to live as an integral part of the Gentile world. Their downfall, it is argued, proves the failure of emancipation as a Jewish way of life.

It is the aim of the present study to refute this argument by showing that it is based on a confusion of sequence with consequence, on the fallacy of *post hoc ergo propter hoc.* Events follow each other, events also give rise to each other. But those events which seem to follow each other most naturally are not always those which give rise to each other. The expulsion of the German Jews followed their emancipation and integration. But it will be our endeavour to show that it was actually brought about by circumstances which were peculiar to the Germany of the post-war period, and therefore cannot be adduced as a proof of the " Failure of Emancipation " in general.

False ideas on this subject can be particularly harmful in the present situation of the Jews. After the second World War the Jews were left in a more desperate plight than ever before in the two thousand years of their Dispersion. Not only were they hurled from a height never reached before into the lowest depth of misery, but at no time in their history have they suffered such a horrifying loss of life. The emergence and recognition of the State of Israel has since given new hope to Jews everywhere. It has brought into the sphere of practical politics that new approach to the solution of the Jewish problem which for years was only a Zionist dream. Already it has greatly improved the possibilities of helping and rehabilitating the survivors of the European catastrophe.

But however auspicious the future which lies before the new State of Israel, it will not alter the fact that Jews will continue to form an integral part of the Gentile world. Well over ten million Jews live still in the Diaspora, among them some six million and a half who enjoy legal emancipation in the Western sense.[1] Not counting the Jewish communities in Soviet Russia and her zone of influence who are emancipated in conditions not fully comparable to those of the West, this means that considerably more than half of all living Jews still cling to a social status the very basis of which, according to the defeatist view outlined above, has been utterly shattered by Hitler's orgy of destruction. If their life is to be raised above the level of weary resignation to an inexorable doom, if they are to regain some of the idealistic belief in human goodwill on which their way of life was based, this defeatest view must not remain unchallenged. Jewish life in the Western world must be vindicated.

We may draw a lesson in this matter from the defence of democracy. When certain traits of superior efficiency in the post-war dictatorships became manifest, numerous writers came forward to oppose the challenge. They weighed the advantages and disadvantages of the respective systems and were not afraid to acknowledge the weaknesses of democracy. But they were not content with criticism alone. They essayed to re-establish democratic ideas on a new basis. While recognising the obvious imperfections of democracy, they sought to save those elements which in their opinion made it superior to any other political system,[2] and showed how the defects which had come to light might be remedied.

Contemporary literature on the Jewish question has until now largely taken the opposite direction. It has answered the challenge of Nazism with discouragement and—at least theoretically—has advocated that emancipation should be finally considered as a failure.[3] Intelligible though this attitude is as a psychical reaction to the profound disillusionment caused by the destruction of Eastern and Central European Jewry, it can be neither scientifically upheld nor politically justified.

It is vital that before the threat to their very survival Jews do not weary in searching after ways and means of safeguarding their future. Any vagueness or failure to grasp the full implications of every possible solution would almost certainly bring about new disaster.

I

ANTI-SEMITISM: A SPECIAL CASE
OF GROUP TENSION

In this chapter we shall examine the connection between the Jewish way of life in general and anti-Semitism. It will be shown that only in special circumstances is the complex phenomenon of anti-Semitism accounted for by a genuine group antagonism which in itself gives rise to social tensions. This genuine antagonism is gradually overcome by Jewish-Gentile integration. But the group tensions do not generally decrease in proportion. Rather do they tend to become accentuated by collective feelings of hostility emanating from quite different sources. The Jewish group, which will be shown usually to preserve its coherence longer than could have been expected at the time of emancipation, represents for a number of reasons a particularly suitable outlet for collective aggressiveness.

One reason why the catastrophe of the Jews in Germany produced so crushing an effect was that the precariousness of the position of the Jews had not been sufficiently realised. People were inclined to be just as over-confident about it as they are now unduly pessimistic. They laid too much stress on the fact of legal emancipation, the importance of which now tends to be minimised. They did not realise that legal emancipation is only a beginning, a programme which raises considerably more problems than it solves.

Emancipation was not the solution of the Jewish question, it only shifted its focal point from the legal to the social field. Before the emancipation, the legal inequality of a group of fellow countrymen was increasingly felt as undesirable by an intellectual *élite*, while to the man-in-the-street it seemed in perfect accordance with the actual social inequality—apart from a small upper section. Legal emancipation brought confusion to the man-in-the-street. The Jew was now a citizen with equal rights, but for some time to come he continued to differ socially in nearly every respect from the Gentile. " The Jew is a human being like ourselves and yet he has not the same rights " was the feeling of part of the *élite* before the emancipation. " The Jew has equal rights and is still an inferior being " became the feeling of broader sections of the population during the early period of emancipation. The feeling was not confined to this period. The strangeness of the Jews, it is true, steadily diminished. But nowhere among emancipated Jews has it disappeared so completely as to amount to a loss of their identity. Although on the periphery of the Jewish group individuals constantly went over into the majority groups by conversion, intermarriage, etc., the Jews nevertheless survived everywhere as more or less distinctly separate entities.

We are not concerned here with the question whether this consummation was desirable or not. We shall, on the whole, refrain from a valuation of the facts we are going to point out. The continuance of the identity of Jewish groups is relevant to this work only as a sociological fact. As such it will be seen to cause certain difficulties in the field of Jewish-Gentile relations. No doubt from the Jewish point of view there is a large measure of compensation for these difficulties, the survival of Jewish group characteristics being the pre-condition of any Jewish survival. But this study deals primarily, not with the problem of Jewish survival, but with the following questions : Does the catastrophe of German Jewry indicate that the way of life of Jewish emancipation and integration has proved a failure? Must the fact that roughly 43 per cent of the German electorate voted for the Nazi Party in 1933 be attributed to a breakdown of the Jewish-Gentile relationship? If the answers to these questions are in the negative, then to what other causes can the catastrophe be attributed?

There is no doubt that the anticipations—often more or less unconscious—formed by both emancipators and emancipated at the time of the emancipation concerning the future of the Jewish group character did not altogether correspond to the development which this group character has actually followed. On the presumption that the character of the Jewish community before the emancipation was essentially, if not solely, national and religious, it was expected that after the act of emancipation the national segregation would cease while the religious would become legally irrelevant. The first

23

expectation was almost entirely fulfilled, the second to a large extent. In spite, however, of the removal of barriers, in spite of the insignificance of the remaining religious differences, the character of the Jews as a distinct group of the population remained.

The question how this was possible is, of course, part of the larger question of the survival of the Jewish people for thousands of years after the loss of its territory, which is one of the riddles of history. The seeming regularity with which friendship and hostility between Jews and Gentiles have followed one another at different times and in different places, the tremendous losses which Jewry has been able to endure without being annihilated, have made people imagine that there is an inner law which imposes the fate of permanent suffering upon the Jews as the price of their eternal existence. This study seeks neither to support nor to refute such a philosophy of history. Suffice it to state that the survival of the Jewish group during the period of emancipation can be explained without recourse to metaphysics. We shall confine ourselves mainly to the development of Jewish emancipation in Germany, as in its success and failure this has come to be regarded by the Jews in other countries as something approximating the " ideal type " of Jewish emancipation.

Apart from a negligible minority, the Jews in Germany, as everywhere, had conserved their medieval way of life till the beginning of emancipation. They lived on German soil, but in religious, cultural, legal, social, and local segregation. The disadvantages of this segregation were compensated to the very last by the liberty which it allowed for the development and preservation of the Jewish ethos. Practically all the Jews in the ghetto clung to Jewish culture and its values. The intensity of the Jewish ethos, which was frequently looked upon by the Gentiles as either stubbornness or arrogance, may have varied in direct proportion to the severity of the penalisation to which the Jews were subjected. In any case, the contempt was mutual. When the doors of the ghettoes were thrown open, the new liberty found the mass of the Jewish people in a state of unpreparedness. They understood, it is true, that they were given the chance of enormous progress in many respects. But unlike the small *élite* whose members had attained social even before legal emancipation, they differed widely from their fellow citizens whose equals they were now to be.

In other words: the German Jews set out on their way into their social environment still carrying with them the full content of their Jewish tradition and still burdened with its full weight. At every stage of the journey, parts of the tradition were discarded, the burden of the Law was eased. First to disappear were the national peculiarities of speech and dress, local segregation, separate law. This was followed by a mitigation and adaptation of the religious precepts, until in the end practically all that remained of Judaism in certain Jewish circles was a nominal adherence to the Jewish community, and, not infrequently, even that was ended by conversion or severance. None the less, even when the fourth emancipated Jewish generation was growing up in Germany, this complete abandonment of the Jewish community was still exceptional in German Jewry, and the losses which it caused, particularly in the big cities, where the Jews congregated more and more, were compensated by the influx of new recruits from the provinces. The numerical strength of the German Jews and the strength of their Jewish feeling at the time when they entered upon the process of emancipation had proved sufficient to carry the overwhelming majority of them through 120 years of continuous exposure to alien influences.[4]

Two points may be noted in this somewhat over-simplified account. First, the Jews were subject to the natural attraction exercised on a minority by a majority among which it lives. Decisive in this process was not their active influence on it, but rather their passive adjustment to it.[5] The second point is that the extent to which assimilation took place was largely dependent on the length of time during which the Jewish community in Germany was exposed to the process of assimilation. During the period of Jewish emancipation in Germany the attraction which the Gentile majority exercised on the Jewish minority was constant, if not always equally forceful. If the process had continued beyond three or four generations and if no other factors had supervened to hamper or reverse the natural development, then the Jewish will to live would probably not have been strong enough to prevent an absorption of the Jewish minority into the Gentile majority.

There were, however, other factors, the most potent of which was the attitude of the Gentile society towards the Jews. It soon became evident that the masses of the German people— and also parts of the *élite*—were not prepared to accept without opposition the integration of the Jews as their equals into the community. This resistance with its effects and reactions forms the essence of the whole history of emancipation. Emancipation is bound to create group tensions corresponding to the character of the society in which it takes place. If the emancipation occurs in a competitive society, the impact of the newly emancipated minority will usually be felt as a sharpening of the competition, except where the minority follow trades not yet known to the majority. Even in that case there is a danger that the majority may take over these trades more quickly than the group character of the minority disappears and that the competitive factor may thus come, though tardily, to increase the group tension. This was the case with the Jewish group. Its early monopoly in money-lending and petty trade was gradually broken down both by the Jews themselves, who took up other occupations, and by the Gentiles who turned towards commerce and financial business. The incursions made by each side into what had previously been the other's exclusive territory increased the fear of competition on the part of the majority. Nor was this competition the only thing which prevented the Jews' desire for acceptance into Gentile society from being met by an equal desire on the part of all Gentiles to absorb them. There was a general attitude of resistance with which we shall have to deal later in more detail. This resistance lost both its real and pretended grounds precisely to the extent to which, in spite of all its impediments, the process of integration succeeded. But even so, it delayed this process not only directly by the refusal to accept the members of the minority, but also indirectly by hindering the readiness of the minority to co-operate. Feeling itself repelled, the minority replied by emphasising its differences and so, in turn, strengthened the will to repulsion on the side of the majority. In this way a series of mutual reactions was set up like the swing of a pendulum; but like a pendulum they tended gradually to lose their force. They retarded the process of integration without bringing it to a standstill.[6]

Both these factors, the tradition on the one hand which only slowly loses its segregating power, and the resistance to the acceptance of an alien group on the other hand, stand in the way of the social integration of any newly emancipated minority. At the same time, they safeguard the coherence of the minority group for a considerable time after the enactment of the formal emancipation. As long as they exist, even in so attenuated a degree as to be hardly felt by the individual members of the group, the group character of the minority persists.

In view of what has just been said it should be self-evident that the Jews will continue to constitute a separate group even after their legal emancipation. The same features which make them Jews serve also to separate them as a group from their environment. They lose their group character only when they have stripped off their last remaining vestiges of Judaism, that is to say, when they have ceased to be Jews.[7] If this statement will come as a surprise to many naïve observers, the more so if, later on, its far-reaching consequences will become apparent, this only shows how little Jews were wont to see themselves as a social problem. Most of them were aware of their group-distinctiveness in the religious field, but, apart from that, thought of Jews only as individuals. They denied any solidarity with persons within their group of whom they disapproved. Only when some member of his community distinguished himself did the isolated Jew awake to a somewhat bewildered group pride.

The process of integration has been carried to varying lengths with the various Jewish groups and has left them with varying degrees of coherence. This is apparent when we compare the characteristics of Jewish groups in different countries. As against the small, quickly dissolving group of the Jews in Italy, we see, for example, the considerably more solid group of the Jews in Great Britain. With regard to Italy, Ruppin [8] says that " the Jewish religion has almost entirely lost its significance and that mixed marriages decimate the Jewish community. In Trieste not more than 10 per cent go to the synagogue on the highest festivals. Mixed marriages are more frequent than marriages between Jews." What is left of group consciousness is described by Ruppin in the following sentence : " To my questions why the Jews of Trieste remain nominal Jews at all, one of the members of the board of the Jewish community answered : ' It does them no harm and they want to be buried in the Jewish cemetery '." [9] By contrast with the Italian Jews, the Jews of Great Britain, notably those who have immigrated since the 1890's, exhibit, not only in their occupational and local distribution but also in their average adhesion to Jewish tradition, a far higher degree of cohesion.

A similar variation is found in the features in which the Jewish groups differ from their respective enviroments. These are determined more or less precisely for each group by the distance it has travelled from the ghetto towards the goal of complete integration with its environment. On their release from the ghetto the Jews exhibit differences in nearly every field, from religion to the external habits of daily life. Language and education are exclusively Jewish. In the second stage of development, which usually sets in with the first generation born after emancipation, though the Jews still form a rigidly separated group, their education is no longer exclusively Jewish, an assimilation of habits is slowly proceeding among them, and they are bi-lingual, speaking both Yiddish and the language of the country. Religious life, however, with its tradition is still almost intact. The Jews are slowly broadening their economic basis by taking up occupations from which they have been formerly excluded. In the third stage the language struggle has been definitely decided in favour of the language of the country. Education is almost entirely non-Jewish. The Jewish culture has been almost completely replaced by the culture of the environment. The Jews of this stage feel themselves linked with Judaism only by their religious creed, and even this has been permeated by many elements imbibed from the environment. It has been increasingly " westernised ". In this stage the occupational distribution of the Jews is much more diversified, but it still shows the effects of their former concentration on money-lending and petty trade. We see the Jews again grouped together in a limited number of occupations, among which trade and commerce continue to hold pride of place, though in addition manufacture and the liberal professions are well represented. Thus in this stage also the occupational distribution of the Jews, although broader and more differentiated than before, still shows great anomalies. Both this fact and the urbanisation of the Jews account for most of the peculiarities by which, apart from their religion, the Jews of this stage still differ from their environment.

It was to this third stage that the overwhelming mass of German Jews belonged when Hitler appeared on the scene. A small number, particularly in Berlin, before, during, and after the first World War, carried assimilation a stage further and became utterly indifferent to Jewish tradition and Jewish group problems; and this was the prevailing attitude in some small communities, such as those of Italy, France, and the Scandinavian countries.

While some of the effects here mentioned are produced fairly generally by every contact between minority and majority groups, the Jewish minorities were affected by a factor peculiar to themselves which gave their contact with the majorities a special character. This was the factor of migration.

Jewish history is a record of perpetual migration. This fact is one of the many peculiarities of the Jewish existence. It is closely related to the great enigma of the Jewish survival. Not by chance does the legendary figure of the " Wandering Jew " bear the traits of eternal life.

Till about the middle of the 17th century Jewish migration flowed mainly from West to East. With the year 1648, and more definitely with the beginning of the 19th century, this direction was reversed.[10] At the end of the 18th century, 1·5 millions of the then living 2·5 million Jews, or 60 per cent, lived in Eastern Europe, *i.e.* in the Kingdom of Poland and its neighbouring countries.[11] When by 1850 the number of Jews had increased to 4·75 millions, the proportion of the Eastern European Jews amounted to 3·4 millions, or as much as 72·1 per cent. In 1925, however, only 7·6 out of 14·8 million Jews, or 51·2 per cent, still inhabited the same territories.[12] Yet, though by that time nearly four million Jews had joined in the great stream of the East-to-West migration between 1880 and 1925, the Eastern European part of the Jewish population had still retained its numerical predominance.

Throughout this period of westward migration, the Eastern European Jews were distinguished from the Jewish communities to which they came by a lower standard of living. It was, indeed, their economic plight which, apart from intermittent persecution in the countries of their origin, set the stream of migration in motion. The Eastern European Jews were, for the most part, not yet politically emancipated; and of those who were emancipated the bulk continued to live in purely Jewish settlements isolated from their environment. Their cultural status was that of the " first stage " mentioned above. Consequently, the contact between Eastern European Jews and the existing Jewish communities in the countries to which they immigrated, had everywhere the effect of retarding the process of assimilation. Although the old communities, in their fear of being identified with the newcomers, behaved with a certain measure of reserve towards them, they were neither able nor willing to avoid all association. Even if this contact was at first limited to the giving of charity, the very fact that new Jewish communities and associations sprang up, that new Jewish settlements were established in certain towns or districts, —even the mere increase of Jewish population could not leave the former Jewish inhabitants unaffected. In some places these patent signs of Jewish life reawakened in the Gentiles a consciousness of the Jewish problem, and the older Jewish inhabitants found themselves again regarded by their neighbours as Jews, as members of a different group. And this was not the only way in which the immigration of unassimilated Jews accentuated the Jewish problem. It also helped to revive the Jewish ethos which had been commencing to fade away among the old settlers.[13] Already in the second generation some rising families of new settlers usually succeeded in establishing social relations with the old community. And, although the process of assimilation had by this time begun to tell on these newcomers themselves, their way of life was still substantially Jewish, and they exercised a Judaising influence on their more assimilated fellow Jews. While perhaps arousing anti-Jewish feeling among the Gentiles, they prepared, so to speak, a line of defence against it by strengthening the Jewish ethos which compensated the disappointed Jewish assimilant for his failures.[14]

There are thus three factors which can be held to account for the conservation of Jewish groups even in the state of legal emancipation : the comparatively brief period during which the Jews have enjoyed emancipation, the attitude to them of their non-Jewish environment, and the Jewish migration.

We have now to discuss the consequences of the retention by the Jews of their group character, viz. anti-Semitism.

Anti-Semitism has been repeatedly described in terms of the usual reactions to each other of different groups when brought into contact.[15] As a rule those who see in anti-Semitism only an instance of group hostility take the view that it is not due to any faults on the part of the Jews.[16] They are, therefore, pessimistic as to the ability of the Jews to combat it, and see no possibility of their escaping it, short of the radical solution of liquidating the Diaspora.

Though group hostility *per se* is undoubtedly one of the

causes of anti-Semitism, it is a mistake to concentrate attention on this to the neglect of other essential points. It is true that group characteristics may serve as a peg on which to hang hostile sentiments of a quite different origin, but to regard the anti-Semitic ideology as a mere invention without any objective foundation whatever,[17] is to overlook the fact that the co-existence of divergent groups may very well involve an objective social problem. The treatment, as identical of anti-Semitic phenomena which differ in their historic backgrounds, is the besetting sin of the theory. Anyone who seeks to deny that the largely alien Jewish group at the beginning of the 19th century in Germany, or the constantly renewed immigrant groups in the United States of America represent real social problems, obscures the issue. While it is true that group contacts and group tensions may serve as outlets for an aggressiveness springing from entirely different sources, this is, by no means, their only significance.

The contact of one social group with another automatically creates hostility between them. Sigmund Freud regards this fact as axiomatic :[18] " Of two neighbouring towns each is the other's most jealous rival ; every little canton looks down upon the others with contempt. Closely related races keep one another at arm's length ; the South German cannot endure the North German, the Englishman casts every kind of aspersion upon the Scotchman, the Spaniard despises the Portuguese. We are no longer astonished that greater differences should lead to an almost insuperable repugnance, such as the Gallic people feel for the German, the Aryan for the Semite, and the white race for the coloured. . . . In the undisguised anti-pathies and aversions which people feel towards strangers with whom they have to do we may recognise the expression of self-love—of narcissism. This self-love works for the self-assertion of the individual, and behaves as though the occurrence of any divergence from his own particular lines of development involved a criticism of them and a demand for their alteration. We do not know why such sensitiveness should have been directed to just these details of differentiation ; but it is un-mistakable that in this whole connection men give evidence of a readiness for hatred, an aggressiveness, the source of which is unknown, and to which one is tempted to ascribe elementary character."

Similarly Trotter [19] sees the resentment against any dissimilarity as the natural consequence of his hypothetical human herd instinct: "Anything which tends to emphasise difference from the herd is unpleasant. In the individual mind there will be an unanalysable dislike of the novel in action and thought." [20] Trotter regards the happiness felt by the individual when he succeeds in identifying himself with his group as the essential feature in the idea of the legendary Golden Age.[21] It goes without saying that it involves the exclusion of strangers.[22]

We need not have recourse to the hypothesis of the " herd instinct " to convince ourselves that when a fundamentally homogeneous group is brought into contact with another group, it undergoes psychical repercussions which disturb its absolute or relative equilibrium. The group, therefore, instinctively strives, either by separating itself from the new group, or by assimilating it, to restore its equilibrium. Where the second of these methods is used, the new equilibrium will differ from the old in proprtion to the extent of the interference set up by the new elements, that is to say, to the size and degree of difference of the group with which contact has taken place. The new equilibrium may also be reached by a compromise between separation and assimilation. If, however, the compromise is not strictly observed, the equilibrium will tend to be unstable.

This state of affairs constitutes the genuine kernel of what we are accustomed to call the Jewish question. Nor is it restricted to Jewish experience, but it is found wherever different groups come into continuous and vital contact with each other. The part which it plays in the Jewish question has sometimes been overlooked by Jewish apologists who should know better. Even Professor Hugo Valentin in his extensive study of anti-Semitism [23] neglects it in his presentation of the problem : " It is not the case ", he says, " that one group after objective enquiry arrives at the result that a certain other group is harmful or inferior. The primary thing is hatred. The argument furnished by reasoning is secondary." This is largely true, but it is not the whole truth. A social conflict does not cease to exist, because it is produced not by " objective enquiry ", but by spontaneous hatred. The presence of an irrational hostile reaction does not exclude the existence of a real social conflict, and may in fact be its symptom. Though the social grounds of the group conflicts may be obscured by subsequent rationalisation, this does not alter the fact that such grounds may exist.

The impulse in the individual to preserve the homogeneity of his group and his sensation of challenge on being brought into close contact with a different group must be reckoned with as an elementary fact of social life.[24] The principle of homogeneity, however, need not be the same as it was in the original organisation of the group. In essentially religious periods, *e.g.*, religious homogeneity was considered indispensable for States which owed their existence to dynastic or military causes. After the French Revolution the demand for homogeneity shifted to the national field.[25] In Soviet Russia the principle of class homogeneity was for the first time embodied in the State system, and this fact no doubt contributed to the possibility of dispensing with the principle of national homogeneity in that country. In modern States which do not coincide even approximately with nations, *e.g.* Switzerland and the United States, which are inhabited by more than one nationality, and not less in the German territorial States before the foundation of the German Reich which were inhabited by only part of the German nation, for the principle of national homogeneity there is substituted that of the homogeneity of the State. This demands the fulfilment by the citizens of voluntary obligations which go beyond those imposed by law and thus create a consciousness of political homogeneity. The German Professor Richard Thoma defines this as the " unconditional loyalty to the State which cannot be brought about by rational calculations only ", but without which no State can permanently exist.[26]

Unlike the State whose political and social aspects can be sharply defined, modern society is a diffuse structure which has received some sort of reflected homogeneity only as State society. According to Herbert Spencer, social evolution is a continuous process of differentiation and integration. But not infrequently the actual interdependence of the elements produced by differentiation does not create in them a corresponding consciousness of interrelation. Although, *e.g.*, employers and employees depend on each other and are in constant mutual contact in work, on the labour market, in the institution of collective bargaining, etc., they are conscious of a deep gulf separating them from each other; so much so that in periods of economic and political strain their co-existence within the same State or nation may become problematical. Likewise there co-exist in modern society innumerable groups and sub-groups which, though dependent on each other, are nevertheless opposed to each other. Fundamentally, this lack of homogeneity in modern society favours the admission of the Jewish group. Where a comprehensive unity of consciousness no longer exists, the degree of adaptation required from an alien group will diminish as a matter of course.[27] In two respects, however, the differentiation may cause increased difficulties for the Jewish group. For one thing, it may create a general feeling of discontent which makes people apprehensive towards any further danger of disruption and induces them to cling more closely to the remnants of homogeneity. In this case, the contact with a group which, though economically heterogeneous, is ethnically and religiously homogeneous may make the majority group more keenly aware of its own ethnical and religious bonds by which it is separated from the newcomers as a whole in spite of internal subdivisions. Further, the differentiation of modern society causes the Jewish-Gentile group antagonism to manifest itself in widely varying spheres; not only in the national, in the political, in the religious field, but equally between Jewish and Gentile tailors, students, athletes, doctors, Freemasons, etc. Even though in modern society, therefore, homogeneity exists only in a very restricted sense, yet the striving for the lost homogeneity on the one hand, and the homogeneities of the several sub-groups on the other, cause the Jew who desires to be incorporated to be still regarded in all spheres as " the " stranger, " the " intruder, " the " enemy.

Nor is it only the striving of the majority for homogeneity that keeps alive the conflict between the groups. In our case there is another factor which works towards the same end, namely, the fact that individual members of the Jewish group are constantly moving towards and into the majority group. In some group relations tension is mitigated by a certain amount of stability—as, for instance, in the relation of a State church to a sect of long standing or the relation between two sports clubs of equal reputation. In others, again, no tension arises because one of the groups is by its own will exclusive— here we are thinking of socially privileged groups like an aristocracy. The emancipated Jewish group, however, is in a state of continuous motion. By abandoning some of their group characteristics—the linguistic, etc., by preserving others—the religious, and by developing still others along lines largely independent of their intentions—the economic, its members constantly set new problems of adjustment. These problems are the inevitable concomitants of the process of social integration, on the desirability of which both emancipators and emancipated agree, since, as has been pointed out before, the progress of integration is the real gist of the " objective ", the " genuine " Jewish question.

In Western and Central Europe the inhabitants of the ghetto were at a lower stage of development than their neighbours, both in the socio-economic field and in the process of spiritual liberation from medieval ties. When the ghetto doors were thrown open, the Jews started at once to make up the lost ground in order to attain the standard of the environment. They were stimulated to do so by the outspoken desire of the emancipators to see the Jews assimilated, as well as by the general contemporary hostility to corporations.[28] In consequence, the initial resistance to the emancipation offered by some Jewish circles who feared its disintegrating effects on the Jewish group [29] was overcome, the rights offered were accepted, and the gradual but steady process of integration of the Jews into their Gentile environment began.

Fundamentally the same process will be set going wherever Jews live as a scattered minority among a Gentile majority culturally superior to them. It makes no difference whether the initial contact is due to immigration or emancipation, for emancipation may be regarded as a kind of vertical immigration and shares most of its characteristics. Since the Jews everywhere represent an underprivileged, if not always a backward, community, they are striving for an improvement of their status, no matter whether their penalisation is due to actual laws or merely to the fact of their being a minority.[30]

It is necessary to mention here that in this connection numbers play a peculiar and tragic rôle. That is to say, it is of considerable importance whether a few individual Jews, a small number or a large number, pass over into the majority group. The penetration in the 18th century of a small number of Jews into spheres which had hitherto been closed to them helped to pave the way for the emancipation. It created more sympathy for the Jews who were discriminated against than opposition against them as intruders. This may, it is true, be partially attributed to the high achievements of the successful bankers and scholars of this time, but the fact that they were a few isolated individuals must also be borne in mind. Their contemporaries looked upon them rather as economic and intellectual pioneers than as competitors. This attitude changed towards the middle—and more markedly towards the end—of the 19th century, when more and more Jewish business men and students entered into competition with Gentiles. They, too, were still the products of a fairly strict social and intellectual selection, and they had for the most part a remarkably high standard of ability and conduct. The relations between them and their Gentile colleagues were still not very seriously marred by prejudices and the fear of competition. But when towards the end of the 19th and at the beginning of the 20th centuries Jews, taking advantage of the economic development of Germany and following their specific Jewish inclinations, began to flock in large numbers into business and the liberal professions, opposition became more general. It was more and more felt as an opposition between groups, and new reasons were sought to justify anti-Jewish feeling.

Undeniable as is the relation between the number of Jews and the resistance against them, this relation cannot be expressed in exact figures. The capacity of absorption and the point of saturation change with the circumstances, and an attempt to put the limit at 4 per cent [31] must be considered arbitrary. One of the factors which influence the capacity of absorption is, *e.g.*, the degree to which the accepting group itself is integrated or striving for integration. A loosely knit group, such as that, *e.g.*, formed by the inhabitants of an urban residential district, will have a higher capacity for absorbing Jewish members than a business association, and a business association a higher one than a circle of friends. In the economic field the absorbing capacity is dependent furthermore on the prosperity of the Gentile group and on its fears of competition. The saturation point will be somewhat lower in a depression, and in a crisis it will be so low that a movement will arise to expel even previously tolerated members of the minority. Another factor is the rate at which Jews are being integrated into the majority. A slow and steady integration is able to raise the saturation point, while a quick and sudden penetration can precipitate resistance. Finally, the extent of dissimilarity between the accepting and the accepted group is an important factor.

These points have been made with the object of refuting the opinion that because anti-Semitism can be explained as a case of group tension it therefore need not be regarded as a serious social problem. The phenomenon of anti-Semitism is not exhaustively dealt with merely by unfolding its psychological origins. The assertion frequently heard of late that anti-Semitism has no connection whatever with Jewish conduct and way of life is nearly as one-sided as the anti-Semitic assertion that it is solely due to this factor. It is, for instance, only natural that the Gentiles should resent the Jews observing two moral standards, one within and one without their own group—a practice which is likely to survive among them from the ghetto into the early period of emancipation. Even if anti-Semitic feelings which have been aroused by an experience of this kind, are subsequently accentuated by a latent aggressiveness not due to Jewish-Gentile relations, they must primarily be attributed to an objective group antagonism. An entirely different problem, however, is raised when this " double morality " has long been abandoned in the more advanced stages of emancipation, but anti-Semites still allege it in order to procure an effective slogan for an anti-Jewish boycott. " Genuine " and " sham " motives of anti-Semitism may be mixed up in many ways.

The objective group antagonism tends to diminish with the decrease of group differences. It gradually ceases in itself to disturb the social equilibrium. But it disappears only with the disappearance of the Jewish group character, that is to say, with the end of Jewish life. Group tension, however weak it may be, or the existence of an " objective Jewish question " is inherent in the existence of the Jews.

The actual Jewish question, however, is of far wider scope than this objective kernel; and to understand it we must have recourse to the theory against which we have been arguing so far without explaining what it stands for. The psychological theory of anti-Semitism maintains that anti-Semitism originates essentially if not entirely in characteristics of the anti-Semites themselves. It is held to have its roots in the need for hatred, aggression, and self-assertion on the part of the Gentiles, passions which are only accidentally vented on the Jews. It cannot, therefore, be avoided by the Jews except by total

37

segregation.[32] One-sided as it is, this explanation represents a remarkable advance on the opinion formerly prevailing that the arguments used to justify anti-Semitism were more or less identical with its causes. In this belief people thought they had adequately refuted anti-Semitism when they had proved that the arguments put forward by anti-Semites were not, or not sufficiently, borne out by facts. However indispensable in the fight against anti-Semitism is the refutation of false allegations, it is without doubt insufficient. The new psychological explanation of anti-Semitism insists, on the contrary, that it is not only a matter of indifference what the anti-Semites say about the Jews but also how the Jews react to their accusations.

The defect of this theory is its one-sidedness. It overlooks the fact that if the antipathy between groups were not, as stated above, the symptom of a real social problem, it would not be so easily capable of drawing to itself grievances of a different origin. It is, of course, also true that if these other grievances were not of considerable force, the objective social problem would only rarely result in a grave conflict.[33]

Sigmund Freud has asserted that the process of civilisation involves the suppression or sublimation of primary human impulses, and that though this may be achieved temporarily or permanently, the impulses continue to exist.[34] The process of repression is accomplished only at the cost of great strain and not infrequently it leads to nervous disturbances, malformations of character, etc. For instance, to overcome aggressiveness, which Freud considers a primary impulse of human nature, it was necessary to bring into play an immensely powerful instrument like Christianity, the moral demands of which involve a radical reversal of human instincts.[35] This complete overriding by civilisation of original human nature imposes so great a burden on the individual that fresh conflicts may be the consequence. " What an overwhelming obstacle to civilisation aggression must be ", Freud finally exclaims,[36] " if the defence against it can cause as much misery as aggression itself! "

Apart from the painful renunciation of primitive impulses which humanity had to undergo in the cause of progress and civilisation, there is in the smaller issues of daily life no lack of grief, sorrow, and continuous frustration. These miseries likewise tend to transform themselves into aggressiveness [37] so that it becomes of secondary importance whether we regard aggression with Freud as a primary urge, or with Suttie [38] as the outcome of frustrated love. What matters is that civilisation disapproves of it, and that therefore it must rely on outlets which are admissible according to the accepted standard of morality. There is, then, no necessary connection between the cause of the grievance and the object of aggression. Aggression directed against objects which have not been in the least responsible for the frustration can produce the same feeling of relief. Psychology speaks in this case of a " displacement " of aggression. This is usually accompanied by the psychological mechanism of " rationalisation " by which the would-be aggressor persuades himself that the object of the displaced aggression is in reality the cause of it.

Granting that there exists, on the one hand, in every individual some latent aggressiveness seeking for an object and, on the other, that acute group tensions are to be found in every society, it will be readily understood why this aggressiveness should by preference find its outlet in these tensions. If even a normal person can hardly help regarding the co-existence of a group of " strangers " as a challenge to his own striving for the preservation of his way of life and thought, then for the over-aggressive individual this challenge must amount to a virtual instigation to violence. The normal resentment of the unlike is then enhanced by the innate fighting spirit which is gratified in defence of what are considered high ideals. For the danger of group hostility is the extreme facility with which it can be rationalised. Group existence, group homogeneity, the alleged or actual threat from a neighbour group, the significance of group loyalty—all these factors lend themselves easily to idealisation. Whoever has seen how such a thing as, *e.g.*, a shorthand system could be represented as a " philosophy of life ", a criterion to separate not only blockheads from intelligent persons, but also the wicked from the good (as was the case in Germany between those who had adopted the shorthand system of Stolze-Schrey and Gabelsberger respectively), will be convinced of the usefulness of practically any group difference as an instrument of self-assertion and an outlet for aggression. Love for one's group is socially admissible self-love; group hatred is socially admissible aggressiveness. Both are not only tolerated, they may even be glorified as self-sacrifice, devotion, and heroism.

The Jews, it is true, form only one of many sub-groups in modern society, but they have a number of characteristics which

39

mark them out as the ideal target for collective aggression. The Jews are not only different, they are considered strangers. They are nowhere autochthonous, and before the foundation of the State of Israel, they were, even in the land of their national history, exposed to the reproach of being intruders. In the lands of the Dispersion, at any rate, they are everywhere " late-comers ". Everywhere they find their claim to share the country disputed by a native majority. Doubtful as the claims of the so-called " old settlers " may in some cases be owing to the fact that they themselves may to a considerable extent consist of immigrants, the evidence is all in their favour.

The Jews are everywhere weak—not only because they are a minority, but because of the absence of a powerful political centre which might safeguard their rights. In the psychological mechanism of displacement, however, weakness amounts to an invitation to aggression.

The Jews live nearly everywhere. They live not only in almost every country but—in the countries of emancipation— also in all districts and, although unequally distributed, in almost every town and many villages. Their ubiquity multiplies the number of their contacts and hence the possibilities of hostility between them and other groups.

Physiologically the Jews present a type more or less different from that of the Gentiles. Although recent research has shown that they cannot be considered a race in the strict sense of the word, the Ashkenazic Jews at least form an ethnical community and, as a result of intermarrying, a certain similarity of type exists among them. Although many Jews do not conform to this type, it is sufficiently common to be regarded as a distinctively Jewish stereotype. That it is a dark-haired type renders it— according to the psychologist Peter Nathan [39]—all the more liable to arouse dislike in a fair-headed environment. The fact that it still partially bears the marks of several centuries of an unhealthy ghetto life has no doubt equally contributed to making it inferior to a predominantly Nordic ideal of beauty.

On the other hand, the Jews do not differ in any decisive way, notably not in the colour of their skin, from their European and American environments. They thus show just that degree of similarity which makes people all the more sensitive to remaining differences, especially when these differences are only the bodily symbol of other divergencies. " Racial in- tolerance ", says Freud,[40] " finds stronger expression—strange to say—in regard to small differences than to fundamental ones." [41]

The same characteristic of similarity combined with difference is found in the religious sphere. Jews and Christians have an essential part of their ideas and holy scriptures in common. But they are separated by the central figure of Christianity who has not only been rejected by the Jews, but—what is infinitely worse—was abused and crucified by them—so at least Christian tradition has it. The antagonism created by this difference was a long time the decisive factor in instigating Jew-hatred. And even to-day, when the hold of religion on society has been weakened, the place it still occupies in the education of children makes it a greater influence on the subconscious life of adults than might be expected.

The religious opposition is deepened by the fact that it is from their religion that the Jews draw the main justification for their self-valuation, namely the conviction that they are God's Chosen People. True, that conviction is not peculiar to the Jews. We find a secularised version of it in every modern nationalism. But while people are inclined to accept national self-exaltation of a State inside its undisputed frontiers as the inevitable consequence of its normal existence, they resent it as annoying, even as intolerable, if it is displayed by a small, weak, despised minority, whose circumstances seem to require rather a humble submissiveness. In such a minority their claim to be " chosen " must appear as unseemly arrogance. It cannot, therefore, be surprising that the notion of the " Chosen People " has been hurled against the Jews in scorn and fury by the anti-Semites of all times and countries. [42]

It is one of the many paradoxes connected with the Jewish problem that the Jews, who were originally predominantly a religious community and whose religious separateness is even to-day their most manifest peculiarity, should recently have become an object of attack because of their apparent lack of religion. It is, indeed, quite intelligible that to members of a group suppressed for centuries for religious reasons, religion should appear as a disability of which they would fain rid themselves. But not content with this, some Jews in their efforts to free themselves from the ties of their own community tend to defy the general cultural standards also. While freeing themselves from the bondage of the Jewish tradition they are apt to throw over tradition as such; while denying Jewish values they may deny any objective value whatsoever. This is a process characteristic of all aliens in their first contact with their new country. The German sociologist Georg Simmel [43] values it highly as the pre-condition of greater liberty, objectivity, and detachment, although he does not overlook its inherent dangers.[44]

Closely related to the reproach of irreligion is another factor apt to excite group antagonism against the Jews, viz. that of political extremism. This is no more a general Jewish characteristic than irreligion. Not even a considerable minority distinguishes itself by extremist views. But the reproach of Jewish extremism has become one of the standard themes of anti-Semitism. Plausibility has been given to it by the fact that some very prominent representatives of political and cultural extremism have been Jews. The reason for this lies unquestionably in the difficulties experienced by Jews at a certain stage of the emancipation process in adjusting themselves to their environment. It results also frequently from their resistance to persisting discrimination. But these explanations are too subtle to be grasped by the man-in-the-street who sees only the bare facts and even these in a form exaggerated and distorted by propaganda. Thus it is no wonder that simple-minded people who desire passionately to preserve their way of life, are bound to resent the disturbers of their peace.[45]

In the enumeration of factors which make the Jewish group a natural target for aggression we have purposely so far ignored the economic, although these provide, above all, particularly striking explanations. We wished to show that reasons independent of economics would in themselves have sufficed to make the Jewish situation very precarious. Considering the predominant part played by economic factors in modern society, if we now proceed to take these into account, hardly anything inexplicable will remain in the phenomenon of latent anti-Semitism. It will rather have to be regarded as " over-determined " in the psychological sense.[46]

Professor Arnold J. Toynbee,[47] in his chapter on the " Range of Challenge and Response ", examines the laws according to which physical or human challenges are transformed into positive stimuli. He first formulates the law : " The greater the challenge, the greater the stimulus ", and then modifies it by the so-called Law of Compensation, under which a compensation takes place in the same field where the challenge is offered. In this context he says: [48] ". . . we again found our 'law of compensation' at work in the most extreme example of Challenge and Response in the human realm that can well be imagined : the example of the Jewish 'Diaspora' ". The following is, in his opinion, the compensation : [49] " The exercise of holding their own in a hostile human environment has not only stimulated the Jews of the Dispersion to activity. It has also enabled them, in diverse Gentile societies in successive ages, to keep their footing in the market-place and their seat in the counting house, and to take their tribute from the golden stream of commerce and finance. . . ." These words show that Toynbee regards the preference with which the Jews flocked into commerce and finance as the direct result of their penalisation. Similarly Simmel [50] calls the history of the Jews in Europe the " classic example " of the fact that commerce is the " appropriate field of the stranger ", because it can at all times occupy more persons than primary production.

This disproportionate distribution of the Jews, which was a natural consequence of their pre-emancipatory concentration in money-lending and petty trade, contained further elements exposing the Jewish group to particular dangers. We need not examine here whether the situation of Palestine at the crossing of important caravan routes, whether the Dispersion and the preservation in it of a common language and a common law gave the Jews a bent towards commerce. It may well be assumed that several circumstances worked in the same direction, so that, when at length the medieval potentates forcibly limited their activities they only intensified a tendency already existing. This is not to deny that Jews for a time occupied a prominent place in many of the crafts and that here and there they were also to be found in agriculture.[51] These occupations were, however, nearly always only additional.[52] In recent times it is only in Eastern Europe that conditions have been somewhat different, above all in Poland, where there were a considerable number of Jewish artisans. There were even Jewish guilds competing with the Gentile guilds and entering into agreements with them concerning their customers.[53] But even there most of the Jews were petty traders, and there were also among them a large number of innkeepers and agricultural middlemen.[54] Often the Jews did not exercise a real occupation at all, but were now traders, now workers, now teachers—in fact what the Jewish writer Max Nordau called " Luftmenschen ". At any rate, here as elsewhere, the Jews were almost entirely excluded from owning landed property, and those who wished to climb on the social ladder found openings elsewhere, preferably in commerce, finance, and certain branches of manufacture, where they consequently acquired a disproportionate prominence.

Commerce, however, and still more finance, are late-comers in the realm of economics. Agriculture and craftsmanship were first, and it was only when the economic activities broadened and became increasingly complicated and difficult to understand that the work of the middleman became an independent occupation. In consequence, he always laboured under a certain stigma which has been reinforced by his apparent unproductiveness. Deep-rooted in human consciousness is the idea that in bygone times people were able to do without commerce, that commerce is unproductive, that it increases the prices of articles without adding to their value.[55] We are not concerned with the economic error involved in this opinion. What matters is its wide diffusion. True, there are differences between the esteem in which commerce is held in different countries. No doubt it is more respected in England than it is in Germany. In Germany, at any rate, where army and bureaucracy kept commerce in a position of social inferiority even during the industrial period, commerce was regarded with a disdain which has survived to the present day. This is why the National Socialists were able to make such play with their distinction between " creative ", *i.e.* industrial, and " rapacious ", *i.e.* commercial and financial capital.

Even more widespread are the dislike and contempt of everything concerned with pure finance, whether money-lending on interest or against pledges, or more complicated transactions through banks and stock exchange. The connection between such transactions and the creation of goods is even less evident, since finance is not even concerned with the distribution of commodities, but only the manipulation of the abstract sign of purchasing power, viz. money. What is earned in this way appears still less justifiable, if not positively immoral. Book-keeping and money-counting seem to deserve the name of work even less than the buying and selling of concrete goods. It is not an accident that the Jewish Law and the Roman Catholic Church restricted or forbade the taking of

44

interest, and that hardly any other economic function has been subjected to such continuous regulation. Furthermore, this much abused activity, equally hated and indispensable, seems to place in the hands of him who exercises it complete power either to save or to ruin his client. And it was in this occupation that the Jews were destined to play so important a part as to become virtually identified with it.

But finance was not only unpopular for the above reasons. There are other occupations which are despised and even suspect, but which arouse pity rather than moral indignation. What in contrast to these makes finance utterly odious is its relatively high returns. True, its profits to a large extent were merely an optical delusion on the part of people who saw only those Jews who had actually become rich by money-lending, but did not think of the many others who had been robbed and expelled while doing the same kind of business. In reality, the relatively high profits of the successful money-lenders represented premiums against the risk of arbitrary interference with their way of business and life. It is the insecurity of their trades and lives which accounts for their earnings. The general average over a period or over a large area would have been considerably lower. But it was hardly to be expected that the mass of the public should take all these points into consideration. What they saw was that an allegedly immoral occupation, involving little work, yielded profits such as the peasant or the artisan, in spite of hard work, could never hope to attain.

Why did not this precarious economic situation fundamentally change after the opportunity for free development had been ensured by the emancipation? After legal and economic discriminations against the Jews were abolished, it became theoretically possible that the first liberated generation would " normalise " itself, that is to say, would take up all branches of employment roughly in proportion to their numbers. There is no doubt that the emancipators expected a development of this kind. One of the main arguments of the friends of the emancipation was that the legal act was a necessary preliminary to the economic and social normalisation. Their opponents, on the other hand, made the socio-economic anomaly of the Jews the ground for withholding emancipation, while the advocates of a medium solution desired to grant emancipation only as a reward for a previously achieved normalisation.

45

The expectation of a speedy normalisation was not fulfilled. It could not be fulfilled because of certain trends which were inherent in the original position of the Jews, and which led to the preservation of the group characteristics, even in the changed circumstances.

One of the main obstacles to normalisation was the fact that the Jews were chiefly town-dwellers. Whether this must be attributed, as Max Weber [56] suggests, to an innate dislike for agriculture on the part of the Jews—a dislike which found expression in, and was in turn deepened, by the specifically urban Jewish ritual—or whether their frequent exclusion from landed property was the chief reason, need not be discussed here. Certain it is that the Jews were mostly traders, even in rural districts. This gave them a mobility which made it particularly easy for them to flock into the growing urban centres. Certain other factors worked in the same direction. For their religious life the Jews require a community, both for their services and for the observance of their ritual laws. But not only in this positive sense did they depend on each other. To associate closely with peasants whose life was dominated by the Church and its customs would have been extraordinarily difficult for them. The town, on the contrary, is a place where the notorious strangeness of the Jews, the primary cause of so many of their sufferings, may be a positive advantage to them. So at least Louis Wirth suggests in his study of " Urbanism as a Way of Life ".[57] " It [the town] has not only tolerated but rewarded individual differences. It has brought together people from the ends of the earth *because* they are different and thus useful to one another, rather than because they are homogeneous and like-minded." But even if we cannot go so far as to accept the author's opinion that the town offers a premium for dissimilarity, we can readily agree with him that if the handicap imposed by dissimilarity can be mitigated at all, it can be so mitigated only in the town. In contrast to the daily neighbourly supervision which the rural community exercises over each of its members, urban contacts are transitory and superficial, and in no case extend to more than part of the activities of the associating individuals. This power of passing unnoticed in the town eases the burden of strangeness, and is therefore bound to exercise a strong attraction on the "vertical" as well as on the " horizontal " immigrant.* It is not, there-

* See p. 35.

fore, surprising that immigrants in general concentrate in towns, even if they come originally from rural districts.[58]

Many other peculiarities of town life favour the immigrant in general and the Jew in particular. The village can find room for one or at the most a restricted number of strangers only on the tacit but inexorable condition that these strangers develop into complete villagers and abandon all their essential peculiarities. The town, on the other hand, allows for the preservation of such peculiarities. The slight contact between town-dwellers is not notably impaired by them. It is even possible for strangers to concentrate in special town districts on account of their peculiarities. In one word, the town is less exacting than the village in its demands that the inhabitants should adapt themselves to their environment. It is this loose association which makes it easier for the newcomer to settle down. He is, in any case, by his emancipation or emigration in the middle of a process of disengagement from previous ties, and this process is favoured by the laxer control exercised by town life. The possibility, furthermore, of living with one's equals, of benefiting from the help of those who have arrived earlier, and at the same time of getting into economic touch with the broader environment, appears to the immigrant as an ideal solution of his problems. That there is no contradiction between the striving to rid oneself of too strict controls and the endeavour to utilise the advantages inherent in the old community will be obvious to all who have studied these " marginal " situations.[59] If, finally, we take into account the fact that urban existence with its permanent contacts between individuals who are not bound to each other by sentimental ties favours a spirit of competition, of self-advancement, and of useful co-operation, that in a word it demands and develops the very characteristics which the Jew as a rule possesses, we shall come to regard the Jewish tendency to urbanisation again as psychologically " over-determined ".

Those, however, who have once settled down in the town, do not as a rule go back to the country. Leaving the town for the country would be a re-migration, in view of the fact that in the industrial period, which roughly coincides with the Jews' right to move freely from place to place, there is spontaneous mass migration generally only from country to town. The town population does not reproduce itself and has to rely on continuous recruitment from rural districts. This is given only

47

too willingly. " Landflucht " is a serious problem in most industrial countries; " migration from the towns ", however, usually ends at the farthest in the suburban districts, which expand more and more. Coercive measures would be needed to reverse this natural tendency.

Thus the Jews, in the lack of any effective counter-attraction, remained town-dwellers. They concentrated increasingly in the big cities where all the advantages pointed out above were most fully to be obtained.[60] True, their strangeness diminished with every generation, and with it diminished their need for keeping aloof. They no longer wanted special dwelling districts, but on the contrary desired to be distributed over the whole town.[61] The craving for freedom from control which was acute during the first stages of severance from the Jewish community was gradually replaced by a higher degree of self-confidence. Nevertheless, the traces of their former mentality endured for a long time, and were from time to time accentuated by anti-Semitism. The broadened occupational basis comprised likewise only urban occupations. The traditional Jewish attitude towards profit made the Jews seek for the greater opportunities in the greater business centres, and the facilities which the large cities afforded for gratifying the cultural and aesthetic inclinations awakened in them by their relatively high educational level added to the attraction which these exercised over them.[62]

The town, however, in spite of the supreme socio-economic function which it has fulfilled since the breakdown of feudalism, has not escaped the strictures of social moralists. Certainly the blessings of town life are not unmixed, and the social politician has to grapple with its undeniable dangers for health, morality, and reproduction. But it is a mistake to condemn it for sentimental reasons instead of trying to effect constructive reforms. Unfortunately, comparisons between town and country life often take the form of condemnation of the former and glorification of the latter. Among a people fundamentally so healthy as the English, this attitude merely produces such wholesome manifestations as the country house of the well-to-do and the gardens of the middle and petty bourgeois classes. But in a country like Germany, too quickly industrialised to adjust itself properly to the new conditions, the morbid longing for the lost state of nature became both a cause and a symptom of the feeling of discontent with contemporary civilisation as a whole. It became, *e.g.*, one of the characteristic features of Romanticism. While such expressions as " the dirty human stream of the metropolis ", or " the glowing, barren asphalt of a bestialised sub-humanity " [63] to be found in the big towns, need not be regarded as typical, yet we find everywhere in popular literature and public opinion condemnation of the cities and longing for the countryside. A characteristically German phenomenon like the Youth Movement before and after the first World War, which in its aversion from civilisation shows so many similarities to National Socialism, was primarily based on feelings of this kind. To look on the country as a paradise of purity and to live in the town but to see in it the incarnation of evil—these are only extreme manifestations of a feeling widespread in all industrial countries. And once again we find the Jews inhabiting those quarters which public feeling holds in low esteem.

The urbanism of the Jews was one of the principal obstacles to their economic and local normalisation. There was no compelling reason in the town to divert them from giving preference to commercial occupations. Commerce continually increased in importance and offered considerable prospects. Owing to their experience and their freedom from anti-capitalist prejudices, the Jews took full advantage of them.

The upward path from petty trade and hawking as well as from money-lending was well marked out from the beginning. It led to shopkeeping, to wholesale trade, to department stores, to banking, stock exchange, and the many middleman activities of every stage, as represented by commercial travellers, estate or insurance agents, etc. It is safe to say that there is no single activity in the commercial sphere which has not been taken up by Jews.

It was different in manufacture, which also absorbed part of the Jewish energies. Here infiltration took place mainly in three ways, out of which only one favoured normalisation.

The Jews developed, to begin with, the crafts which they had exercised before industrialisation.[64] This led to their great prominence in the clothing industry in its widest sense, for large numbers of Jews who had previously worked as tailors found this the easiest way of making progress.[65] Arthur Ruppin, who limits the term " Jewish industries " to those branches of industry " whose employers and employees are exclusively or mostly Jews ",[66] mentions as " Jewish industries " only three,

49

two of which belong to the clothing industry, viz. the textile industry in Poland and the manufacture of clothing and underwear in Paris, London, and the United States.[67] For our own purpose the less exact statement is sufficient that, of the Ashkenazic Jews everywhere, an extraordinarily high percentage go into the textile and clothing industries, including all their sub-industries, such as leather and fur manufacture, cap and button-making, etc. As a third " Jewish industry " Ruppin mentions diamond-cutting in Amsterdam and Antwerp, for which the Jews were suited by their former prominence in glass-cutting as well as by their trade in jewels during the Middle Ages. A certain disposition for this branch of industry may be found also in another traditional Jewish craft, the working of precious metals.[68] The Jewish predominance in these industries applies both to employers and employees, with the qualification that in Central and Western Europe there was a greater proportion of employers and black-coated employees, and in Eastern Europe of manual workers.[69] In those industries which developed from crafts where there had been hardly any Jews, such as iron-founding and machine-making, only few Jews are to be found.[70] In this way, the original distribution was largely retained even among the Jews who rose on the social ladder.

The second way which led into industry was from commerce and finance. The capital earned there was used for the foundation or purchase of industrial works. There was no restriction as to the kind of industrial enterprises which could be chosen, so that there is practically no branch which Jews did not enter in this way.[71] In consequence of the money-basis on which their participation depended they usually occupied leading positions. Apart from this remaining social anomaly, this is the one way mentioned above which favoured normalisation.

There is, finally, a third way into industry which was not infrequently traversed by Jews. It follows neither the normal development of trades nor the flow of capital in search of profitable investment. It rather seeks to establish new industries where Gentile competition does not yet exist.[72] The search by late-comers for branches of business which are not yet occupied by those already at the place contributes powerfully to the preservation of the group character, even without conscious desire of segregation on the side of the newly emancipated or immigrant minority. Professor Werner Sombart describes this process in the following words: [73] " Here they are the founders of the tobacco industry (in Mecklenburg, Austria), there of distillery (Poland, Bohemia). Here we find them as leather manufacturers (in France, in Austria), there as silk manufacturers (in Prussia, Italy, Austria). Here they make stockings (Hamburg), there mirrors (Fuerth) ; here starch (France), there cotton (Moravia)." True, the predominance of Jews in an industrial branch often came to an end after it had been successfully opened up, and with it the group structure. But in some of them it persisted. The film industry, particularly in America, presents a typical picture of the consequences of Jewish industrial pioneering.

There remains to be mentioned one more typical feature of the social rise of Jews, viz. their influx into the liberal professions. The reasons for which the learned professions proved specially attractive to progressive Jews in Central and Western Europe, and to a minor degree also in Eastern Europe, are not far to seek. The traditional intellectual inclinations of the Jews found their " Europeanised " expression in this choice. The university played the part of a secularised " Jeshivah ". The careers of civil service and university teaching, however, being still frequently closed to Jews, the liberal professions became the most suitable field for their activities. Even within the liberal professions most Jews chose medicine or the laws, for which they were particularly suited by traditions of long standing. Their connection with medicine goes back to the Middle Ages, when Jewish doctors were in high repute. And the age-long study of the Talmudic law had created in them an inclination as well as a special gift for legal matters. Moreover, the Jews found it preferable to depend rather on their own achievements and the favour of an unorganised public than on appointments by the State or private business where some degree of discrimination had always to be reckoned with. They may also have preferred these professions on account of the fact that the Jews are generally more interested in human beings than in machines.[74]

We have thus established two facts with regard to the social structure of the Jewish community : first, that the Jews tend to preserve their group character even after their formal emancipation ; secondly, that—except for those who entered the liberal professions—they tend to concentrate in those spheres which are generally held in low esteem by public opinion. Both facts make it easier for us to understand why the Jewish group should be singled out as an object of group hostility.

It need hardly be mentioned that this description of the economic structure of the Jewish group in no way claims to be complete and exact. Its purpose was solely to bring into relief certain basic facts bearing on anti-Semitism. Some of these facts, of course, do not apply to the Jewish groups in all countries. To give only one instance, there is not a predominance of Jews in the liberal professions in England. But in England we find, so to speak, as "compensation" for this missing group characteristic, a particularly one-sided urbanisation and a relatively early stage of assimilation as far as the bulk of the Ashkenazic Jews is concerned, corresponding to their comparatively recent immigration. If, in the course of time, one or the other group characteristic should entirely disappear without re-emerging on a higher level, English Jews will have achieved a quicker and smoother normalisation than has generally fallen to the lot of Jewry. But this is only a theoretical possibility, and in war and post-war times, with their tendency to emphasise rather than to mitigate group tensions, it is scarcely even so much.

The list of Jewish group characteristics which tend to create anti-Semitism is, however, not yet concluded. In summing them up we shall have to draw attention to one factor which includes all those mentioned above but adds to them a special significance.

The average Jew is so familiar with his group that he is inclined to regard all its different traits as forming a coherent and intelligible picture. He has a more or less vague idea of Jewish history and the Jewish religion by which, he thinks, the Dispersion is sufficiently explained, and if he ever starts to question, habit and this kind of knowledge will readily yield a satisfactory answer. It is different with the Gentile who sees Jewry from outside. He probably first comes across the Jew during his school-days. The Jewish child belongs then to the close community of the school, but is still distinguished from his schoolmates by a number of differences. These may vary considerably. They may consist in different lessons in religion, in different festivals, but also in the Jewish child's being forbidden to write or play cricket on the Sabbath day. These differences, according to their scope and to his own sensibility, may appear to the Gentile child like a thick, impenetrable wall between him and the Jewish child or like nothing more than a thin transparent veil. They will, however, never cease to be felt in some degree so long as the Jewish child belongs in any sense to his own group and returns to his own orbit out of school hours. The paradox of simultaneous nearness and distance is one which we shall find in many other spheres. In every single one and in them all together there exists an inexplicable remainder, something mysterious and uncanny. In a reply to Erich Kahler,[75] Carl Mayer [76] rightly points out that " the complete loss of understanding by the modern mind of the phenomenon of the Jews " is " one of the main causes if not *the* main cause of modern anti-Judaism ". It is indeed characteristic of the Jewish situation and all its concomitants that the more its details become known to an outsider, the more difficult it becomes for him to understand them.[77]

Just as the Jewish child appears to his Gentile class-mates equal and yet unequal, so the Jewish adult appears to his Gentile fellow citizens equal and yet unequal. The proportions between his equality and his inequality vary widely in the different countries, so for the sake of simplicity we will limit our remarks to Germany, on which in any case our interest is focussed. Conditions in Germany were typical of those of other Jewish communities in a progressive state of assimilation, and, in fact, the problem there differed only in degree from what it was even in Poland and America.

In Germany, through a century of assimilation, the Jew had become very like the non-Jew. While some differences of type remained,[78] the average Jewish individual had many traits in common with the Gentile individual of the same vocational and educational sphere. The overwhelming majority of the German Jews knew no other national loyalty than that to Germany. Their feelings of solidarity with the Jews of other countries and their stronger or weaker allegiance to Palestine did not alter that in the least. Nevertheless, the anti-Semites alleged a contradiction between these loyalties. They reproached the Jews on the ground that their maintenance of international Jewish ties could not be combined with truly " national " feelings towards Germany. To make this argument conclusive they interpreted the term " national " in such a way as to make it inapplicable to the Jews. They artificially narrowed the concepts of " Volk " and " Volkstum ", identified the word " völkisch " with anti-Semitic, defined " nation " in a racial

53

sense, and brought out finally the ill-begotten term " Aryan "
—all this with a view to arriving at a principle of homogeneity
such as would not include the Jews. No wonder that these
terms lost themselves more and more in vagueness and
mysticism. Indeed no one with proper regard for facts could
exclude the German Jews from the German nation. Nevertheless, this kind of argument contributed to throw doubts on the
national loyalty even of the German Jews. Where the Jews are
less assimilated these doubts seem to be even more justified.
The Jew is a newcomer or the descendant of newcomers. He
either does not speak the language of the country or he speaks
it with a foreign accent. He looks different, has other customs
and habits than the majority of the inhabitants, but is himself
one of them. He is a citizen, belongs to the town community,
claims the corresponding rights, and gradually develops a
genuine patriotism.

But these are not the only riddles which the Jewish group
sets for the Gentile observer. Nearly all the above-mentioned
features, which rendered the Jewish group especially exposed to
attack, contain elements of paradox. According to the medieval
classification of estates which still lingers in the public mind,
the Jew represented the lowest estate. But he has risen and
holds some of the prominent places in society. The Jew is
everywhere, but he is nowhere at home—so, at any rate, maintains the hostile propaganda which aims at making the public
aware of all these paradoxes. The Jew believes in the same God
as the Christian, but he is separated by an abyss from him
precisely in the religious sphere. Christ was a Jew, he lived and
taught among the Jews; but the Jews crucified him. To be a
Jew means mainly to adhere to a special religious creed; but
the Jews fill the ranks of the agnostics. The Jews are considered
second rate, they are not admitted to intimate circles of friends;
but they think of themselves as God's Chosen People. In the
face of considerable opposition they strive to get themselves
accepted by the Gentiles; yet at the same time they hold themselves aloof and persist in a voluntary isolation. The Jews are
rich, they love money; but they produce socialist leaders who
aim at abolishing capitalism. The Jews are extremists, they
are prominent in progressive movements; but in the Jewish
sphere they adhere to many taboos, obviously out of date, and
conserve strange customs, thousands of years old.

All these contradictions exist. But they exist only with

54

regard to Jewry as a whole, very rarely in the same individual. The key to these contradictions lies in the fact that the emancipated Jews form a community only in a very restricted sense. They are in the middle of a process of differentiation which has taken all the various lines mentioned above. In reality, all the contradictions derive from the one fact that the Jewish group is rapidly changing and disintegrating. From without, however, it is still regarded as a whole and a much higher degree of cohesion is assumed in it than actually exists. This mistake is partly due to the desire of the ordinary man for neat categories which can save him the trouble of examining the facts too closely. The Jewish group, moreover, suffers not only from the ordinary consequences of this tendency to generalisation, viz. that the mistakes of single individuals are blamed on the community. There are other people who are well aware of the obvious differences within the group, but do not infer from them that the group character is gradually dissolving and that the individual is entirely free to go his own way. They rather draw the conclusion that under the surface of seeming divergencies there is still a secret unity of aim, a conspiracy directing a drama of world-wide scope with cunningly assigned parts.

Thus from the wrong way of generalising, which is greatly encouraged by propaganda, there results a lack of understanding for the Jew's actions. From the lack of understanding follows a feeling of uneasiness in the face of something mysteriously incomprehensible, and from this follows eventually a readiness to accept any explanation however improbable. A similar feeling of uneasiness will in many more instances be found to be at the back of a willingness to accept all sorts of fallacies.

Generally speaking, the growing inconspicuousness of the Jews largely contributed to their acceptance by the Gentiles as part of the general community in normal times. It must, however, be pointed out that in certain unfavourable circumstances this growing similarity may turn into an element of positive danger. It is true that this artificial transformation of normal neighbourly relations into a seeming anomaly depends on circumstances. In a period of general bewilderment, if fervent anti-Semitic agitation gains hold of credulous, unstable minds, the Jewish neighbour who has hitherto been taken for granted may suddenly appear in a new and weird light.

55

In a study of " The Uncanny " [79] Freud expresses the following idea on the origin of the uncanny feeling. There are certain supranatural things such as the omnipotence of thought, a secret power of doing evil, the return of the dead, etc., in which our primitive ancestors believed in bygone times. Later on, with the growth of a superior insight, these beliefs were discarded as superstitions. But fundamentally people have never felt quite secure in their new conviction, and as soon as something happens which seems to corroborate their old beliefs they have the feeling of something " uncanny ". That something very similar applies to the Jewish problem is evident from the researches of Joshua Trachtenberg. In his work, *The Devil and the Jews*,[80] he presents abundant material to prove that in the Middle Ages the Jew was considered the devil incarnate. This belief has in modern times been banished by enlightenment and daily intercourse. But in cognition as in psychological repression, stages which have been overcome have a tendency to re-emerge.[81] When, as in the present case, they are reawakened by an intense anti-Semitic propaganda, the feeling of the " uncanny " is aroused, just as when a gipsy makes a child " ill " by her " evil eye ", or when a dead person is thought to have been encountered. The outworn superstition which has been driven back into the subconscious reasserts itself. And precisely because people were so certain that it was a superstition, because the Jewish neighbour spoke, dressed, and behaved exactly like themselves, they feel something " uncanny ". They cannot help shuddering at the cunning and deceitfulness of the devil if they realise that harmless old neighbour Cohen has yet something to do with him—whether his devilishness reveals itself in rapacity or plotting for revolution or world conquest or similar infamous ways.

This process, however, will be set in motion only in exceptional cases. Generally, we hold to our conviction that daily intercourse will much more frequently produce some kind of immunity from anti-Semitic phantasies. On the other hand, the human mind is sufficiently complicated to allow many stages between total immunity and total acceptance of the Jewish legend. When the judgment is thrown off its balance, as, *e.g.*, in mass meetings or in party training courses of the National Socialist brand, bewildering doubts may emerge with regard to the mental picture of the Jew previously formed. These may be followed by some part of the psychological

56

process described by Freud, leading to a renewed suspicion or even to revival of the old superstition.[82]

Having thus explained why the Jewish group is particularly liable to draw upon itself the subjective elements in group antagonism, *i.e.* latent hostility and aggressiveness, we have now to discuss a social phenomenon which is especially apt to generate such subjective elements, viz. the crisis.

A few words may here be added on the relationship between sociology and psychology. The question how far psychological generalisations can be derived from a socio-economic group situation has attracted much attention of late. There is among sociologists and psychologists a widespread desire for co-operation, but so far only few successful attempts have been made in this direction. Even so interesting a symposium as the special issue on the problem of the *American Journal of Sociology* [83] testifies rather to the reluctance of students to have their own methods interfered with from outside than to their willingness to accept assistance. Particularly, psychologists seem rarely inclined to have their interest in individual cases diverted by social generalisations. A remarkable exception is Karen Horney [84] who has explored the factors inherent in a certain cultural pattern which affect all members of a group equally. Franz Alexander [85] makes a useful incursion into the marginal territory between sociology and psychology by pointing out that despite all individual differences an equal social situation of, for instance, all employees, all employers, all farmers, does result in common psychological traits in the people belonging to the same section. Similarly, Erich Fromm [86] distinguishes between "individual" and "social" character, which he thus defines : " The social character comprises only a selection of traits, the essential nucleus of the character structure of most members of a group which has developed as the result of the basic experiences and mode of life common to that group." [87] This distinction between a general and an individual psychological sphere is, however, only a beginning. It can yield valuable results when it is shown in what way the relation between the two spheres changes not only from individual to individual but from group to group, from epoch to epoch, and from civilisation to civilisation. It may be assumed, *e.g.*, that the general sphere will be relatively extensive in periods of cultural conformity, whether primitive, religious, or post-rational mass-conformity. It will be equally large in groups which are economically hard pressed, and larger in " average " people than in intellectuals. The general sphere will widen furthermore,—always at the cost of the individual sphere—when people are highly excited by common experiences. It will be larger in times of need, but will yield ground to individual differentiation when a greater affluence and the absence of strong emotions allow more choice to the individual in the shaping of his own life. To the same extent as the general sphere enlarges, the application of group psychology in the sense of a generalising psychology of its typical members will be more fruitful. This must be distinguished from a psychology of the typical changes an individual undergoes through association with other individuals in a crowd, an amorphous mass or an ordered one, or in an organised society. Neither is it concerned with the psychology of the so-called social or group-mind.[88]

While the aggressiveness mentioned above was generated mainly by the particular situation of the individual in his family and his personal fate, the advent of a crisis gives rise to aggressiveness in the general psychological sphere. We speak of a social crisis when social relations in one or several fields become so unbalanced that their breakdown seems imminent, or when, while the danger of a breakdown is distant, there is a general slowing-down of normal social functions. In such a situation the general sphere increases in importance. It increases within each single individual and it comprises a larger number of individuals. The psychic energy of every individual is drawn upon to a higher degree than in normal times by the critical events which affect them all. To mention one example : a clerk normally spends ten hours on his work, his journeys to and from work, and his meals. He spends eight hours in sleeping and during six hours he can peacefully enjoy his individual hobbies. His work has become routine and makes no considerable demands on his intellect or emotions, which can therefore be devoted with comparative vigour to his private affairs. As soon, however, as he loses his employment in a crisis, his whole mind is filled with anxiety to find another job. True, he gains time in a formal sense, but only in ex-tremely favourable circumstances will he be able to use this time for relaxation. Rather will it be taken up by the search for a new occupation, by occasional jobs, and by work in the household by which he tries to reduce his expenses. The decisive fact is, however, that his whole thinking and feeling will be centred on his unemployment, that is to say, it will follow exactly the same course as that of all his unemployed fellows. With the people who are still in employment the fear of losing it will occupy an abnormally large place in their thoughts. In a word, people suffering from their economic situation to an extraordinarily high degree will be more affected by it or, for that matter, by general affairs, and concern with these will use up a larger amount of their strength than it will of people who are settled peacefully and satisfactorily in their jobs. Exactly the same widening of the " general sphere " can be observed with a shopkeeper or a manufacturer worried by stagnation of trade.

But not only does the " general sphere " enlarge itself in every individual during a crisis, a wider circle of persons is affected by it. This does not imply that every member of this wider circle will at once share all the traits that have just been described as the result of unemployment. While the unemployed clerk, the unemployed worker, and the merchant who cannot sell his goods suffer from certain similar economic troubles, each group has in addition certain special troubles of its own. Common to all, however, is an increased feeling of insecurity and fear, and as a result an increased need for self-assertion and for an outlet for their grievances. The consequence is that group rivalries which, as has been shown, afford a ready outlet for both will acquire special importance during a crisis. For these rivalries the peculiarities of the Jewish group provide a specially suitable lightning-conductor. So true is this that the strength of anti-Semitism in any given period may serve as a reliable indication of the extent of social disintegration in the society affected—especially in one where the objective tensions caused originally by the Jewish group have almost entirely disappeared, so that the remaining antagonism reflects almost entirely subjective frustrations.[89]

The results of the above enquiry can thus be summarised : (1) there is a psychological sphere which is common to all members of a social group ; (2) this general sphere becomes enlarged in times of crisis, both in depth and breadth ; (3) the general sphere is in times of crisis predominantly the seat of grievances generating the need of self-assertion and aggression ; (4) this need, like the one aroused by personal frustrations, tends to seek its fulfilment by way of group tensions, preferably anti-Semitism ; (5) where the crisis originates in conditions unconnected with the Jews, that is to say, in practically all modern social crises, the resentments worked off through the Jewish-Gentile group relation must be classified as " subjective " or " sham " reasons of anti-Semitism.

During the different periods of the history of emancipation in Germany, " objective " and " subjective " reasons were intermingled in varying proportions and interacted in different ways. Not even in the early period, that is to say, at a time when the newly emancipated Jews presented a considerable social problem through their dissimilarity, did this objective social phenomenon suffice to arouse an anti-Semitic movement. For this purpose it had always to be reinforced by other factors, notably economic, and in most cases the subjective factors had to be deliberately directed by political agitation into the channel of group antagonism. Neither was the purpose of this anti-Semitic propaganda restricted to the Jewish question. Almost every anti-Semitic propagandist and writer pursued other political ends apart from anti-Semitism, which seemed to him to be more attainable in combination with anti-Semitism. In fact, even for the declared anti-Semite the Jewish question was usually not sufficient to make up his whole political programme. Thus we find in the motives of the political agitator, who contributes so largely to the development of the anti-Semitic movement, an element wholly unconnected with the Jewish question.

These generalisations will be made clearer by an examination of some characteristic episodes in German anti-Semitism with a view to determining the parts played by " objective " and " subjective " elements.

Anti-Semitism in the period of counter-emancipation, between 1815 and 1819, opposes the Jews as forming " a State within the State ".[90] The philosopher Jacob Fries [91] points out that the Jews are (1) a nationality of their own, (2) a political association, (3) a religious party, (4) a caste of hawkers and hucksters. The philosopher J. G. Fichte, who first coined the phrase that the Jews are a State within the State, does not bring this accusation against the Jews alone. He reproaches other communities, especially the military, in the same way and justifies at the same time the existence of such " States within the State " from the point of view of Natural Law.[92] But there is no doubt that the existence of a community which showed some characteristics of a State and, because of them, did not readily adapt itself to the real State, was generally felt as disturbing and, indeed, constituted a social problem. A second disturbance was caused by the fact that the majority of the Jews were at that time hawkers and hucksters with what appeared to be an alien, often a lower, economic morality.[93] Both facts seemed to conflict with the equal citizenship granted before the War of Liberation and thus created the nucleus of the objective Jewish question of the time. Likewise the closer contact with the strict observants of an alien religion was fraught with considerable difficulties.[94]

Subjective tensions were created in this period by the general disillusionment about the wars which, although they had ended victoriously, had not brought freedom and unity. Moreover, the years 1816 and 1817 were years of scarcity and high prices, and after a stoppage in business in 1819, a depression set in which Professor Werner Sombart describes as ". . . the first big crash in the 19th century ".[95]

The exploitation of anti-Semitism for other political purposes is less clearly discernible at that time than it became later on. The leading anti-Semites belonged to all parties. Fichte was a Liberal revolutionary, Professor of Theology Paulus in Heidelberg was also a Liberal, Fries a romanticist. They all were united only by the national idea which at that time inspired equally the protagonists of popular sovereignty and of the romantic idea of the " Volkstum ". The national ideal, however, lent itself particularly to a combination with anti-Semitism. At this stage the main connection lay in the fact that the emancipation of the Jews appeared to be some relic of French domination, because, apart from the coincidence in time, the association between its principle and the maxims of the French Revolution was manifest.

The anti-Semitic writings of that time contain all these elements combined into ideologies of various shades. But everywhere the chief stress is laid on the actual condition of the Jews. True, the critics reveal by their impatience that they are largely swayed by passion. They do not want to wait until the development set in motion by the emancipation has remedied the existing defects. No less does the vehemence of their attacks, which frequently overstep the mark, testify to their own lack of detachment, while at the same time it provides the readers with a welcome outlet for their subjective grievances. But, on the whole, the anti-Semitism of the early 19th century is based essentially on the objective tensions between the Jewish group and the Gentile society. This manifests itself also in the sporadic anti-Jewish riots of 1819, called the " Hep-Hep " movement. Its origin in Frankonia, where the Jews were mostly agricultural middlemen, suggests that, apart from all kinds of " sham " reasons, " genuine " reasons for antagonism between a primarily agrarian population and the Jews, whose function appeared both indispensable and detestable, played their part.

We still find both these elements, if in widely different proportion, in the Stoecker movement, sixty years later. What remains of the objective Jewish question in the years of the foundation of the Reich is no longer a tension created by a " State within the State ", the characteristics of the Jews which gave rise to that charge having disappeared almost completely. A considerably slighter group problem consists rather in the ill-proportioned distribution of the Jews in the occupational sphere, notably by their relative prominence in finance, commerce, and the Press. In addition, their still uncompleted emancipation, which continues to be obstructed by the administration, accounts for the Jews' one-sided allegiance to political Liberalism. Both facts give rise to objective tensions, the strength of which can, however, not be compared with that prevailing at the beginning of emancipation. All the more numerous are tensions of a subjective origin. They are generated by the rapid progress of industry from which the craftsmen especially suffer. When in 1873 a bank crash puts an end to the prosperity brought about by the French war-indemnity, a severe crisis breaks out. Years of economic depression follow.

The brand of anti-Semitism introduced by Court Preacher Adolf Stoecker reflects clearly both objective and subjective tensions. His agitation against the Jews is centred in the accusation that they dominate finance and the Press. He finds his followers, whom he seeks in vain among the workmen, in the ranks of the lower middle-class, so that he feels himself compelled to change the name of his party from Christian-Social Workers Party into Christian Social Party. Those who persuaded him to do so pointed out that the " number of workers in the Party is not more than from 150 to 200 ".[96] Thus it is not the workers who flock to him, for though they too suffer from capitalism they see in it also their opportunity.

62

It is rather the petty bourgeois who fly before the menacing trend of capitalist development into a false interpretation of its economic laws—an interpretation which teaches them to attack the concrete Jew instead of the abstract capital.

The Stoecker episode is another clear proof that anti-Semitism frequently serves only as a means to an end. Originally Stoecker had set out to fight the Social Democratic Party. Only after this adversary had been rendered harmless by the Anti-Socialist laws of 1878, and when he became aware of some anti-Jewish undercurrent in his meetings, did he commence to extend his campaign to the Jews.[97] There was all the more reason for this since his chief opponents were henceforth the Liberals, who were led in the Reichstag by the Jews Lasker and Bamberger. As a weapon in the battle against Liberalism, and only as such, anti-Semitism at that time enjoyed even the cautious and indirect assistance of the Bismarck Government.

Anti-Semitism in itself may now and then form the motive for the public activities of a fanatic. But wherever the Jewish question is made into a major political issue it serves in most cases as a smoke-screen. This fact diminishes its significance as a serious problem. But it brings into relief the unpleasant fact that the exploitation of the Jewish question for directing latent grievances into the desired channels seems nearly always successful. The success seems to depend on the sum total of " genuine " and " sham " motives existing in a given period.

What was the proportion of both in National Socialist anti-Semitism ? As described in greater detail in Chapter IV of this study,* only small residues of an objective Jewish question existed in Germany in the 20th century. A certain unequal distribution in the occupational, local, and political spheres persisted. But in itself this would not have been sufficient to generate a sharp mass anti-Semitism. Neither would the tensions resulting from the activities of some Jewish participants in the post-war revolutions and the first appearance of Jews in the higher civil service, which had been closed to them before but was opened by the Weimar Republic. Conversely, more weight than ever attached at that time to both the other factors, the subjective frustrations originating from the post-war crisis, and the deliberate utilisation of anti-Semitism for other political aims, for the overthrow of the Weimar Republic and the Nazis' own accession to power.

* Cf. Chapter IV, " The Catastrophe ".

It would thus seem that, in the course of the 19th century, the objective social divergence produced by the existence side by side of the Gentile majority and the Jewish minority in Germany diminished steadily. But, at the time, both chronic and acute collective discontents originating from other sources increased. Political leaders, recognising the usefulness of the anti-Semitic device, managed with remarkable success to direct these widespread grievances into the river-bed of Jewish-Gentile group antagonism, ever narrowing, but still serviceable.

II

THE EPOCH

WE HAVE, in the previous chapter, placed the objective and the subjective reasons for anti-Semitism in their proper perspective. In this chapter we shall try to answer the question why the epoch of emancipation provided a particularly fertile breeding-ground for the latter. For this purpose we shall briefly renew the economic and spiritual development of the 19th century, showing how it was intertwined with a great increase of population and the political emancipation of the masses, and how it finally entered into a phase in which the achievements of civilisation could be seriously threatened by any disruptive socio-economic crisis.

Among the causes leading to the destruction of the German Jews by National Socialism, anti-Semitism and the Jewish problem play only a subordinate part. The truth of this statement, which at first sounds paradoxical, will become apparent from an analysis of the real causes accounting for the Nazi movement. Nor can the rise of the Nazi movement be explained merely as the consequence of the German post-war crisis or of the endeavour of monopoly capitalism to defend itself against organised labour. These factors simply brought to a head a development which had long been in preparation.

It was a fateful coincidence that the emancipation of the Jews took place within the framework of a competitive society. This was, of course, no mere accident, since the way towards emancipation was prepared by the liberal spirit of the age which, in turn, was closely interwoven with the liberal economy. None the less, this dependence of the liberation of the Jews on a period of this particular character made it precarious and gives it a certain tragic quality. Let us imagine for a moment that the Jews had been emancipated into a non-competitive economy, say that of the medieval trade-corporations. Let us suppose that the guilds had agreed to admit Jewish masters and journeymen with equal rights. Let us furthermore suppose that in spite of a certain prepossession on the part of the Jews for competitive methods, carried over by them from the period of their exclusion, the new arrangement had, after a period of transition, worked smoothly. In the new situation thus created the Jewish members of the guilds would have had their guaranteed living. On the other hand, any attempt on their part to increase their income at the cost of their fellow masters by a breach of regulations would have led to their immediate exclusion and loss of livelihood. Thus the probability of clashes in the economic field would have been considerably reduced.

Nor would this have been the only favourable effect. A static economy which keeps people in rigidly defined spheres but provides them with an adequate livelihood makes them feel secure. It certainly does not prevent private misfortune and it also makes people feel " corporation-conscious ", that is to say, it inspires them with a pride in their own and a contempt for other corporations which may provide pretexts for quarrels totally unconnected with economic interests. Anyhow, in a healthy static economy economic relations as such do not as a rule give rise to vehement grievances. There is no increase of frustrations during a crisis, since in such an economy crises do not occur. Allowing a short time for adjustment, the emancipated Jew might in such circumstances have been accepted with relatively little opposition.

With this imaginary—and impossible—picture in our minds we can see that Jewish emancipation actually took place in far less favourable circumstances. All over Western and Central Europe the 19th century was a period of rapid economic progress. True, the " Industrial Revolution " in England had taken place in the late 18th century, and its equivalent in Germany happened as late as the second half of the 19th. But in spite of this considerable interval, there is this much in common to all the countries concerned that during the period of emancipation economic evolution towards industrialism is proceeding at considerable speed. Transition from manual work to machine work involves a comprehensive rearrangement of economic conditions, rightly called by the English a Revolution. For a static economy a dynamic is substituted.[98] The member of the craft guild no longer has a secure living, guaranteed by tradition and right, and the legislation affecting him is revised in favour of free competition.[99] This portends the struggle of all against all. It involves the abolition of laws which hitherto have not only restricted but also protected economic life. Its effect is that henceforth people will not strive for a living only but for profit. Custom will be replaced by reason, tradition by progress, quality by saleability. Free competition transforms a quiet and secure life into continuous movement, rivalry, haste, and insecurity. Man no longer rests under the peaceful guardianship of ancient inherited rules, nor in the familiar association with his fellow craftsmen. He has emerged from the narrow path assigned to him. He stands alone, surrounded by rivals.[100]

But free competition not only loosens the individual from the ties of a protecting community, it acts equally as an emancipator of economy itself. Economic forces themselves are freed from legislatory fetters and left to their own laws. These economic laws, for reasons which need not be discussed here, lead to trade cycles, *i.e.* to alternations of periods of prosperity with periods of depression. In terms of the labour market this means that periods of high demand for labour alternate with periods of excessive supply.

There are thus two economic hardships peculiar to the industrial age. First, there is the necessity imposed on the individual of adapting himself to an economy in continuous movement, where standing still means going back. The necessity of keeping pace with an increasing number of competitors and of prevailing against them compels business men continually to change, extend, and accelerate the methods of production and sale.[101] But even if the free entrepreneur successfully overcomes such problems of individual competition, he is, secondly, not safe from relapses and possibly from a complete loss of his livelihood. He is still exposed to the danger of business stoppages which threaten the successful business man no less than his unsuccessful rival—and sometimes even more, because he has taken greater risks.

This is roughly the situation of the upper strata of business men, merchants and industrialists, whose difficulties, however, are largely compensated by the chances of profit which they bring with them. The picture grows less favourable when the plight of those sections is considered to which the new economy holds out fewer advantages. Those craftsmen who do not manage to adapt themselves to the technical advance have to compete not only with men in like case but also with the machine. For them the struggle is frequently hopeless, since their economic failure is due not to individual shortcomings but to the very methods of their production. The same holds good for many proprietors of small undertakings, both in the field of production and distribution.

The workers are subject to their own special frustrations in an industrial society. They are both the basis and the ever-renewed product of industrial economy. They have no property and are therefore exposed without protection to the harshness of the system. For this reason, however, they were the first to abandon the doubtful or even illusory advantages of free competition. They broke through the principles of free economy, and combined in trade unions. Nevertheless they remained under the continuous threat of unemployment, which the trade unions were unable to avert. That, in spite of their economic weakness and their general lack of education, they rarely succumbed to the temptation to vent their grievances on the Jews by joining the ranks of political anti-Semitism is the more remarkable since capitalism—the apparent cause of their sufferings—was not infrequently personified for them by a Jewish employer or merchant.*

Finally, industrial capitalism has multiplied the difficulties of agriculture. On this as on the crafts the whole structure of the new economy—or, more correctly, of the new economic policy—presses very hard. Generally speaking, the demand for agricultural products is increased with the economic expansion. But the industrialists, with their increasing power and growing organisation, do not allow the farmers to enjoy for long the fruits of this development. They aim at keeping wages and, for that matter, the prices of agricultural products at as low a level as possible. They prefer cheap foreign products to dear home-grown ones and therefore urge the abolition of import duties. In Germany this controversy was, after a period of free trade, settled for the time being in favour of agriculture through Bismarck's adoption of protective tariffs in 1878; but it was not yet laid to rest. Bismarck's successor restricted the protective policy, and, apart from this, agriculture had to struggle continuously against chronic ills such as debts, the subdivision of holdings, out-of-date methods of production, etc.[102] Big landowners, of course, are affected by this struggle in a different way from farmers. But, in spite of many internal

* Cf. pp. 96 *seq.*

68

differences, both these classes are agreed in regarding themselves as the stepchildren of industrial economy. It was commonly said in Germany that " farmers always grumbled ". It needs stressing that agricultural circles were increasingly compelled to base their arguments in favour of protective tariffs not on economic but on military considerations. They pointed out that, in case of war, Germany would need an agriculture of her own, and that she must therefore keep it going even at a loss, so that she should be able to make use of it if the necessity arose.

This short review of the situation of the essential occupations in the industrial period purposely gives a one-sided picture. It ignores the enormous economic advance made by every single group in itself, the unheard-of growth of material wealth, the progress in material well-being of the lower sections of the population. As we are primarily concerned here with the origin of collective discontent, it has seemed to us necessary to emphasise the drawbacks at the cost of which this economic advance was achieved. Since these cannot be measured by objective standards, as can the growth of wealth, the increase of population, or the progress in technology, they are generally disregarded. Histories of the period are full of admiration for its momentous achievements—and they are right in so far as in its course man has advanced in freedom, wealth, and, on the whole, also in bodily health, apart from the havoc wrought by the shocking labour conditions which marked its inception. These achievements are so outstanding that sentimental lamentations for the " good old days " are utterly out of place. It is, however, quite a different question whether the new time has made man happier. Happiness, as we have said, cannot be measured. But if we take into account the widespread insecurity which the advance brought with it [103] and the nervous strain caused by the increasing complexity of life,[104] we shall find reason to doubt whether the technical progress was accompanied by a corresponding growth in human happiness.

It is not therefore surprising that capitalism has, on the whole, failed to win the sympathy of the epoch it shaped by such enormous efforts. In his apology for capitalism—a work with an element of tragedy, because in spite of the vitality remaining to capitalism the author has no faith in its future— Professor Joseph Schumpeter [105] remarks that " emotional attachment to the social order " it has created is " the very thing capitalism is constitutionally unable to produce ".[106]

He speaks of an " atmosphere of almost universal hostility " which capitalism has created towards its own social order,[107] and declares the " condemnation of capitalism and · all its works " as " almost a requirement of the etiquette of discussion ".[108] Professor Schumpeter's attitude is best characterised by his formula " creative destruction ", which he declares to be " the essential fact about capitalism ".[109] Professor Werner Sombart speaks similarly of capitalism, which he otherwise praises enthusiastically, as a " witches' sabbath " which " Mankind has produced since the beginning of the 19th century",[110] or as a " giant running unchecked through the land " " throwing down everything that stands in his way ". He advises us to take protective measures against it as against a conflagration, to provide fire-buckets, to protect life and limb.[111] He repeatedly mentions as a characteristic of capitalism that it drives people to an ever-increasing effort, that it incites " modern economic man to increase his exertions extensively and intensively up to the limits of human possibility " [112] He speaks of " people working to madness ", so that they are " under the continual threat of breaking down with exhaustion ".[113]

These two critics are typical of many others. Their judgments are significant because they are not the outcome of an anti-capitalist bias, at any rate not of a conscious one. They carry more conviction than socialist condemnations, of which, of course, there is no lack. The fact that these two are fully aware of the achievements of capitalism and nevertheless feel forced to pass so severe a judgment upon it is particularly strong evidence of the inner disharmonies of the system. What lends even more force to their arguments from the point of view of this study is the fact that it is the human sphere where they discover that the greatest harm is done. They do not deny that capitalism opens up tremendous new opportunities for economic progress, but the price which has to be paid for them in psychological strain appears too high. Life has become rich and many-sided, yet affluence and variety have not made it easier but more difficult. Town life, for instance, with its abundance of opportunities and entertainments and with its breathless speed has attracted ever more people from the healthy rural districts.

Life in the industrial age is strenuous and nerve-racking for the business man even when he is doing well. It grows more complicated and nerve-racking with every stoppage and depression. Life is full of frustration and disappointment for the craftsman and small trader, for the farmer and peasant even in good times. The difficulties grow desperate in a crisis. Life is full of monotonous drudgery for the wage-earner, who even in times of full employment laboriously drags out his existence at subsistence level. A prolonged period of unemployment spells for him material and moral ruin. No doubt there were in the 19th and early 20th centuries periods of prosperity from which all groups profited, *e.g.*, during the 1850's [114] and the famous " Founder-boom " in Germany after the conclusion of the Franco-Prussian War in 1871. In the first case, however, the breakdown followed in 1857, after the collapse of American railroad securities,[115] and in the second as early as 1873, after a bank crash in Vienna. Between 1873 and 1901 there were three more waves of reverses followed by recoveries.[116] Thus, fear of another crash poisoned all satisfaction in the economic success of the moment.

The above considerations go half-way to answer the question why the 19th century was such a fertile breeding-ground for collective frustrations or, for that matter, for " sham reasons " of anti-Semitism. Where, as Milton Steinberg puts it,[117] " the hand of each man is against his brother ", where " every advance on the part of one individual is possible only at the expense of another ", latent hostility is bound to increase everywhere. Where in such circumstances people feel the immediate competition of Jews, as is the case with the lower and middle bourgeoisie and the intellectuals, they become increasingly attracted by theories which open up a prospect of getting rid of the whole group of competitors at one stroke. This wish, it is true, might be fulfilled by the removal of any group of competitors. It aims at the competition, not at the Jews. The fact, however, that the Jews are " alien " or " different ", or rather that they can still successfully be presented as such, makes it suddenly appear possible that the latent wish might be fulfilled. It even provides an " idealistic " rationalisation of crudely egoistic motives.

The cry of " Jewish competition " has from the beginning been a kind of *leitmotiv* in the anti-Jewish campaign. In the period of early emancipation it was struck quite frankly,[118] while later on it assumed all kinds of variations. This charge roughly indicated its transformation from what has been called a

71

" genuine " into a " sham " element of anti-Semitism. That is to say, where competition with aliens is concerned, or where the competitors use unfair or untraditional methods,[119] legitimate opposition may result. The native group, or the group applying fair or traditional methods, will justly try to get rid of the competitors. When, however, as was the case with the emancipated Jews, both the alien characteristics and the unfair or untraditional methods simultaneously disappear, the removal of the competitors is demanded with an increasingly bad conscience. The allegations that the competitors, or part of them, are still foreigners, that they still use unfair methods, will be felt to be insufficient; and people will talk of the alien group's " excessive influence ", " predominance ", or " control " in order the better to base their opposition on apparently objective reasons. They will finally resort to all kinds of rationalisations and slogans in order to gloss over the economic motive which, however, will still appear plainly enough through the disguise.

From this it is clear that every newly emancipated or immigrant group within a competitive society has to reckon with certain difficulties. The Jews, however, are not any ordinary group in this respect. Their habitual occupation as middlemen as well as their exclusion from the medieval corporations gave them a long experience in competitive methods well before other people were allowed to apply them. They thus had a considerable start. One need not regard them, as Professor Sombart does,[120] as the creators of capitalism, and explain this by their religion and early history, in order to appreciate fully their outstanding contribution to the development and expansion of capitalist methods. Their very aptitude for a system which has given rise to so much hostility among men made it all the more tragic that their emancipation should coincide with, and indeed depend on, the development of that system. The Jews acted everywhere as pioneers of capitalism. They were not average competitors in that economy of which the hall-mark was *homo homini lupus*, but they were especially able, mobile, and progressive competitors. Untrammelled by the medieval tradition which they had not been allowed to share, free from sentimental ties of all kinds which continued to restrain their Gentile rivals long after capitalist views had officially prevailed, the Jews applied logically the economic principles which were now not only accepted but intrinsically required. They thus became, whether they liked it or not, the instruments of " creative destruction ", the apparent symbols of an era setting man against man and threatening whole sections with ruin. " The more Jewish ways assert themselves ", says Sombart—to quote only one passage from many others—" the more exclusively capitalist organisation is applied." And he goes on : " This Jewish mission, to promote the transition to capitalism, becomes especially manifest where it is a question of abolishing the remnants of pre-capitalist organisation, hitherto preserved, in the disintegration of the last handicrafts and in the craft-like petty trade. We can justly say that, *e.g.*, tailoring, shoemaking, joinery, the building trade owe their decline to the restless activities of Jewish business men." No wonder Sombart concludes : " For this reason a spontaneous anti-Semitism has developed in the circles of the declining craftsmen which, as is usually the case with such blind popular movements, seizes upon the concrete form (Jewry) instead of the inward kernel (capitalism) ".[121]

Life is growing more difficult. At the same time the mass of the Jews enter the social life of the wider community. Life is not growing more difficult on account of the Jews, but the persons affected by its increasing strain are at times likely to think so, because the changing conditions are not infrequently personified by Jews. True, the Jew became constantly more similar to his Gentile neighbour as far as his outward appearance, his thinking, feeling, and behaviour were concerned. He no longer spoke a foreign tongue, often had not even a distinct accent, he dressed like his neighbours, he became less and less conspicuous within the framework of society.[122] But old prejudices survived, new antipathies were born, and a general demand arose for a suitable object on which to vent the aggressiveness bred of an increasingly arduous life.

Motives of this kind were bound to reinforce each other. They were the never-failing source of latent anti-Semitism from which during the 19th and 20th centuries writers and politicians were able to draw whenever this seemed desirable for one reason or another. And this source was like the miraculous pitcher of the legend of which it was said that the more that was drawn from it, the more it yielded. So the more anti-Semitism was mobilised for political purposes, the wider did it spread. This, however, only showed how effectively propaganda managed to canalise more and more latent

73

aggressiveness, *i.e.* more and more " sham " motives of anti-Semitism, into the stream-bed of the Jewish problem. At times the anti-Semitic symbol prevailed victoriously over other symbols. If, during such periods, that part of the population which had been hardest hit by the economic development, viz. the working class, had not been under the influence of superior symbols leading them towards humanitarianism and education, anti-Semitism would very probably have found supporters there also. Things being as they were, however, the lower middle-class remained its main reservoir, because they felt themselves hopelessly squeezed between capital and labour.[123]

But important as were these material conditions, there were also spiritual factors which greatly influenced the course of emancipation. Let us suppose, for the sake of argument, that the increased complication of life which accompanied the development of industrialism had taken place in a society the foundations of which were still solidly based on a universal religious belief. This supposition is not entirely unreal, as such conditions actually obtained to a considerable extent in England. The Industrial Revolution happened here at a time when religion was still a dominant force. Professor Karl Mannheim [124] attributes great importance to this fact, which, in his view, explains why in England both the conservative and the progressive parties developed their programmes within a religious framework, so that up to the present day there has been no radical severance between progress and religion. To the same fact may, perhaps, be ascribed much of what appears moderate, fair, humane and accepted among all classes in present-day life in Britain. And, though this point should not be unduly stressed, it is worth while to ask, in passing, whether the survival of Christianity in England, not only into the period of enlightenment but beyond it into a period of post-rational paganism, may be in part due to the fortunate circumstance that here the most serious social controversy was dealt with within the framework of Christian ideas and not from the standpoint of rationalist radicalism.

On the Continent the complication of life by the Industrial Revolution coincided largely with the weakening of religious values. This spiritual process, like the economic, had actually commenced with the Renaissance, and in the 18th century in France with Voltaire and the Encyclopaedists it began to influence broader sections of the population. It is this broad influence with which this study is primarily concerned. For its purposes spiritual development is important generally only in so far as it bears on public opinion.

It may be pointed out that, generally speaking, this socio-psychological aspect of ethics makes for pessimism with regard to human progress in general. This pessimism, however, does not contradict the more optimistic view held, *e.g.*, by Professor Morris Ginsberg in his paper on " Moral Progress ".[125] Professor Ginsberg asserts that *sub specie saeculorum* a slow but steady process of moral development has taken place as far as both intellectual concepts and social institutions are concerned. It is, however, different with the reception and effect of spiritual concepts among the public. The reception by the masses of ideas and fragments of ideas is, at best, not promoted by their morality and truth. It depends essentially on their psychological appeal. Pure ethics, *e.g.*, may represent a definite moral progress as against religious ethics, but they may, nevertheless, be unable to exert as good an influence on man. Moreover, while moral progress is going on on the highest intellectual level, other philosophies of a lower moral standard, even of an amoral or anti-moral character, are continually conceived and given publicity. These are frequently more attractive in a psychological sense than more difficult and exacting systems. And the readiness with which these are accepted will increase in proportion to the size and the mental inertia of the public exposed to their influence.[126]

The deification of Reason during the French Revolution marked the transformation of Enlightenment from a philosophical concept into an element of public opinion. It was a visible sign of religious decay. The movement spread across the neighbouring German frontiers. Here, it is true, enlightenment did not march victoriously onward, unchecked. Here it met, on the contrary, its strongest adversary in romanticism, which was, among other things, professedly religious. But no religious creed remains quite the same after it has passed through a stage of enlightenment. The romantic tendency towards Roman Catholicism thus bears all the symptoms of its origin as a reaction against rationalism.

The coincidence of the emancipation of the Jews with secularisation is no more an accident of history than is its

75

coincidence with industrialism. All three phenomena are closely interrelated. The details of this relationship need not be followed here, but this much should be observed. However strongly the standard-bearers of emancipation in both camps emphasised the principle of religious tolerance, however definitely the demand for assimilation stopped short of the Jewish religion—the very possibility of this tolerance betrayed the growing religious indifference. It became possible to advocate the admission of a group differing in religion only because Christianity itself had in the eyes of its followers lost its character of uniqueness, because it had come to be regarded as one religion among others.

However surely this secularism and religious relativism prepared the way for emancipation, it is equally certain that this necessary combination involves obvious dangers. Man's release from the religious determination of his thoughts and actions made him freer and richer in opportunities in the same way as industrialism did in the economic field. It made him self-dependent and gave him the chance of shaping his life according to his own insight and sense of responsibility. But this new freedom also put a heavy load on his shoulders. The Promethean self-reliance of the revolutionary bestowed buoyancy and energy upon the genius. But for the average man irreligion and doubt spelled only increased confusion. This was felt all the more since the striving for the good and the true, that is to say for the values established by religion, long survived the actual religious guidance.[127] Thus man had to rely essentially on himself in the difficult task of overcoming those instincts which drew him in the opposite direction. He had to make his own choice among the multitude of theories presenting themselves to him. When he had just thought that he might save for himself some remnants of faith and beloved ideals in the system of Deism which, purified of mystic dross, might pass the tests of reason, then the next book borrowed from the library would perhaps inform him that it was precisely by adhering to such relics of " slave morality " that he made himself guilty of the real sin against the real god, that is against the deity of " Superman ". And if, consequently, he fell a prey to perplexity, he was in the right mood to be carried away by enthusiasm for the concrete Fatherland which, deified by the German State philosophy, revealed itself to him with all the attributes of god-like glory.

No doubt it is only in rare cases that the problem of values creates so definite a crisis in the life of the individual. On the contrary, what strikes us about the general public in the 19th and early 20th centuries is rather its lack of a clear consciousness of what was happening to its spiritual orientation. Not frequently was the individual aware of his helplessness and embarrassment among the many spiritual and moral roads open to him. Had this been the case, then he might have deliberately taken refuge in the security of one single system of thought, though knowing it to be inadequate. But even in the rare cases when men did find their way back into the protective enclosure of a unified philosophy, this philosophy often involved a step back from the ethical standard of the former religious creed. A greater part of the people, at any rate, felt immensely superior to any firm belief and enjoyed the widening horizon as an addition to their inner liberty and a first stage in the lightening of their moral obligations. With even greater numbers the confusion and complexity of values resulted mainly in the creation of a vast inner void, which only in times of national enthusiasm was filled with the national and State ideals.[128] These made far more concessions to human egoism and more and more replaced the religious standards.[129]

Life is growing more difficult—in this formula we may sum up the effects of the spiritual development as we did those of the economic development during the period of emancipation. Life is growing more difficult when I still feel under the obligation to be good but no longer know what is " good " or how I can achieve goodness. Life is growing more difficult when I want to recognise the truth but no longer know what truth is or whether, indeed, truth exists. Life is growing more difficult when no authority takes the burden of decision off my shoulders —even a slight compulsion is borne more easily than full freedom combined with aimlessness. Life is growing more difficult when I am no longer allowed to justify my deeds by reference to a generally recognised system of ideas, but when the system I have chosen is opposed by a multitude of other systems, each of them claiming equal authority. Life grows more difficult through its vaster dimensions, through its increasing intensity, through man's lack of adequate understanding. Life certainly grows more difficult.[130]

It has been emphasised above that it is the survival of the religious values which makes the absence of religious guidance more keenly felt. It must be added that the importance of the value of " truth " is even considerably enhanced after it has become secularised. In a religious culture truth is at once inherent in the religious tradition and limited through it. An unrestricted, unprejudiced striving for truth becomes possible only after religion ceases to define its beginning and its end. Through the decay of religion the 19th century becomes a century of research and unparalleled scientific progress. It spreads belief in science as a substitute for religious belief among large sections of the people. School and university education expand rapidly. The hopes attached to this development by a rationalist age are immense. People follow the schemes for popular education with expectations derived from the standards of the 18th-century educational aristocracy. They forget that the intellectual independence of a few well-to-do members of a learned *élite* cannot be attained by a mass living in straitened circumstances and sharing only a fragment of the educational facilities. The results of popular education, therefore, fall far short of the general expectations. It produces few independent minds, but crowds with just sufficient knowledge, or ignorance, to fancy themselves omniscient.

The typical product of general education is the half-educated person. The hope that ever greater numbers would perpetually approach objective truth, that they would become more and more capable of making logical inferences—this hope has not been realised. Thus Hobhouse admits with resignation that " education itself must in large measure be ranked among our failures ".[131] Bertrand Russell presents the issue as follows : " In the world as it used to be before we had compulsory education, there were two rather sharply distinguished classes in every community—one of people who had a great deal of education and one of people who had absolutely none. Now, on the other hand, there are still people who have a great deal of education . . . and the other people have some. And that is where the trouble comes in. They have just enough to have acquired susceptibility to propaganda ".[132] The most remarkable description, however, of this critical stage is given by the Dutch philosopher J. Huizinga. He draws attention to the fact that the half-educated mind has lost humility without gaining wisdom. It professes to understand life and claims the right to order it according to its lights, but it is not capable of doing so, and in its mistaken idea of its own capacity it easily falls a victim to pseudo-scientific fallacies. But let us hear Huizinga himself: " The peasant, the mariner, or the artisan of earlier times had in the sum total of his knowledge the pattern in which to view the world and its life. He knew himself unqualified to judge what lay beyond his ken (unless he were one of the professional talkers common to all times). He accepted authority knowing his judgment to be defective. In his acknowledged limitations lay his wisdom. It was the very limitation of his power of expression which, leaning on the pillars of the Holy Book and proverbial lore, often gave him style and eloquence. Modern organisation of knowledge-distribution is only too destructive of the beneficial effects of such intellectual limitations. To-day the average inhabitant of the Western hemisphere knows a little of everything. . . . Even where there is a genuine desire for knowledge and beauty, the noisy obtrusiveness of the modern cultural apparatus still makes it very difficult for the average man to escape the danger of having his notions and values forced upon him. A knowledge which is as diversified as it is superficial and an intellectual horizon which is too wide for an eye unarmed with critical equipment, must inevitably lead to a weakening of the power of judgment ". " Our time, then, is faced by the discouraging fact that two highly vaunted achievements of civilisation, universal education and modern publicity, instead of raising the level of culture, appear ultimately to produce certain symptoms of cultural devitalisation and degeneration. The masses are fed with an hitherto undreamt-of quantity of knowledge of all sorts, but there is something wrong with its assimilation. Undigested knowledge hampers judgment and stands in the way of wisdom ".[133]

It goes without saying that neither Hobhouse nor Russell in any way pleads for a discontinuance of the educational efforts. The aim of their criticism is rather to improve the methods of education and to steer it clear of the dangers besetting it. Nor is Huizinga's criticism, which results from his religious outlook, meant to shake confidence in the diffusion of education.

To explain the catastrophe of the German Jews it is necessary to survey and analyse all the factors which contributed to bring it about, even where—or, rather, just where—their analysis is bound to challenge concepts generally held in high esteem. We often hear the question asked : How could it be that " the nation of thinkers and poets " succumbed to a political system like National Socialism? To answer this question it is not sufficient to complain about the betrayal of a great heritage and to lay the blame on corruption of human nature. Rather is it necessary to examine the tendencies at work in this nation during nearly a century and a half, the changes they brought about, and the reasons why eventually those sections of the people that were most fatally affected by these changes became responsible for the nation's decisions. As such decisive tendencies have been mentioned above the factors which made life more complicated, increasing frustration and aggressiveness. Another such tendency is the broadening of education without making it adequate, so that it fosters in man the desire to understand and control the powers on which he depends, but fails to furnish him with the means of doing so.

In discussing the changes which these tendencies brought about, it will again be necessary to generalise widely. In face of the increasing differentiation which took place during the 19th century, it may seem somewhat hazardous to disregard the differences between the various strata of the population and to speak of general effects. There is, however, sufficient material available to justify this procedure.

We hear on all sides complaints about the lowering of the intellectual and moral level in recent times.[134] It is, of course, the tendency of every epoch to seek its model in the past, sometimes also in a Utopian future, and to censure its own imperfections. Yet when every allowance has been made, there remains something in the strictures passed on the 19th century that demands serious attention. This is a connection which is rightly found between the signs of decay and a social development that cannot be reversed. To us it would seem, in addition, that the universal lowering of standards might be attributed to a widespread physical and mental fatigue.

Let us once more apply the psycho-analytical theory of civilisation. According to this, civilisation demands a continuous repression of primary impulses in favour of the social standards which are taken over and internalised by the individual conscience or "super-ego". Freud states repeatedly [135] that this process demands considerable sacrifices from the individual, who is originally eager to satisfy his impulses, and that it can be maintained only through a persistent effort. No matter whether the individual, the "ego", really succeeds in driving his urges back into the unconscious, the "id", or whether he becomes a hypocrite, only pretending for the sake of material advantages that he believes in good deeds—in either case civilisation brings about an estrangement between man and the basis of his instincts. In individual cases, this leads to neurotic diseases and malformations of character. But even in so-called normal persons, social adjustment is made possible only at the expense of continual nervous strain.

If—in free application of Freud's concepts—it is asked how is this unstable equilibrium to be maintained, the reply will be : The moral standards, internalised as individual conscience or super-ego, together with the control of the ego over the unconscious or id must be strong enough to check effectively the lower human urges. When either the super-ego or the ego weakens, the balance is disturbed and the primitive instincts, which have never been annihilated but only repressed, reassert themselves.

Both these changes occurred in the period under consideration. The established values of society were vehemently assaulted. Religion was undermined by scientific and technical progress, while its standards survived in a secularised form. Although opinions may differ widely as to the correctness of Freud's view [136] that nothing is so much opposed to human nature as the command to love one's neighbour as oneself, there will be pretty general agreement that even its approximate fulfilment is extremely difficult. The strength to live up to it can only be imparted by strong emotions, such as love of, and devotion to, God and faith in Him. To realise such a commandment a much greater firmness of purpose is needed than can be attained by intellectual speculation alone. As soon as the supernatural anchorage of religion is loosened and emotional motives begin to lose their force in the process of intellectualisation, religious values are likely to lose much of their power over more primitive minds. As soon as people are taught to " understand " why mutual forbearance between neighbours is indispensable for the existence of society, they are no longer safe against " understanding " an equally scientific theory arguing that just the opposite behaviour, namely the struggle of all against all, is necessary and desirable. They will then perhaps be able to withstand the new idea for a while, possibly for a lifetime. But the claim of their consciences, which at first was unconditional, will become less absolute. Only where no doubt penetrates, only in an unchallengeable faith, does there exist a source of strength powerful enough for such an extraordinary effort. Thus the weakening of the super-ego will become a collective phenomenon in proportion as religion is secularised and intellectualised.[137]

But the ego, in its struggle with the id, has not only been weakened indirectly through the diminishing support of the super-ego, it has suffered directly from an increasing loss of its own vital energy. To put the matter in terms of the personal experience of the average adult human being, we find that the task of living up to spiritual and moral ideals is far easier the stronger and better rested we feel. When we are tired, worried, and despondent we lose interest in matters which do not concern our personal lives. Only with an effort and perhaps from mere force of habit do we keep up to our usual intellectual and moral standard. But when we fall into a state of exhaustion and helplessness all our remaining energy will be required for the task of self-conservation, and then we may not be too scrupulous about the choice of means to this end. In the competitive industrial economy, as has been shown, strain, worry, and at times exhaustion and despair, everywhere increased. It is therefore not surprising that the barriers erected against the lower urges, already weakened as we have seen above, proved in an increasing number of cases not sufficiently strong to check them.

In this condition a greater number of the impulses previously repressed or sublimated will manage to find access to the consciousness. By so doing, however, they will arouse feelings of guilt as long as the human conscience rigidly maintains its high standards. Man, therefore, when he is too weak to satisfy his conscience by renewed repression or sublimation, will be inclined to regain his peace of mind in another way. He will abandon some of his most exacting standards and replace them by others which are more tolerant to his instincts. The result will be a further weakening of his conscience, and this time in a more direct way. This is the process by which moral standards are lowered in the individual. When it takes place simultaneously in a great number of individuals it will lead to a lowering of the general standards of a civilisation.[138]

This psychological process is matched by an intellectual one. Whilst the weary masses, unable to lighten the burden of material life, seek for some relaxation, at least of their moral obligations, intellectual leaders have seen to it that this wish should meet with fulfilment. Many of them have, it is true, begun only by re-interpreting the old values. But the multitude of interpretations which all, at the same time, claim to be " the " truth, has led the way to scepticism. It has created relativism, degraded the concept of truth, and exposed its various explanations to the criticism of the many. And some of the intellectual leaders have gone further. They have thought out systems which are more plausible and at the same time more convenient than many of the older ones. Kant's exaltation of the concept of duty, for instance, or Schiller's and Humboldt's radical universalism leading almost to national self-sacrifice [139] are superseded by Fichte's nationalism, Hegel's deification of the State, and Darwin's theory of evolution. In the light of such teaching, people found it easier and more attractive to seek the meaning of life in a crude struggle for existence both in the individual and in the national sphere. They particularly rejoiced that the ideals of Reason, which was attainable only by so great a mental effort, and of the Equality of Men, which could be realised only by so great a moral effort, should be replaced by the concepts of " historical traditions " and of " nationhood ". These, after all, were achievements which they possessed and for which they were under no obligation to take further pains. Instead of visualising future ideals for which they would have to strive with ever-renewed sacrifices of natural impulses, people preferred to hang on to concepts which gratified human passivity by glorifying ideals of the past. When, as was the case with Darwin's theory, the concept was focused in the notion of evolution, it favoured the instinctive desires even more, since it proved that evolution was effected by the working of instincts. No wonder that nationalism and Darwinism joined hands and later led to the fatal combination of imperialism and racialism.

In the substitution of a passive for an active outlook on life which took place during the 19th century, romanticism played a special part. It was the prototype of a number of ideas— or, rather, compounds of ideas—which during the industrial era found ready acceptance because they served to ease the increasingly troublesome burden of social obligations. In what way romanticism answered to certain specifically German needs will be seen later.

It has often been suggested, both by Jews and non-Jews, that romanticism and anti-Semitism are closely related. Not infrequently the German romanticism of the beginning of the

18th century is actually alleged to be the origin of anti-Semitism. This is, however, an over-simplification. It is contradicted, to begin with, by the fact that the famous romantic *salons* in Berlin of Rahel Lewin, Dorothea Veit, Henriette Herz, etc., afford some of the most perfect examples of unprejudiced social intercourse between Jews and Gentiles that are recorded in the history of Jews on German soil. Apart from that, it may be said that while a number of romanticists were anti-Semites (Achim von Arnim, Brentano), others kept entirely aloof from this aberration of their newly discovered national feeling. Nevertheless a relation between both conceptions does exist. It lies, however, in another plane. Romanticism, particularly in the form in which it became an element of German public feeling, is, like anti-Semitism, a reversion to a stage of civilisation which had already been left behind.

Romanticism defies by its very character a precise definition. This fact already puts it in a different category from enlightenment to which it is the reaction and antithesis. The contrast between them can be brought out by juxtaposing some essential features of both, those of enlightenment being shared by it, broadly speaking, with rationalism and humanitarianism.

Enlightenment	Romanticism
Reason	Sentiment
Objective norms	Subjectivity
Rigid forms	Lack of form, fragmentarism
Universality	Nationalism
Man	Co-national
Secularism	Religion
Protestantism	Catholicism
Freedom	Authority
Responsibility	Obedience
Modernism	Medievalism
Clarity	Obscurity
Manliness	Femininity

A glance at these pairs of concepts will leave no doubt as to which alternative places in each case the greater strain on those human powers which have lifted man out of his original primitive state to the highest spiritual level so far achieved. This, however, is no criterion of their respective social effects. It may well be that the demands made of man by enlightenment exceeded the powers of human nature, at any rate for the ordinary hard-worked person who came more and more to represent the cultural level of the age. Compared with these demands, the romantic standards may represent a wholesome compromise which made civilisation attainable and progress endurable to the masses. If this be so, romanticism would have to be regarded as the better cultural pattern, in so far as it is better suited to man as he really is. None the less, it would continue to signify a regression from a height previously reached, a relaxation of spiritual effort, the restitution of a state nearer to nature that had previously been overcome.[140]

The most marked contrast in these pairs of concepts is that between Humanity and Nation, involving as it does the abandonment of a high moral ideal in favour of one closely connected with human nature. If man, instead of being taught to regard his fellow-man as a brother, is permitted to regard only his " brother ", viz. the member of what may be called his national family, as his fellow-man, then the progress of humanity towards ever wider spheres of mutual responsibility has been reversed at a decisive point. What has been said above about group-love and group-hatred, namely that they are the particular kinds of self-love and aggressiveness sanctioned by society, applies first and foremost to nationalism and its more radical expressions.[141] This, again, is in itself no condemnation of nationalism. It may well be that the natural love of man for his likes is the best basis for his achievements for mankind. And the ethical limitations inherent in the national idea form by no means the central problem of this very complex and momentous phenomenon. Neither should the fact be disregarded that, in the medieval world of Christian and in the enlightened era of secular universalism, the lives and the thoughts of many people were actually restricted to their own narrow environment; to these, not only persons coming from another country and speaking a different language, but those coming from a neighbouring county and speaking another dialect were suspect as strangers and potential enemies. Compared with this state of mind, national integration meant in practice a widening of the outlook. Just as this had been made possible by the improvements in communications, so social integration might have been carried beyond national boundaries as technical progress continued to narrow distances. But it is here that the lowering of standards comes in. If universalism had been able to survive into an age when the consciousness of world-wide interrelation became general, it might have helped to prevent wars—at any rate, in so far as the outbreak of wars is stimulated by aggressive nationalism. But there was no expansion of ideas corresponding to the growth of interrelation, and this did much to prevent the fruits of general human interdependence from maturing into whole-hearted co-operation.

On the other hand, this ideological limitation was a psychological advantage. It increased the attractiveness of nationalism to 19th-century people striving for more comfortable spiritual concepts. One sign of this is the fact that nationalism had a certain tendency to become gradually more exclusive and aggressive, and that this tendency asserted itself particularly in those countries where economic and national frustrations were most strongly felt. Although, according to the conclusions of a most competent symposium on the subject,[142] nationalism is not inevitably bound to follow this line of development, there is a grave danger that where it becomes dominant the path of mankind will lead, as the Austrian dramatist Franz Grillparzer put it, " from humanism via nationalism to bestialism ".

A significant description of such development is given by the German historian Friedrich Meinecke in his book *Weltbürgertum und Nationalstaat*.[143] He shows how one German protagonist of the national idea after another dispenses with more and more of its universalist ingredients. Originally, universalists and early nationalists had hardly differed in their sense of world-wide responsibility. From the standard of Humboldt and Schiller, the national idea sank via Novalis and Friedrich Schlegel to that of Fichte and Adam Müller. But even Fichte still dreams of a republic of the united peoples, and Müller, a true romanticist with economic ideas derived from medieval feudalism, recoils before the consequences of unbridled nationalism ; his conversion to Catholicism is explained by Meinecke as a kind of " fear of death " which Müller experienced in face of his idea of the State left entirely to itself.[144] Likewise the historian Niebuhr, although he earns high praise from Meinecke for his " national realism ", upholds the idea that " the Christian States of Europe form a unity which it would be nefarious to damage ".[145] The decline went on beyond the convert from Judaism Friedrich Julius Stahl, the founder of Prussian conservatism, who still paid homage to Christian universalist ideas, to Hegel, Ranke, and Bismarck.

These three men are highly praised by Meinecke for having liberated political thought from " unpolitical universalist ideas ".[146] But even Hegel he still finds blameworthy because of his universalist leanings towards the " world spirit ".[147] No less did Ranke " reach downwards in depths and upwards to heights where universalist powers work ",[148] and it was only Bismarck who emancipated the national idea from the last relics of universalism. It was he who declared unambiguously in his speech at Olmutz : " The only healthy foundation of a great State . . . is State egotism,—it is unworthy of a great State to fight for a cause which does not directly serve its own interest ".[149]

Meinecke's exposition is instructive as illustrating how the intellectual leaders in one special sphere tended more and more to abandon the obligations of self-denial and comprehensive mutual responsibility. Instead, they preached and justified collective egotism. No wonder that the German public were only too willing to accept the doctrines so convincingly and alluringly set forth. Among the interpretations of the national idea offered to them, they chose increasingly those which appealed to their more primitive urges, since there seemed to be no ideological ground for suppressing them. Through such co-operation of teachers and public the national idea degenerated eventually into a caricature of its original self. No service for mankind, no universal ties, no international legal inhibition remained at last. Self-love, widened into national love, and superficially justified as such, triumphed over all previous restraints.[150]

Although romanticism and nationalism will have to be discussed again in connection with special German problems, it was necessary to mention them here as significant examples of the transition from higher to lower standards in the epoch under review. Romanticism combined all regressive human leanings in a kind of unsystematic system. All those who rebelled against the higher laws of social existence, those who wanted to indulge their craving for rest and to escape from certain intolerable burdens of civilisation, turned to it for justification. Those who found it easier to base their judgments on their uncontrolled emotions than on connected thought did so in the name of romanticism. Those who desired to be released from obligations to humanity at large, and to give free rein to their instinctive affection for their own kinsfolk, pretended to act according to romantic principles. Those who took refuge from individual responsibility in the sheltering authority of the Church, or in a " divinely ordained dependence ", claimed to follow the same guidance. The vagueness of the idea permitted many interpretations. It was therefore only natural that in its protective dimness many people should recover their good consciences who had no longer been able to face the blinding clarity of reason.

Romanticism, however, produced only the protagonists in the great struggle to relieve the qualms of conscience. The German historian Franz Schnabel emphasises the rôle played by Hegel in this process.[151] Hobhouse mentions the effect produced by Darwin,[152] and the responsibility of Nietzsche and the French philosopher Bergson.[153] We need not stop to consider which of the many writers who might be mentioned in this connection are to be included within the flexible concept of romanticism and which not. There is no doubt that there were more than sufficient of them in the period under discussion, and whoever desired an ideology which should justify an easy life had not to search long for it.

The influence of ideologies on the development of public morality should not, however, be over-emphasised. The spiritual outlook of a people is determined only indirectly and partially by philosophical systems. We are not to suppose from the above statements that, e.g., an overworked clerk who has been annoyed by a domineering colleague will sit down at night over philosophical books in search of a system which will justify him in complaining about his colleague to his employer or in boxing his colleague's ears; that, in doing so, he may read that life is not, as he had learned at Sunday-school, all charity towards one's neighbours, but that it is a ruthless struggle of all against all, in which the stronger is likely to win and in which the victory of the stronger is sanctioned by the duty to preserve and improve the species; and that when he further reads that what he had deemed to be Christian duty is in reality slave morality, inimical to culture and by all means to be repudiated, he will next morning go into his office with the best possible conscience and struggle there for his own life with all available means. It is not in this simple way that the influence of the few on the many is exerted. This asserts itself rather indirectly and without being realised by the people. The influence is exercised at universities, from which a more or less vulgarised version of the original philosophy is passed on to the educated classes. School teachers embody it in even more primitive doctrines and hand it over to the youth. The same philosophy is furthermore preached in certain churches where the parsons try to curry favour with an enlightened congregation by showing their accessibility to modernism. It is diffused through books, in public lectures, in theatres, and, above all, by the Press. All these agencies act in the opposite manner to a sieve, holding back the finer elements of the original concepts and allowing only the coarser ones to pass through and reach the mass of the people. Bismarck's glorification of "blood and iron", Nietzsche's "re-valuation of values", Ibsen's exaltation of the amoral Hedda Gabler exercised a pernicious effect on a public weighed down with labour and moral restraints and craving for a release of their primitive vitality.[154]

The lowering of standards led, consequently, to a recrudescence of violence in public life which is observed with consternation by modern thinkers.[155] In his critique of his own time, to which we have frequently referred,[156] Hobhouse describes this relation as follows. After man had renounced reason and made will his sole guide, he soon went a further step back, from will to instinct, to emotions and impulse which he "shares with the brute creation. . . . Reason, that we were taught for ages to place at the summit of human faculty, was degraded, and instinct, which men spent painful generations in seeking to subdue, was set upon the throne." " The idea of violence was in the air." Similarly Ortega y Gasset [157] speaks of a promotion of violence from the place of " ultima ratio " to that of " prima ratio " and even " unica ratio " : " It is the norm which proposes the annulment of all norms . . . it is the Magna Charta of barbarism ". Nor after what has been said above need we be surprised at this development. Violence, *i.e.* the radical expression of aggressiveness, is only one of many primitive urges repressed in the course of civilisation, which was restored to its " rights " with the gradual undermining of the established system of values.

Another gratification of primitive desires, resulting from, and leading to, a lowering of general standards, can be seen in the way in which politics came to be determined more and more by economic interests. The historians of the 19th century agree that the world became in it materialistic, that people no longer acted according to principles but to their economic requirements. Some of them are inclined to attribute this fact to the increase of wealth brought about by capitalism.[157a] We should rather suppose the contrary. The preponderance of economic interests over spiritual ideals is the consequence of a lack of wealth, not absolute, but relative, combined with the increased effort required by every individual in the more strenuous struggle for existence. By the relative lack of wealth we understand the fact that in the face of a virtually unlimited material advancement the individual feels more keenly the limitations of his own possessions. Since the dynamic force of capitalism knows no limit to the increase of material riches, the striving for this increase is infinite. This does not deny that sensible people are content with what they have obtained and reduce their material interests in order to cultivate ideals. The rule remains, however, that man continually pursues a fuller satisfaction of his greed for commodities, and so for money or productive goods. People of every social stratum look with envy on the one next above them and when they have reached it make the next one their goal. When all luxury goods that can be thought of stand actually at the disposal of a person in an elevated social sphere, he will still be stimulated to greater efforts by the prospect of winning influence and power. Among the working classes again, who form the bulk of the people, the effort necessary to procure a mere subsistence is such as almost entirely to prevent their thoughts ranging beyond the economic sphere.

It is thus the expansion of the economic sphere in every individual life as a consequence of capitalism which puts the economic interest into the foreground of human motives. The upper classes in the pre-capitalistic and also in the early capitalistic period worked little and slowly, while the working-classes were excluded from political and cultural activities. For the upper classes to have worked harder and more quickly would have been a breach of the existing laws and customs. Apart from this, the prize to be gained by such overwork was not alluring. People had their living, they neither desired nor were able to acquire more. They could, therefore, devote their large amount of leisure and surplus energy to the beautiful things of life. In the creation and promotion of these they saw the real meaning of life. True, in the striving for ideal aims they did not actually run counter to their economic interests. They were fully conscious of these and knew how to stand up for them very effectively in times of real or supposed danger.* But many of the matters with which they were concerned did not touch the economic sphere at all. Among these they were free to choose.

As the struggle for existence became more severe, economic considerations intruded more and more into all spheres of life. Every political decision meant, above all, a choice between different economic policies, and gradually almost every literary and aesthetic judgment had some connection with the political outlook. The respective merits of the philosophy of Kant and Christianity had once been a matter for a few thinkers to decide according to their own convictions. But whether a person espoused Natural or Historic Law was very nearly identical with a political decision. Later on, not only was the choice between historic idealism and materialism strictly bound up with one's economic interests, but nearly every urban district in which one resided, every health resort where one spent one's holiday, every style in hats one preferred, became an expression of one's economic situation. The spheres that remained independent of economic interests shrank more and more.[158]

It is very instructive to examine the way in which the public conscience of the epoch reacted to this process. In a society bent on gain, people engaged in business have always sought their advantage. But for a long time they wrapped up this crude impulse in a multiplicity of religious and traditional rules meant to restrict the profit motive in favour of the general good. They were inhibited egoists, egoists with a bad conscience. When economic opportunities increased, nothing fundamental changed in the attitude of man, who continued to seek his advantage. But when his advantage increasingly conflicted with the advantage of his fellow-men, the prohibitive rules did not withstand the challenge. First the qualms of conscience continued to be felt. But when religion and tradition, whose precepts conscience reflected, lost their coercive power, then it underwent the same process in the economic sphere as has been previously described in general. It was trimmed in such a way that it should no longer withhold its sanctions from actions which had become so manifestly necessary in capitalist economy. With the widening of the

* Cf. the resistance against Jewish competition mentioned above, pp. 71 *seq.*

economic sphere, and under the influence of Darwin's theories and of Marx's discovery of the economic basis for every political idea, people lost their reluctance to admit their egoist motives. In the course of the great controversies of the 19th and 20th centuries between Liberalism and Conservatism, later on between Liberalism and Socialism, and still later between Socialism and Fascism, the dependence of principles on economic considerations was admitted with increasing frankness. True, the workers could still claim that by means of a socialist order the ideal of justice on earth would be fulfilled. Neither were the champions of other political creeds at a loss to prove that their private interests were the true interests of the community. But these justifications declined more and more in importance, and it was eventually mainly during electoral campaigns and party celebrations that these weapons were dragged out of the political arsenals. For all practical purposes the sway of economic interest was considered as no less legitimate than that of any supreme truth or any sublime ideal had previously been. The need of self-preservation had dislodged more general values from their pinnacles. The walls of civilisation were crumbling.

There were, however, two factors, closely connected, which tended to counteract the general lowering of standards. These were individual prosperity and general economic expansion. In tracing the psychologically unfavourable consequences of capitalism, we have intentionally under-emphasised the fact that under its sway numerous individuals and, during periods of prosperity, large sections experienced the satisfaction of a rapid advance. In such good times the exhausting effect of business life temporarily diminished. The success which so quickly rewarded every effort made people feel less of the strain and stimulated energies which could be used for "higher" purposes. He who was successful himself could afford to be generous and help others to get on. In this fact lies no doubt one of the most essential socio-psychological causes of the growth of political Liberalism with its ideal of "Live and let live". But here lies also the clue to the oscillations of anti-Semitism corresponding so closely to the economic cycle.[159] And here lies finally an indication which will help us to understand the irresistible decline of standards in the German post-war period.

It appears that a considerable amount of psychical energy

is needed to preserve and uphold social ideals, particularly after people have been shaken in their belief that these ideals were imposed by a supernatural power. Where the necessary energy is available, that is to say, where strain and misery do not absorb the psychical reserves, moral concepts are more likely to be adhered to than in adverse circumstances. Strong props are needed to keep, as it were, ideals at the summit of civilisation, where their own potential energy corresponds to the effort needed to lift them to this height and to keep them there. As soon as the support grows weaker, the ideals tend to fall and, while falling, to lose part of their potential energy. If, eventually, all energies are used up in the struggle for life, and none of them is available for the support of established values, social ideals collapse. Their potential power is completely spent. This description is only a metaphor taken from mechanics. But it illustrates in terms familiar from natural science the development which took place during the 19th and 20th centuries. When the expansion of the markets met with increasing obstruction, when the existing markets were gradually saturated and the tendency towards rationalisation and monopoly resulted in economic contraction, when competition became keener and a rapidly growing population flooded the labour market—then the economic struggle absorbed more and more of the psychical power which had previously served other purposes.[160] The well-tried method of easing the burden of conscience was applied more radically. Men soon ceased even to choose every time the " easier " of two opposing theories as their guidance in life. They began to renounce all objective principles and followed only *their* will, *their* sentiment, *their* intuition. If any external or internal protest was made against such behaviour, the moral and intellectual plane was exchanged for the aesthetic, and one was bidden to admire the beauty of the beast freeing itself from its fetters. Every standpoint had become possible, and therefore no general standard remained.

What bearing have these observations on the Jewish problem? It might be assumed that the Jews as a group which had little or no share in many traditions of the majority could only profit from their gradual disappearance. Where now so many different opinions, classes, organisations existed side by side, it could well be expected that there would be room for the Jewish brand as well. This assumption, though not entirely incorrect, does not contain the whole truth. The homogeneous world of the Middle Ages offered indeed considerably less prospect for an admission of Jews as members with equal rights than the differentiated world of the modern age. However, here lies again one of the tragic coincidences which have been repeatedly mentioned before. The Jews, as has been pointed out, create an objective social problem. This in itself does not distinguish them from the proletariat, from the women, from the Non-Conformists, and from the innumerable other groups in modern society that give rise to more or less acute social tensions. But it has also been pointed out that the objective tension created by the Jews decreased in importance to the extent to which the Jews were integrated into the Gentile majority, that the Jewish problem tended steadily, in spite of obstacles and retardations, to become neutralised. And, thirdly, it has been emphasised that the character of the Jewish problem is such as to make it, out of all proportion to its genuine tensions, a vehicle for subjective resentments, which originate in frustrations entirely outside the realm of the Jewish-Gentile relationship. Where people live under the influence of well-established moral values, there exist also conventional channels through which resentments are generally disposed of. People will either blame themselves or some immaterial devil. So long as these moral values hold sway they can be relied upon to counteract any tendency on the part of the masses to look for innocent scapegoats on which to vent their anger. A lowering of common moral standards, however, weakens their power to resist the exploitation of the objective Jewish problem for the abreaction of the subjective discontents. This does not imply that anti-Semitism is bound to become a permanent feature of such a society. But it does mean that every economic crisis will probably bring on an anti-Semitic movement.

This analysis, it is true, holds good, for the most part, only under two conditions. First, public opinion must have the possibility of expressing itself more or less spontaneously, which is not the case, for instance, in a clerical or secular despotism. Secondly, the respect felt for the existing moral standards must not be compromised by their own standard-bearers, as was done during the Middle Ages by churchmen who instigated the persecution of Jews, heretics, and " witches ". In the conditions existing during the period of emancipation, that is to say, in countries which are, or are becoming, democratic, the appearance of anti-Semitism will largely depend on the degree to which moral standards are generally recognised, apart, of course, from the volume of objective and subjective elements of anti-Semitism existing in a given society. It may be assumed that in a crisis as severe as that through which Germany passed after the first World War, the masses in Britain would have shown more power of resistance against a vehement Jew-baiting campaign, although—and this makes the assumption even more significant—the objective Jewish question in Britain was still generating more acute tensions than it did in Germany at that time. In Britain the people have still to-day many moral principles in common which in Germany were already crumbling long before the assault of misery and propaganda razed the last bulwarks to the ground. The British conventions regarding what " is done " and what " is not done " may seem arbitrary to the outsider, at times even out of date and absurd. But they derive from a common style of life which demands a high degree of altruism and self-denial in order to realise such generally accepted moral concepts as " fairness " and " kindness ".[161] Closely related to this feature of British life is the superior vitality still exhibited by Christianity in Britain. That Christianity, once the bearer of anti-Jewish resistance, should to-day nearly everywhere form a common front with Jewry against the recrudescence of violence can come as a surprise only to those who have not grasped the essence of this struggle. It is no longer a struggle between ideas, not even one between ideologies and vested interests. It is a struggle between the mastery and the indulgence of primitive instincts, between civilisation and barbarism.

That in the course of this struggle certain groups with common interests have thought it to their advantage to ally themselves with the forces of barbarism does not diminish the significance of the phenomenon of re-barbarisation itself. Its protagonists had first to show their mettle, *i.e.* to gather a following around their disgusting banner, before they became a desirable ally in the struggle for power. It was the number of his adherents which recommended Hitler as an ally both to the military and the industrialists. Each group would have preferred to see one of the old political parties triumph. Each decided, with great reluctance, to back the petty bourgeois, who was socially and educationally their inferior, but each, in the end, yielded to his overwhelming success among the masses. Thus it does not suffice to explain Fascism as the political consequence of monopoly capitalism. This definition applies only to part of the phenomenon, namely to the subsidies granted to the Fascist movements by heavy industry. It does not explain in what way the movement came into being and became a mass movement. Here, however, lies what is fundamentally new in Fascism, what distinguishes it from the reactionary movements of the past. Until the emergence of National Socialism as a powerful factor in politics, big business and Reichswehr regarded the German People's Party and the German National People's Party respectively as the representatives of their interests. But only what distinguishes Nazism from these parties makes it " Fascist ". Rauschning [162] was the first to point out that this distinction is not a different ideology but the total lack of any ideology, a radical nihilism. How this nihilism, posing as heavenly idealism, managed to get hold of the masses is the actual problem.

Here is the place to deal with an obvious objection. While the great parts of the hard-working masses of the people were impelled by moral and mental weariness to seek for a relaxation of moral standards, the working-class proper formed an exception. Although the urban proletariat has been one of the sections most badly affected by modern conditions, suffering as they have been from long hours, from insecurity of employment, and a wretched standard of living, they have shown a remarkable resistance to the decline of moral values. In particular, they did not resort to anti-Semitism. On the contrary, they distinguished themselves, even in times of general demoralisation, by remaining faithful to such " difficult " ideals as humanitarianism, education, and international solidarity.

How is this to be accounted for? As far as Germany is concerned, the answer must be that popular Marxism in its influence on the German workers' movement combined in an extraordinarily felicitous manner the gratification of some primitive impulses with the subjugation of others. In other words, Marxist Socialism appealed to primitive instincts just sufficiently to gain wide support, but at the same time it imposed on its supporters high ethical obligations. If Professor

96

Ginsberg describes as the great difficulty of thought " that it can make no progress without subduing passion—yet must remain ineffective unless it can arouse passion "[163] then the Marxist workers' movement has managed to overcome this difficulty with remarkable success. Professor Schumpeter [164] rightly points out that the scientific value of Marx's theories has nothing to do with their success. He is even sceptical as to the lasting influence of the highly effective slogans of Marxism, the " white-hot phrases " as he calls them. He sees the secret of Marx's influence in the fact that he exercised a certain prophetic function. His strength, he says, lay in the supreme art with which he wove together the rationalist and materialist tendencies of the time with those extra-rational cravings which receding religion had left running loose like masterless dogs.[165] In this way he succeeded in implanting a deep faith in a paradise on earth in the minds of the workers.

Marxism restored the badly shaken self-esteem of the proletariat by saying to them in effect: You, the Fourth Estate, will be the foundation of the new society. Let the other people deny it. It is you who are in possession of the infallible truth. Let the others boast of their education and let them exclude you from the sacred places where this is acquired. In reality it is you who have the knowledge, because you possess the scientific weapons of Marxism. The others are ignoramuses blinded by their interests.[166] Marxism appealed, furthermore, to the craving for property. You are poor, it said. But in this capitalist system your poverty is an intrinsic necessity, and at the same time the essential preliminary to a revolution which will bring about your triumph. Under the socialist order, you will be those in possession, because you will be in charge of the new society, and society will own the means of production. Marxism knew equally well how to harness the spirit of aggression for its purpose. The bourgeois, the exploiters, those in whose grasp you are to-day, will be expropriated. Down with capital ! Long live the revolution ! In this way it enlisted hatred and envy in its service. And Marxism finally found its most potent means of influencing the masses by playing on both their eagerness to fight for their rights and their actual inability to do so. Marxism explained to them that the advent of Socialism was inevitable. True, it created a " revolutionary " movement. But at the same time it taught them that the actual motive force was the " productive power ", to whose mysterious and yet scientifically ascertainable guidance the individual might abandon himself with full confidence. Thus it gave the workers the thrill of marching with flying banners into the State of the Future, while at the same time it spared them the hardship of the march. It gave them a feeling of security as could only emanate from a power outside themselves, and which they would never have derived from reliance on their own feeble force.

That Marxism appealed to human passions does not distinguish it from other movements which solicit the favour of the masses. What does distinguish it is the way in which it linked this appeal to the subjugation of passions in the service of civilising ideals. Marxism, it has been said, enhanced the self-esteem of the proletariat. But it enlisted this self-esteem in society as a whole by promising the working-classes fair and honourable conditions, free from the incubus of class struggle. Marxism did promise the workers that they would own the means of production. But it connected this hope with the obligation to employ the means of production for the benefit of all. It demanded the renunciation of private property also from those who, having been excluded from it, desired it most vehemently. Again, in appealing to the aggressiveness of the workers, Marxism sought to direct it solely against the system of capitalism, and it demanded disciplined behaviour towards the bearers of the system, the individual bourgeois. He who realises how weak a substitute is the hatred of an abstract order of things for the hatred of living beings will be able to gauge the severity of the restraint which this limitation placed on the primitive impulses. It has no doubt not always been strictly observed in the propaganda of the local branches. But the official standard set by the party programme and the central party organ remained authoritative.

Thus Marxism combined all its promises with moral obligations. It successfully linked interests with principles. It imposed on its followers loyalty to mankind and humanism, to the rights of minorities, to truth in propaganda even where it was not conducive to the extension of the party membership,[167] to solidarity, discipline, and intellectual training. The effort which these objectives, especially the last, exacted from toil-worn people, unaccustomed to this kind of work, can hardly be sufficiently commended. The proletarian educational idealism is one of the most significant signs of the Marxist allegiance to the standards of civilisation. Even if one regards its results with scepticism and suspects that the knowledge which it spread was defective, the motive as such and the effort which it called forth merit unstinted praise.

If it is asked how it happened that a class at a comparatively low level of civilisation accepted this " difficult " ideology while later on an amoral or even anti-moral nihilism met with mass support in approximately the same circles,[168] it must be answered : The attraction of Marxism depended on the one hand on its effective psychological appeal to the mass already mentioned above, and, on the other hand, on its excellent choice of slogans. Apart from this, the " difficulty " of its ethical values was mainly a matter of the future. For the time being, the workers felt mainly that they were the class to derive benefit from such reforms as common rights, freedom for all, abolition of discriminatory laws, and international co-operation. The stage in which they themselves would feel the obligations inherent in these reforms lay far ahead in the distant future. But all this explains only why the socialist loyalty to the values of civilisation did not prevent the spread of Socialism. It does not yet account for the fact that these values came to form the undetachable background of the socialist system of ideas and consequently of the struggle for proletarian interests. It must therefore be added that in this respect Marxism is only a particularly important variety of the socialist concepts of the 19th century, in all of which socio-ethical responsibility was an essential element. To understand this we have to consider the spiritual environment in which the socialist idea took shape. Marx carried on faithfully the tradition of enlightenment and liberalism, his attachment to which was not impaired by his Hegelian training. When he, the son of a Jewish bourgeois, made the proletarian class struggle his own, he instilled into it the moral values of his time, and of his class, and the zeal for justice and learning which he had inherited from his old community. These elements which he intermingled with the proletarian cause were, strictly speaking, alien to it. But they gave it its *raison d'être* in a civilised world. They did not facilitate the acceptance of Marxism by the proletarians. On the contrary, they added to the danger that, in revolutionary times, watchwords demanding less moral restraint would catch the public ear and lead to cleavages and a weakening of the movement.[169]   But wherever they were accepted as party ideology they exerted an elevating influence.[170]

It is thus no mere accident, but a direct consequence of the elaborate ideology of Marxism, that it fought anti-Semitism. Its loyalty to those values which were primarily unconnected with a struggle for proletarian interests, prevented it from employing this cheap propagandistic device.   The fact that the workers seldom encountered Jews as competitors in their own sphere was probably also not without effect.   But this was to some extent balanced by the other fact that they did meet them as " exploiting " capitalists and " sharp " traders. Marx's Jewish lineage may also have played its part.   But Friedrich Julius Stahl's Jewish extraction was not able to prevent the Conservative Party, which he inaugurated, from taking an anti-Semitic turn.   Apart from that, Marx, in his pamphlet on the Jewish question, had taken Jewry so severely to task that it might easily have been made the justification for an anti-Jewish attitude.   The socialistic doctrine, it is true, was a consistent whole and was incompatible with anti-Semitic views.   But doctrines are extremely flexible in the hands of those who wish to transform them, and no great difficulty would have been involved in giving even " scientific Socialism " some anti-Semitic accessories.   The conscious avoidance by the champions of Socialism of any such deflection stands in favourable contrast to the methods of the later National Socialists who had no scruple in combining the most contradictory ideas.   The central importance which Socialism attributed to changeable social conditions as against unchangeable hereditary qualities is, strictly speaking, in contradiction to the racial doctrine.   But propaganda does not take this so seriously and the Social Democratic leader August Bebel betrays in his controversy with anti-Semitism [171] a fairly wide sympathy with the racial theory.   But in spite of this he takes the anti-Semitic bull by the horns and removes it once and for all from the socialist stable.   While doing this he points out repeatedly how plausible it would appear on the evidence available to identify capitalism and Jewry.[172]   He also shows a remarkable understanding of the attraction anti-Semitism is bound to exercise through its power of satisfying the latent need for sensation and excitement.[173]   However, to all these psychological advantages of anti-Semitism, Bebel—and with him the rest of the socialist leaders—opposed the responsibility for upholding what had been accepted as truth. How profoundly true was the remark that " anti-Semitism is the Socialism of the blockheads " was probably not fully realised by the Austrian Social Democrat Pernerstorffer, to whom it is attributed. But it was an expression of that loyalty towards the moral principles of the movement which enabled German Socialism to accomplish its work of education and which saved it from anti-Semitic degeneracy.

In referring to the question, so frequently asked, how could it happen that the " nation of thinkers and poets " succumbed to a system like National Socialism,* we said that to answer this question it was necessary not only to show what tendencies were at work on the German people, but also to examine this further question : In what way did those sections of the people which were most critically affected by these changes eventually become responsible for the national decisions. This latter point will now be discussed.

There were three important trends in German life during the epoch following that of the " thinkers and poets ", all of which contributed to the rise of National Socialism. First, there was the descent of the intellectual *élite* from spiritual heights into more earthly regions; secondly, the emergence of a very numerous class of people suffering from serious frustrations in virtue of their economic situation; and thirdly, the rise of these people to politcal influence. The spiritual decline and the economic frustration have already been discussed. The emergence and political rise of this new social class remain for consideration. These points have to be elucidated in view of the decisive rôle played by the National Socialist movement in bringing about the catastrophe of the German Jews. Without Nazism this catastrophe would never have occurred, but without the tendencies on which this analysis tries to throw light, Nazism would never have come into being. The very fact that these tendencies have apparently little to do with the Jewish problem, that their pro- or anti-Jewish implications are in each case only a side-issue, is especially illuminating for the character of the catastrophe. Paradoxical as it may seem, to seek for the causes of the Jewish catastrophe in the Jewish question as such would be to seek them where they cannot be found.

The century of emancipation was not only a century in

* Cf. pp. 79-80.

which life became harder and in which moral and social values disintegrated, it was also a century of an enormous increase of population. This increase, like other general conditions of the period, had its own bearing on the Jewish problem, since the need for more people created by the new methods of production had no small share in bringing about the emancipation of the Jews. Yet this same need leading, as it did, to an enormous increase of population did much to endanger the permanence of emancipation. Here again it was the tragedy of emancipation that the conditions which made it possible contained at the same time dangers for its success.

If the emancipation of the Jews had occurred at a time when the birth-rate was static, an increase of the population by roughly one per cent would have been probably quickly digested, perhaps even welcomed. But to the above-mentioned need of hands the peoples of Europe replied with an increase of one and a half times their former numbers. From 1800 to 1914 they increased from 180 to 452 millions.[174] In Germany the increase during the same period was even larger, it amounted to 171 per cent. Germany's population increased from somewhat over 24 to 65 millions.[175] This rise becomes still more astonishing when it is considered that the greater part of it occurred during the second part of the 19th century. While from the beginning of the century till 1846 the population of the regions which later made up the German Reich increased by 44.6 per cent, from that date till 1907 it increased by 77.8 per cent.[176] During the same time there took place in Germany the process of urbanisation which brought this growing population together in towns, and chiefly in large towns.[177]

The most important cause of this sudden increase is to be found in the growing need for labour which accompanied the age of industrialisation. To this other factors were added, as e.g., the improved hygiene. But on the whole we are probably right in following Professor Götz Briefs who suggests that the lower age at which the early factory workers married and the early age at which children could be set to work mainly accounts for the growing Western European populations of that time. "The boundlessness of capitalist expansion results in the infinity of expansion of the population, particularly of those sections which capital needs." [178] This is also the view of Professor Sombart. The disproportionately large share which the highly industrialised German provinces, Saxony and the Rhine Province contributed to the growth of the population, was a sign of the same trend.[179]

This growth of population of which the proletarian class contributes a relatively high proportion, brings about a fundamental change in the structure of Central and Western European society. The proportion of the upper middle-class and of the aristocracy declines. The age of the masses sets in.

From the end of the 19th century this process takes an important turn. The lower and middle-bourgeoisie begin to increase more rapidly than the actual working-class. The concentration of industry and the extension of State, municipal, and judicial administration, the expansion of schools and public services, create an ever-growing class of employees with small incomes.[180] At the same time, the prospects for this new stratum decline, as well as those of the older one of shop assistants, which likewise grows in numbers. The hope which had previously inspired every black-coated employee at the start of his career, that he would one day become an employer himself, was realised now only in exceptionally favourable circumstances. The bulk of the employees remained dependent wage-earners and were even threatened with impoverishment, as the higher age-groups were frequently worse paid or did not find any work at all. The greater security of the career of officials was counterbalanced by a still smaller immediate income.

It is not the task of this study to examine why no leader arose to inspire the lower middle-class with political self-respect and a sense of social responsibility. There was nothing in the nature of things to prevent this from happening. The black-coated workers and lower officials consisted not only of middle-bourgeois who had sunk in the social scale and were therefore full of resentment, but also of proletarians who had risen. Their economic outlook was not, as is frequently maintained, hopeless. This was the case only with part of their class, viz. a portion of the small shopkeepers and of the remaining craftsmen. It would not have been difficult for a political leader to turn to account the progressive bureaucratisation of society in order to emphasise the present and future importance of the black-coated staffs. He might thus have created in them a healthy self-assertiveness, a collective hope for social advancement, and a certain spirit of generosity derived from such satisfactions. These could have been amalgamated into a specific ideology for black-coated workers and made the foundation of a political education, similar to that of the socialist workers' movement. In fact, however, no such attempt was made that met with any measure of success. The different trade unions of black-coated employees followed in the wake of the political parties and fought each other. They did not succeed in securing joint representation in Parliament, still less in developing a common ideal that might have inspired them with zest and enthusiasm.

We must, therefore, regard the lower middle-class, which became so important in numbers, as the " normal " case, as it were, of a thwarted and exhausted social group, in danger of losing its moral principles.[181] As their anxious striving for a somewhat larger share of earthly happiness was not balanced by class-pride, it became an even more distressing source of frustration. Their fear of sinking into the proletariat was not compensated by any assurance that such an unhappy consummation would at any rate lend confirmation to their political philosophy—a satisfaction which was not denied to the workers when they sank into the ranks of the unemployed. They therefore tried to banish this fear by keeping proletarian society and ideas strictly at arm's length. If they had nothing positive to boast of, they could at least take a pride in not being proletarians. They fancied themselves to be something superior and vented no small part of their aggressiveness on their proletarian fellow sufferers. In their misguided efforts to attain a higher station, they developed all the faults of the semi-educated. As no one arose to explain to them their true place and function in society, or rather since the majority of them would not listen to such explanations when given, they fell victims to all kinds of social quackeries. They became vegetarians, anti-vaccinationists, agrarian reformers, sectarians —according to the doctrine instilled into them in a weak hour by some colleague or superior or cleverly written booklet. They were thus the predestined supporters of anti-Semitic agitation which should be launched at any future time.

Thus the demoralising tendencies of the period, unchecked by any spiritual influence, played havoc with the lower middle-class. The numerical increase of this class in proportion to the total population was ominous for the future of society as a whole.

Three results have so far been noted in examination of the

social trends of the 19th century : (1) An extremely large increase of the population takes place during the period of emancipation ; (2) this increase is to a high degree accounted for by " proletarian reproduction " [182] and changes therefore the proportion of the different classes largely in favour of the lower strata ; (3) among these lower strata the lower middle-class increases relatively since the end of the 19th century. With it a class gains in importance whose social and psychological deficiencies are not mitigated by " class-consciousness " and its wholesome effects.

The direct consequence of this transformation of the social structure is the increase of the mere number of competitors with whom the Jews had to reckon. The fact that the class which has actually expanded most is that with whom the Jews, owing to the circumstances of their entry into general economic life, do not, as a rule, enter into competition is of little importance. The increase of population made itself felt in all classes. Thus in 1835 just as in 1875, there were in Germany 38 university students in every 100,000 inhabitants, but in 1880 there were 46, in 1885 57, in 1899 60, and in 1911 there were more than 100.[183] This shows for one sphere how the " overcrowding ", concerning which complaints became general, came about. As is well known, in the academic sphere the " overcrowding " led also to direct competition with Jewish candidates. The growth of competition in the different sections of the labour market is, however, only one of the developments of modern mass society bearing on the Jewish problem. Another more important development is the gradual transference of political power—as represented by Parliament—to these new or, at any rate, enormously enlarged lower classes.

The fame which the German nation acquired of being " a nation of thinkers and poets " was won for it by its intellectual and artistic *élite*. Their achievements were certainly outstanding. From Leibniz to Kant and Fichte in philosophy, from Bach to Mozart and Beethoven in music, and from Lessing to Schiller and Goethe in literature, they maintained an exceedingly high standard. But in thinking of the admiration which the works of such men naturally excited, it must not be forgotten that these were the only achievements contemporaries thought of as specifically German. There were neither political nor military nor other achievements to which Germans at home or abroad could point as achievements of the nation, as distinct from its separate States.[184] There were no other common representatives of Germany than her writers and artists. The German Reich hardly survived even as a phantom. Within its political organism the people had no place whatever. As far as the estates exerted any influence at all, they did so within the territorial States, which were often hostile to each other and fought now in this and now in that coalition. The fact, therefore, must not be overlooked that the German people became known as a " nation of thinkers and poets " not only because some of its outstanding members thought and wrote, but also because no other group could at that time challenge their position as " the " German people. Similar intellectual achievements during the era of the new German Reich would have been hopelessly overshadowed by the figure of Bismarck, and the remarkable advances of German technology and scientific research after the first World War will not prevent this epoch from being known in history as the era of the Weimar Republic and of the rise of National Socialism.

The distance which the Western European countries travelled in the period during which Germany degenerated from a " nation of thinkers and poets " into Hitler's Third Reich was, fortunately for them, not quite as far, for both England and France were already national States at the beginning. Nevertheless, their political representations also underwent a remarkable transformation. While the parliamentary suffrage in Engand was till 1832 dependent on the tenure of land, and in France—according to the Bourbon Constitution of 1814—on a high property qualification, privileges of property had in this field been practically abolished by the end of the first World War. A broad democratic franchise had been established.

In Germany, too, national unification led eventually to a central political representation. The Reichstag, although it had no executive power, expressed fairly adequately the will of the people.

The expression of the will of the people is the basis of democracy. The most exact possible representation of the opinions of the greatest possible part of the nation is the theoretical basis of democratic government. In the too logical application of this idea there are, however, certain dangers which we shall have to discuss in the following pages. This implies no condemnation of democracy itself. If a doctor in making a diagnosis discovers that the illness of the patient has been aggravated by a morbid disposition common to members of his family, he will feel it necessary to give some warning on this matter. In doing so he does not act against the family, but definitely in its interest. If it is found that the main culprit for the catastrophe of the German Jews, *i.e.* Nazism, sprang from a germ which is likely to exist in every democracy, it is the duty of the investigator to urge the democracies to turn their attention to possibly weak spots in this hitherto most perfect political system. It would not only be unscientific but cowardly to shun such a course. Not only from loyalty towards the Anglo-Saxon democracies, which, in the most crucial time, acted as the guardians of the Jewish community's rights, but from a deep religious and historical allegiance to the ideas of humanity and justice do the Jews regard the fate of democracy as their own fate. But this feeling makes it all the more incumbent on them to lay bare certain potential dangers in democracy which have in one country contributed to the doom of the Jews.

Anti-Semitism, it may be objected, has existed as long as Jews have lived in Dispersion. At times anti-Semitic riots have been organised by both clerical and secular Governments, at times both have tolerated them, and at times both have prevented them. The German catastrophe was brought about by a Government as despotic as any that has ever been guilty of a pogrom. To attribute the catastrophe to certain concomitants of democracy, *i.e.* to a political system which the Jews have mainly to thank for their emancipation, it may be argued, is absurd.

Such an objection would be justified if we could simply attribute the events in Germany to a dictatorial Government. It must not, however, be overlooked that this Government rose to power after the Nazi Party had been able to organise not much less than 50 per cent of the German people into a popular movement. The subsequent exclusion from the Reichstag of part of its members by means of the trick of the Reichstag fire must not blind us to the fact that the rise of Nazism took place within democracy and largely by democratic means.

In a very illuminating study on anti-Semitism [185] Professor Morris Ginsberg puts the question whether perhaps " recent anti-Semitism is something radically different from ancient or medieval anti-Semitism ". It may well be that the answer to this question is in the affirmative if by " recent anti-Semitism " the total phenomenon of mass anti-Semitism in modern democracy is understood. It is not that the motives affecting individuals have changed. Superstition, envy, and hatred against the real or alleged stranger play their part to-day as they have always done. Neither can the change be attributed to anti-Semitic theories, for this would be to exaggerate their importance, considering that they have tended to become increasingly mere pretexts. The question whether anti-Semitism professes itself to be religious, social, cultural, or racial may be important for determining its symptoms. Whichever theory is adopted may also be sincerely believed in by a small circle of ardent supporters. It would, however, be a misunderstanding of the true nature of anti-Semitism to regard the emergence of racial anti-Semitism as indicating a new anti-Semitic epoch.

The difference between modern anti-Semitism and its former varieties lies rather on the same plane as that between modern European barbarisation and primitive barbarism or—in a psychological analogy—that between neurotic infantilism and the mentality of real children. It is one thing for men at the dawn of history to look for booty and slay the enemy who would deny them their prey, and quite another for men brought up under European civilisation, who have learned—either from religious or political teaching—to respect the life and property of their fellow-men, to abandon these principles without external compulsion. When an infant destroys his toys and picture books in the unrestrained enjoyment of his hardly realised strength, he is passing through a phase of natural development; but when a grown-up loses control over his destructive impulses and abandons himself to vandalism he is mentally defective. When a group of people who have been kept in mental dependence and have never known political responsibility commit acts of violence against Jews, such a proof of their immaturity will need far less explanation than the approval of such acts by people who had been taught to think more or less for themselves—even if this had done no more than fill them with the dull pride of having thrown off the fetters of a dogmatic creed. If people who have attained spiritual and political emancipation relapse into the state of mind of their pre-rational, pre-civilised ancestors and in consequence turn against the Jews, this kind of anti-Semitism may indeed be regarded as a fundamentally new variety. Anti-Semitism is only an especially effective means of unfettering asocial impulses which had been subdued by civilisation.

It makes all the difference whether those who indulge in such an act of unfettering have had a civilisation imposed upon them or have largely created it themselves.

It might be objected that there have always been both educated and civilised persons among the anti-Semites. Of that there is no doubt. But as far as their anti-Semitism has been the outcome of considered and deliberate choice, it has differed radically from German post-war mass anti-Semitism. They too, in becoming anti-Semites, gratified certain feelings of hatred and envy which would have had to be suppressed if they had chosen another political allegiance. But the way they chose was still not the indiscriminate setting free of primitive impulses. Only where this ceases to be the by-product of a rational process and becomes the focus of an irrational process are we brought face to face with the phenomenon of modern mass anti-Semitism.

We are now in a position to realise the decisive importance of the fact that National Socialist anti-Semitism owes its emergence to democratic propaganda methods. It is this fact more than anything else which makes it imperative for democrats to define their attitude to this possible aberration of their system. The fact that in former times the Jews were attacked with blind savagery, that popular rage against them was instigated, tolerated, or restricted by the respective authorities, has been frequently explained. But that people in a modern democracy should, in the name of the democratic right of self-determination, have turned against the Jews—against Jews, that is, who had identified themselves to so great an extent with their fellow citizens—is proof of a tendency which might compromise democracy itself. It is, therefore, all the more urgent to discover how this degeneration came about. Only in this way can a repetition be prevented.

The contrast between " easy " ideologies, those near to the instincts, and " difficult " ones, those which demand a good deal of suppression of instinct, has already been pointed out. If these criteria are applied to the idea of political democracy, it must be classified as a " difficult " political conception. True, for the French revolutionaries the watchwords " Liberty, Equality, Fraternity " contained appeals to their instincts, because they had been suffering from servitude, aristocratic contempt, and oppression. But the second generation in a democracy is already likely to take the democratic achievements for granted, while the new governing class may find its obligations increasingly burdensome. As soon as the disadvantages which the democratic system has removed fade from the memories of the citizens, they become increasingly aware of those features of democracy which do not appeal to the instincts. When an individual forgets that the absence of bondage is in itself a great positive gain, he becomes indifferent to the value of freedom. A self-determination exercised once in several years in the diluted form of a general election does hardly suffice to inspire him with enthusiasm. Parliamentary routine, after the excitement generated during an electoral campaign, appears intolerably slow. The results are nearly always compromises, which are not infrequently arrived at after unpleasant " bargaining ". Very often their effect cannot be easily assessed by the man-in-the-street. On the whole, democracy is characterised by sobriety. It tends essentially to produce a sound average type, lacking in brilliance. The outstanding, unforeseeable, incalculable is not in its line.

But it is not only the renunciation of such quasi-aesthetic values in government which democracy expects of its citizens. It also makes high demands on their sense of justice and powers of reasoning. Equality of rights is an alluring slogan for the under-privileged. But it is a renunciation for the privileged. Consideration for minorities is not always popular with majorities. The acceptance of majority decisions is not always popular with minorities. To see the value of the great cumbrous State machinery, to realise that bureaucracy, indirect procedure, compromise, and respect for the rights of one's opponents are necessary, require much insight and good-will.

Healthy people, with good hopes and prospects, are in general well capable of such an effort, particularly if democracy evolves gradually and succeeds in creating an emotional allegiance towards itself. People who are conscious of their own shortcomings and recognise the superiority of experts will not become inveterate grumblers. People who have reached a secure position or are convinced of their future success will be generous enough to give a chance even to their adversaries. People to whom democratic self-government is an object of civic pride will be able to put up with the defects of the system as well. But insecurity, anxiety, despair, and lack of understanding are the enemies of democracy. Where these get the upper hand, anti-democratic tendencies are likely to come to the fore.[186]

Democracy is an exacting political system. It demands in a high measure reason, morality, sense of responsibility, and adjustment to the social whole. It forbids the indulgence of anti-social impulses. It has been pointed out above that the development of industry brings into being a political class whose members are less capable of keeping in check their primitive impulses than the economically better situated class that led society before. It will now be clear why democracy is insecure in the hands of this new class. They will be its champions as long as they expect it to yield them immediate advantages. They fall a ready prey to disappointment when these advantages fail to appear. Only those who have taken the trouble to educate themselves politically will retain their self-possession in the inevitable disillusionment, because they have learned to think and to wait. But among the mass, among those whose frustrations, desires, and exhaustion have not found any compensation, the tendency will arise to turn away from democracy because its demands are too " difficult " of fulfilment.

In the course of democratisation as it proceeded in Western and Central Europe during the 19th and 20th centuries, the new social classes only gradually attained full political equality. The process may be most clearly followed in the several stages by which in Great Britain the franchise was extended to ever larger sections of the nation. In Germany this extension was not so gradual. Here, universal and equal suffrage with secret ballot was established by law when the constitution of the North German Confederation was embodied in the newly founded Reich in 1871. But the Reichstag lacked the actual parliamentary responsibility of its Western models. Besides, other political institutions, such as the Prussian Diet with its Three-Class franchise, helped to prevent the real democratisation of Germany. It was only with the foundation of the Weimar Republic in 1919 that Germany became a democracy, in which practically all men and women over twenty years had the right to vote.

However, the influence exerted by the lower classes depends not only on the extension of the franchise, but also on the use which they make of it. In peaceful times there is a kind of tacit understanding that politics are the concern of a group of professional politicians and journalists. The broader masses take part in them only during electoral campaigns and even then many of them abstain from voting. The failure to make use of democratic rights is certainly not in accordance with the democratic ideal, but it is the lesser evil as long as it keeps only the incompetent from the poll and does not spring from hostility to democracy itself.

This attitude is likely to be adopted when the hopes built on the democratic system fail demonstrably. Benedetto Croce [187] points out that an anti-parliamentarian feeling spread throughout Europe in the 1880's. People made " great discoveries with great airs, such as that of the ' lie ' of the electorate and the parliaments where there was, indeed, no other lie, but the difference that always exists between the juridical form and the historical reality ". One might call the difference also that between reality and idea, which is the tragedy inherent in any realisation.

In general, disappointment at the working of democracy makes itself felt in three ways. First of all, the possessing classes are disappointed when the alliance between them and the proletariat, which existed at the time of the common struggle against feudalism, eventually breaks up. They then feel that their property is threatened by the political emancipation of the masses. To the extent to which the workers proceed to strive for " economic " as well as " political " emancipation, a clear-cut difference of interests arises between them and political Liberalism. In the resulting antagonism the propertied class are a minority, and thus at a hopeless disadvantage as long as the struggle is fought out on a strictly democratic basis. But the proletarians are also disappointed. Relying on their majority, they regard their right to vote only as the first step towards economic equality. But they soon find that their predominance in numbers is far from securing them a political predominance. Workers continue to help their " class-enemies " to seats in Parliament. And if their own representatives become numerous enough to take part in the Government, the result is even more discouraging. The political *élan* of the party is blunted by inevitable compromises. Its accession to power leads to controversies within its own ranks, not infrequently to splits and a fatal weakening of its strength. Once more, ideal and reality are in conflict, and the ideal suffers.

Finally, certain intellectual believers in democracy are also disappointed. To this Professor Graham Wallas in his book *Human Nature in Politics*, which was first published in 1908,[188] offers almost alarming testimony—alarming not only on account of its clear recognition of the largely emotional motives which govern political decisions, but equally by its almost prophetic insight. Professor Wallas has to admit, first of all, the importance of the irrational in politics. He foresees, furthermore, that under the strain of an intense social conflict democracy might degenerate in such a way as to exhibit all the characteristics later known as Fascist.[189] The author warns democracy against the dangers arising from the modern achievements of civilisation,[190] and he points with deep concern to the possibility that modern half-education and the irrational motives of the electorate might be systematically misused for dangerous political ends.[191] If Professor Wallas's experiences and insight can be regarded as representative, we may assume that as early as at the beginning of the 20th century the wine even of the most ardent democrats had already been considerably diluted.[192]

But the critics of democracy were not content with mere words. Property continued increasingly to stem the flood of the big numbers by tightening its grip on public opinion. Part of the workers changed to an anti-parliamentarian outlook. In 1908, the year in which Professor Wallas published his book, the French political philosopher Georges Sorel attacked both reformism and parliamentarianism in his *Les Réflexions sur la violence*.[193] For Sorel the declaration of the Rights of Man is " only a colourless collection of abstract and confused formulas without any great practical bearing ".[194] His tendency to abandon all other " difficult " standards along with them is obvious. He rebels against reason and the belief in progress.[195] He criticises the indirect methods of democracy and opposes to them " Direct Action " and the " myth " of the General Strike. He pours scorn on political routine and praises enthusiastically the " idea of greatness " for which the present age is uncongenial.[196]

The writings of Sorel mark an important stage in the recrudescence of violence.* A faithful interpreter of Nietzsche's " master morality ",[197] Sorel regards the reintroduction of violence into politics as a momentous step forward.[198] Surprisingly naïve but equally significant is Sorel's view of violence as a higher kind of morality. He calls his *Réflexions sur la*

* Cf. p. 89.

violence a " moral philosophy ",[199] and assumes that in civil war moral strength will spontaneously unfold itself.[200] He goes so far as to declare that a " high civilising value " is inherent in the doctrine of revolutionary syndicalism [201] which he would substitute for parliamentarism. Sorel played a great part in leading the workers' movements in France and other Latin countries away from reformist trade-unionism to revolutionary syndicalism, and his influence penetrated still farther. True, syndicalism did not at any time spread very widely among German workers, who were rendered immune by Social Democratic training. But some very characteristic syndicalist trends which appeared in Germany during the first post-war years proved that primitive ideologies, demanding no intellectual or moral effort, but flattering to human instincts, could in time of bewilderment be extremely dangerous rivals to Socialism in the fight for the soul of the proletariat.[202] Even without the official claim of Fascism to have taken over the syndicalist heritage,[203] it is obvious that both the Italian and the German brand of Fascism have many features in common with syndicalism. That Sorel should have prefaced his *Réflexions sur la violence* with a letter to the French Jew Daniel Halévy, thanking him for many " inspirations ", strikes one as a piece of unconscious irony. For, in reality, the path which he advocated led logically to anti-Semitism and National Socialism.

Syndicalism is an unmistakable symptom of the general lowering of political morality. With its anti-democratic maxims it undermined loyalty to democracy among the workers, who, by reason of their numbers, were naturally predisposed to find democracy attractive. It aggravated, on the other hand, the other mass leanings towards lower standards, that is to say, it helped to obliterate the more difficult social duties,[204] which at the same time had been partly written off by the ruling classes. This is emphasised by Hobhouse, who expressly denies that the lowering of the political level can be attributed to the extension of the franchise. " The corruption ", he says, " has in fact spread from above downwards." He continues, however : " All classes alike give way to Jingoism, and shut their ears to reason and humanity ".[205] And this description is correct. It was the concurrence of the two processes which lowered the general political level.

These tendencies can be seen at work in all democratic

societies, and it cannot even be said that their destructive power was particularly great in Germany. For, although the social disintegration had gone farther there than in Western Europe, it was partly compensated by the comparatively high power of resistance of the working-class. In Germany, however, three special factors were at work which fatally combined with those mentioned above to bring about the overthrow of democracy: the peculiar nature of the German national consciousness, the lack of democratic tradition, and the disruptive effect of the German post-war crisis.

From the preceding analysis it will be clear that the anti-democratic bias began to take root before the masses had commenced to make use of their potential democratic power, *i.e.* before they seriously challenged private property. When in the elections for the German National Assembly in 1919 the masses made themselves effectively felt by a poll of 82·68 per cent, and the ruling classes felt seriously threatened, the decay of democracy was already on the way. It was thus not surprising that in Germany, that country without democratic tradition, disappointment with democratic achievements did not lead to renewed democratic efforts, but to the gradual abandonment of the idea of democracy. When finally the democratic potentialities of the people were once more exerted almost to their limit, viz. in polls of 82 per cent, 84 per cent, and 88·7 per cent,[206] it was for the purpose of overthrowing, not supporting democracy. The three factors adverse to democracy were now working in conjunction. The masses were tired of a freedom which seemed to avail them nothing, the cynical politicians who had been Graham Wallas's nightmare did not scruple to exploit this state of weariness, and big business, impelled by fear, financed the politicians.

With this last stage of development we shall deal more fully later. For the moment we are still concerned with the stage preceding it and with the characteristics of the transition. Leaving aside various possibilities of combination and gradation, the relations of governments to their subjects are fundamentally as follows. In an autocracy one main task of the ruler and his ministers is to give orders. They demand obedience from their subjects. This demand will be readily complied with as long as the belief of the subjects in the necessity of the existing order is unshaken. In a constitutionally restricted monarchy or an aristocracy the function of giving orders will be increasingly supplemented by that of guiding the emancipated part of the people. To the extent to which the governmental functions have been transferred to popular representatives, these too and those who wish to join their ranks will have to exercise the function of guidance. Guidance consists in an appeal to political ideas and interests, and an attempt to bring these into agreement with each other by means of rational or seemingly rational arguments. The aim is to convince the public that the programme of the Government, or alternatively of the would-be Government, is in accordance with their specific ideas and interests. The instruments of guidance are political organisations, lectures, public meetings, and the Press. This is practically the state of affairs prevailing also in the early stage of unrestricted democracy, and on the whole it remains characteristic of quiet democratic periods. It changes fundamentally only when in times of political or economic unrest the masses make use of their latent powers. They will then tend to throw off the guidance of professional politicians which they had so far accepted, and to exert a more direct influence on their own political fate. They will transfer their confidence to new, more or less untried, politicians of whom they have not yet had time to grow tired. These new would-be representatives, as also the old ones who want to retain their power, will, in such a crisis, have again to change their method of working on public opinion. They will have to replace political guidance by mass propaganda. They will have to appeal to emotions and desires, and the more completely they apply their reason to the task of influencing these irrational motives, the more successful will they be.

Such conditions, in which the masses are definitely on the move, will normally arise only in periods of acute crisis. But the possibility of mobilising at least part of the habitual non-voters and thus of tipping the balance in favour of one's own party is also in ordinary times a temptation to employ propagandistic methods of the above-mentioned kind.

The paradoxical consequence is that democracy becomes. endangered when its latent potentialities become effective to a high extent. Democracy is safest when those who are not politically minded leave the exercise of political rights to the better informed and abstain from voting. When they are awakened by the impact of great economic and political events or by powerful propaganda, they are likely to influence political decisions towards the more primitive. If in such a crisis democracy does not command sufficient unquestioning loyalty among the nation, the call for a " strong man ", which can always reckon on a certain emotional response, can become an acute danger.[207]

But the debasing influence of the entry of the masses into politics does not affect the concept of democracy only. Many other concepts suffer similarly when they are manipulated by the political technique not of guidance but of propaganda. Some of the more general trends of mass reaction upon political ideologies may be thus formulated :

(1) The more primitive the ideology, the greater the likelihood of its acceptance by the masses.

(2) When the masses are presented with an elaborate, or what has been called a " difficult " ideology, they accept only its primitive, its " easy " elements. Those elements which are accepted by all members of a certain group of people will be the more primitive, the larger the numbers who accept them.

(3) An ideological element is felt as the more " easy ", the fewer demands it makes on reason and morality, and the more immediately it appeals to the lower human desires. Some of the general impulses which determine the masses in their selection of ideologies are self-assertion, preservation of species, craving for enrichment, aggressiveness.

This formulation merely sums up much of what has been said before about the debasement of principles. Guidance and propaganda differ chiefly in the attitude which each takes to this downward " gravitation ". As long as its implications are reluctantly recognised and the desire is still strong to counteract them as much as possible,* it is still the technique of rational guidance which prevails. Only if politicians begin deliberately to exploit the above-described conditions in order to produce as great an effect as possible on the masses, do they pass from rational guidance to irrational propaganda. This transition runs parallel with the awakening of the masses in a democracy. As this awakening takes place intermittently, quickens in times of crisis and slows down in times of prosperity or peace, the change in the technique employed for moving the masses is likewise not a steady process. But despite hindrances and interruptions it still asserts itself. And those who, in a period of severest crises, drove it ruthlessly to its crowning point,

* Cf. what has been said above about Professor Graham Wallas, p. 113.

achieved thus the greatest mass effect known in history—the Nazi movement.

The German post-war crisis was a striking example of the lowering of the propagandistic level going hand in hand with the awakening of the masses. By the time the poll had reached the figure of 88·7 per cent, viz. in March 1933, propaganda had become a veritable orgy. Both reason and self-restraint were entirely cast to the winds. This was the situation in which the last elections for the Reichstag, which were still to some extent a free expression of the voters' wills, were held. After the composition of this Parliament had been further manipulated by the exclusion of the Communists, it became ossified in so far as no further elections were permitted which might even approximately have reflected public opinion.

With this ossification the change in the political representation of the German people had, for the time being, reached its limit. It had passed from an intellectual and artistic *élite* through a group of professional politicians to the disappointed and frustrated masses. An intellectual *élite* still existed, even though it no longer consisted of world-famous thinkers and poets, but of scientific specialists. This change, though no doubt a step back,* is not sufficient to account for the rise of National Socialism, still less for the catastrophe of the Jews. However much it may be regretted that the intellectual leaders replaced universal wisdom with limited specialism,[208] the political effect of such a development must not be overestimated. The modern intellectuals may have been one-sided, even mediocre as compared with their predecessors, but they still retained some independence of judgment, they were prepared to listen to arguments and capable of testing them, and they recognised, as a matter of course, a minimum code of morality. The catastrophe of the Jews would never have happened if the national representation had continued to rest with an intellectual *élite*, even one which had deteriorated. Many of the members of the learned professions in Germany were fervent nationalists, not a few of them were jealous and ambitious. In this they were only normal Germans and human beings and as far removed from the average level of the Nazi politicians as normal beings are from a thoroughly anti-social attitude.

It was much the same with the professional politicians and journalists, who had hitherto been the recognised spokesmen

* This is the first of the three processes mentioned on p. 101.

of the masses. It is not difficult to condemn them if one applies to their actions the criterion of any ideal precept. But when all their limitations have been taken into account, the same is true of them as of the intellectuals. Many who have had dealings with them can testify to the fact that even the anti-Semites among them never thought of anti-Jewish measures of the kind the Nazis carried out. But steadily the influence of both these groups diminished. The intellectuals counted for precisely the number of voting papers they put into the ballot-box, and the former party leaders lost their hold on the masses. When, finally, the politically indifferent—especially women—aroused by Nazi propaganda, flocked in overwhelming numbers to the polls, it was of no avail that the Social Democratic bulwark and the Catholic Centre Party withstood even this propagandistic assault, retaining respectively 120 out of 121, and 70 out of 73 seats. The Nazis had definitely managed to harness the extremely widespread feelings of anxiety and despair to their own party wagon. For the first time the broad mass of petty bourgeois who had formerly swayed from one party to the other had been united on one political platform, where they were joined even by unemployed workers who in their misery turned against Socialism as too " difficult ". No wonder the Nazi success was overwhelming.

Thus it came about that that section of the German people which was least capable of civilised conduct came to be the determining factor in German political life. They were not aware of their anti-social leanings. They did not consciously approve of murder and theft. They had no idea of the extent to which their power of moral resistance had been paralysed. Neither were they any longer able to judge what kind of people their votes had presented with a licence for arbitrary acts. Nazism had given expression to their fears, their envy, and their hatred, and had thus achieved its resounding success. No longer did the appeal to these mass emotions serve ultimate moral purposes. Even the idealistic trappings of Nazism originated almost exclusively in the primitive amoral sphere.

If up to that time representatives of the masses had entered the Government, they had accepted without hesitation the social, and thus to a considerable extent also the moral, standards which prevailed there. In the case of socialist workers' representatives, this adaptation had resulted not infrequently in tragic conflicts, as the proletarian voters were inclined to regard what was a more or less external adjustment as an abandonment of socialist principles. The Nazi voters could at the most experience the opposite disappointment. Their parliamentary representatives had not pretended to be bound by the Western European moral code, and they made full use of this liberty. Those among their followers and friendly critics who had believed that their brutality, their uncouthness, and their undisguised threats were only propaganda devices which would soon be discarded under the ennobling influence of responsibility, saw themselves deceived. Ruthlessness was a genuine expression of Nazism, and not merely a means for carrying on political agitation.

There are, it is true, evil elements mixed with the good ones in every fairly large group of human beings. But the adoption by National Socialism of an anti-social attitude is no mere coincidence, it is an intrinsic necessity. An anti-social attitude is the logical outcome of the liberation of primitive impulses. By the sheer weight of numbers, those people who were thoroughly tired of their more difficult social obligations determined who was to represent the German State. Their representatives could only be such persons as had taken the lead in this movement of " liberation ". That they were capable of collective crimes thus hardly needs an explanation. Why among their victims they chose to give a horrible preference to the Jews will be further explained in the following chapters.

III

THE SCENE

So FAR, this study has been concerned with the period in which the emancipation of the Jews took place. The tendencies which were shown to endanger emancipation and integration can be found, at least in embryo, throughout Central and Western Europe and beyond in America. It has been necessary to consider these ubiquitous tendencies, since it is they which appear to justify the widespread fears that the events in Germany may be repeated elsewhere. But grave as are these dangers, they would not in themselves have brought about the catastrophe of the Jews had they not been combined with other causes peculiar to the situation in Germany.

Those who, in the explanation of any problem, seek for one central cause round which all the others may be grouped, might, with some justification, explain the catastrophe of the German Jews by the one fact that Germany lies in the middle of Europe. From this, to begin with, certain facts can be derived which are essential for an understanding of the situation of the Jews in Germany. First, their relative density was due to their proximity to the East, while an absence of mass settlements made the structure of their community similar to that of the Western Jews. Secondly, their emancipation had been granted under the influence of Western Europe, but it was partially withdrawn under the influence of the feudal Reaction which still emanated from the eastern territories. Closely connected with these peculiarities was the characteristic mixture of Jewish and German cultural elements in the way of life of German Jewry, which was a synthesis of Jewish traditions and German civilisation.

Germany's central situation plays an equally important part with regard to some of the most intricate of her internal problems. From the beginning of German history this central position has been the source of difficulties—some of them directly affecting Jewish-Gentile relations—far outweighing the advantages it brought. Moreover, this central position was not the only respect in which Germany had been ill favoured by geography. She suffered from two further defects, a lack of natural frontiers, which were so fortunately presented to the British Isles, and a lack of a natural geographic centre, which France possessed in the Seine Valley.[209] A perpetual state of insecurity, inner divisions, and the rise of territorial princes as heirs to the power of the Empire were, to no small degree, the results of these defects. While France, Spain, and England made headway against the territorial potentates towards national unity, while in Italy there emerged only a comparatively small number of separate States, in Germany the territorial magnates prevailed in the contest against the Emperor. They acquired ever greater privileges at the cost of the central power. " German history knows no fact of greater moment." [210] When towards the conclusion of the 18th century the Reich approached its dissolution, it consisted of 314 independent territories and 1475 imperial knights, amounting altogether to 1789 independent authorities.[211]

The narrow-mindedness and submissiveness which were implanted in the German character by the conditions of life in these territories and the personal government of the princes were by no means their most serious consequences.[212] A much more important one was the tardiness of Germany's national unification. Of this and its fatal effects so much has been said and written that it may be regarded as a matter of common knowledge. It must, however, be emphasised that the continuance of German disunity far into the epoch of the European national States was the most potent cause of that abnormal national consciousness in the Germans which is so closely related to their anti-Semitism ; but not only was this condition responsible for the continued immaturity of the national consciousness ; it also gave the national question an unhealthy predominance over the social and political questions which in other countries in the course of the 19th century moved into the foreground of public affairs ; it absorbed the attention of the people at the moment when their interest in politics began to awake, and at the same time diverted it from the struggle for their own political rights. This preoccupation with " unity ", besides overshadowing the striving for " freedom ", likewise obscured its meaning. Just as the War of Liberty, which initiated this epoch, was officially renamed " War of Liberation ", so the whole concept of Liberty received a purely nationalist colouring. Instead of freedom of the individual it came to mean more and more frequently freedom from the external enemy.[213] The unnatural state of national disunity took its revenge, as it were, by concentrating too much of the available energy on its removal.

Some of the specific difficulties of the Jewish emancipation in Germany are connected with this point. The general preoccupation with the problem of national unity hampered the internal development. And the late democratisation of Germany accounts for her complete lack of a democratic tradition, a defect the sinister consequences of which for the fortunes of the Jews can hardly be overrated. Democratic tradition would have been the only force which might have effectively countered the anti-democratic tendencies of the German post-war years. It was precisely its absence which made the Nazi success possible. But long before this fatal climax had been reached, the weakness of the average German citizen's attachment to liberty entailed another difficulty for Jewish-Gentile relations in Germany. While the Gentile citizens gradually became preoccupied with what alone they regarded as " national affairs ", the Jews continued to be primarily concerned with internal progress, as this was, among other things, inseparably connected with the preservation of their rights. This divergence was largely responsible for the anti-Semitic allegation that the Jews were not " nationally minded ", as indeed every progressive endeavour gradually became suspect as conflicting with a " national " outlook.[214]

The lack of natural boundaries had for centuries resulted in almost continuous military clashes on the German frontiers. It had made Germany the battleground of numerous European wars. The frequent transference of border lands from one hand to another, the ability of these lands to enter into alliances either with members of the Reich or with its enemies—all such uncertainties added fresh obstacles to the formation of a healthy national feeling, self-confident without being chauvinistic. As a result of this lack of well-defined boundaries national dreams and ambitions exceeded all reasonable measure. They were governed less by actual political conditions than by the range of the German language and such vague notions as those of " Volkstum " and race.[215] " In the absence of a natural boundary ", says the Belgian historian Henri

Pirenne,[216] " the conqueror only believed in security when he had destroyed the enemy State ". Many German characteristics which later on frightened the world as militarism, expansionism, and ruthless power politics, may thus be explained without bringing in racial mysticism. For a long time such things merely stimulated the imagination. But when new political developments enabled them to exercise their full influence, they precipitated the course of events with the force of a stream that has burst its dam.[217]

Indeed, one need not resort to any kind of cloudy mysticism to explain certain striking features in the German national character.

At the time of the great maritime discoveries Germany's economic development began to lag behind that of Western Europe in consequence of her remoteness from the Atlantic Ocean. Her proximity to Western Europe, on the other hand, rendered her easily accessible to all ideas emanating from that quarter. These ideas, notably in the political field, belonged to a higher stage of development than Germany had yet reached. Thus the contact had far-reaching consequences.

Here again, for the sake of clarity, it is advisable to simplify matters by referring to the ideas which originated in Western Europe in the 18th and 19th centuries and spread to the neighbouring German provinces simply as ideas of progress and civilisation. This is, of course, to ignore the specifically German distinction between culture and civilisation, by which culture, understood as the inner spiritual unity of an age, was exalted at the cost of civilisation, which was mainly taken to mean technical progress. German writers not infrequently, indeed, went so far as to identify the progress of civilisation with cultural retrogression. We, on the contrary, regard enlightenment, rationalism, and the ideas of the French Revolution as definite progress because they have advanced the individual towards greater personal dignity, and raised society on to a higher level of justice.

These Western ideas have never succeeded in penetrating deeply into the minds of the German people. Many writers have pointed this out. Thus Heinrich von Treitschke speaks of the " ugly dregs of barbarity " which come to light at every stage of German cultural development; [218] Hobhouse states that the spirit of the West has only very superficially touched Germany; [219] the psychologist C. G. Jung personifies the spirit of pagan barbarity, persevering in Germany under the surface of Western civilisation, as the old German god Wodan; [220] the German anti-Semite Hans Blueher maintains that Germany is still to-day living in a state of prolonged armistice with official Christianity and nobody knows whether the pagan sacrificial flames have been really extinguished; [221] Professor Friedrich Wilhelm Foerster points out that " Germany was closer to the steppes of Asia than to the Mediterranean. . . . There were therefore far fewer obstacles to its relapse into barbarism " ; [222] and, finally, D. H. Lawrence in an almost prophetic vision sees " the ancient spirit of pre-historic Germany coming back at the end of history, back, back to the savage polarity of Tartary and away from the polarity of civilised Christian Europe ".[223] In the mouth of none of these critics is the allusion to Germany's barbaric potentialities merely a rhetorical phrase. All of them, and the many others who have taken the same line, genuinely feel that the tension between barbarity and civilisation, between paganism and Christianity, between East and West is nowhere on earth so acute as it is in Germany.

A statement of this kind, it is true, cannot be scientifically proved. None the less it admirably serves the purpose of expressing vividly the popular conception of Germany's situation in the middle of Europe. That Germany belongs only half to Western culture, that Asiatic darkness underlies the bright civilised surface, that the perpetual motion, the " Faustic " principle, which has disquieted her Western neighbours, originates in the half-Asiatic chaos that has survived under a thin veneer of order and Christianity—these are the phrases by which Western Europe used to account to itself for the fact that Germany's West-to-East extension was wide enough to comprehend the vineyards of the Rhine valley and the beginning of the boundless steppes of Asia.

There are, however, more tangible consequences of the collision between the progressive ideas of the West and the immature conditions prevailing in Germany. In France, owing to the position of Paris as the centre of administration, court, and army, a demand for manufactured standard articles had already developed there under the absolutist regime. This led to the rise of a numerous and well-to-do middle-class whose members were the natural standard-bearers of the fight against feudalism. In Germany, at the same time, no numerous middle-class existed.[224]   If the literature of the end of the 18th century speaks of a threefold division of the population into aristocracy, middle-class, and craftsmen, it means by middle-class not a distinct class but either all persons of moderate income or educated people.[225]   The ideas flowing into the country from the West were therefore not imbibed by a rising social class which adapted them to its needs, but they influenced in the first place the intellectual leaders of the nation, philosophers, writers, and scholars.   Since the German people was no less backward politically than it was economically, it is not surprising that German thinkers gave to both the liberal and the national ideas an abstract and doctrinaire interpretation.   While they turned them over and over in their minds, they had no background of reality against which they could survey and measure them.   Thus idealist exaggerations and distortions came into being and wrought enduring harm.[226]

Franz Schnabel points out that the part played in France by political lawyers in the promotion of political science was played in Germany by the political Professors.[227]   The difference, he says, was that the French lawyers, by the experience which they gathered in political and legal activities, made learning " open-minded " (*weltoffen*) and, on the other hand, brought broad views to bear on daily practice.   In Germany, however, the shaping of political thought lay in the hands of scholars who had little contact with practical life.   It must be added that the Prussian State deliberately sought to divert intellectual activity from politics to the fields of art and science, where it was considered harmless.[228]   Part of the energies which did not find an adequate outlet in business and politics did indeed follow the desired course.   The unreality of the German present was distinctly conducive to the attainment of intellectual eminence.[229]

It may with justice be held that this German spirit soared too high above the level of ordinary life.   The unattainable standard of duty set by Kant, the glorification of the nation by Fichte, and the deification of the State by Hegel have in the long run been detrimental.   By raising these concepts to a height which could be reached in thought but not in action, these philosophers gave them a dangerously radical character. Moreover, with their excessively difficult style they widened the gulf separating ordinary people from the realm of learning. The proverbial political immaturity of the Germans is certainly due in the first place to their delayed political emancipation. But it should also be ascribed in part to this outrageous intellectualism of their leaders. The German fondness for theories and ideologies, their almost superstitious belief in " scientific " systems has no doubt been greatly promoted by this tradition. Both have had disastrous results in the field with which we are concerned. Furthermore, this intellectual exaltation, from which amoral theories also profited, resulted in a general weariness with ideals. While this affected first the intellectuals, it could not fail to influence indirectly the rising masses as well.[230]

But the rapid advance of German thought had yet another consequence bearing on the subject of this study. It led to a quicker disintegration of Christianity than took place in other European countries. " In no other modern people had pantheism and classical ethics been adorned so enchantingly as in Germany by the immortal works of her poets."[231] When it is added that in no other modern people was the deification of the State and the nation carried so far as in Germany, then the disintegrating influence exerted by the German intellectual *élite* on religion will be understood. In spite of Pietism and romantic conversions to Roman Catholicism, in spite of the religiously tinged quietism which was generated by the weariness following the War of Liberation, there was no really successful religious movement in Germany to counteract the slow slipping-away of the masses from Christianity. To a certain extent, this weakness of the official Church may be due to the frequent connection between Protestantism and reactionary movements.[232] Another potent factor should be looked for in the division between Protestants and Catholics.

Germany, a land without real political life, lacked also a real religious life in so far as this is dependent on the dominance of a single creed. Thus Treitschke declares with undisguised satisfaction that the better minds of the German People " have already outgrown the conflict of religious opinions " and have been uplifted to that religious view " which alone is worthy of free men ", and he calls religion " a subjective need of the weak human heart " ; [233] but he also tells us what part religious dualism played in this development. " The German nation ", he says elsewhere,[234] " was the only one with religious parity among the great peoples, and it was therefore forced to fortify the peace it had won at the price of so much bloodshed by the habit of every new day. . . . The dearly purchased religious toleration prepared the way for a moderate liberty, a cautious audacity of thinking, such as never prosper under the absolutism of a single church." Treitschke thus regards the tolerance and spiritual liberty which were necessitated by the close contact of two different denominations as the prerequisite of German philosophical achievement. But whether the rapid and thorough secularisation is attributed indirectly or directly to the religious parity, the connection itself seems evident.[235]

It will never be possible to estimate with any degree of accuracy the power of religious faith among the masses of the people. Schnabel is of the opinion that a considerable part of the educated classes in Germany had already renounced Christianity in the first half of the 19th century and that many members of the upper middle-class in trade and commerce showed a " profound indifference " towards it.[236] The universities, too, with their academic liberty and their emancipation from clerical influence, were, in his opinion, breeding-places of religious scepticism. From here it infiltrated into the medium and lower strata. " Thus in Germany, more quickly than in other nations, the road of culture led in the direction of religious indifference." [237] It must be emphasised, however, that the Roman Catholic population, which amounts to roughly one-third of the German People, did not succumb to this process of disintegration to anything like the same extent as the Protestants.

This fact has a special significance in relation to the Jewish problem. It contradicts the generally held opinion that the dissolution of dogmatic Christianity has favoured the acceptance of the Jews.* This view seems at first sight plausible, because people are still inclined to regard the Jewish problem as primarily religious. As long as this was actually the case, a relaxation of Christian dogmas did indeed promote tolerance. Enlightenment therefore, as has already been mentioned, did much to prepare the way for emancipation. But after anti-Semitism had become first and foremost a product of mass frustration, the situation changed fundamentally. The primary cause of it is now the inner need for aggression felt by the masses, while the ideology which justifies this aggressiveness is secondary. The masses do not crave for an attack on the Jews

* Cf. pp. 76 and 77.

particularly—any other " enemy " would serve equally well. What matters is only that the object presented to them as the " enemy " should be capable of inciting their aggressiveness to the fullest measure and should then attract it to itself.

In this new stage of the history of anti-Semitism the decline of Christianity contributes to its spread. It makes for the above-mentioned aimlessness* which can become so dangerous. It " leaves extra-rational cravings running about like masterless dogs ",[238] anxious to find shelter and incapable of judging whether they will be offered a hospitable refuge or will be made to chase and hurt human beings. For people who are not simultaneously captivated by some pseudo-religious substitute which obliges them to behave morally, the decline of religion is equivalent to moral decline. Secularised values generally make too few concessions to instincts and phantasy and can therefore, for the most part, attain influence only among intellectuals. They are bound to be ineffective with the masses, because they do not cater sufficiently for their emotions and primitive desires. It is too difficult to be good without being aided by love of God or fear of God, or—more primitive still—by the hope for reward or the fear of punishment in the next world.

The German Catholics, particularly the older generation, who were still supported by these moral props, showed on the average a stronger resistance to Nazism and anti-Semitism. This statement is not contradicted by the part which Bavaria played in the rise of the movement. In Bavaria the mitigating influence of Roman Catholicism was outweighed by the resentment aroused by the rising of revolutionary socialists in Munich after the first World War, in which a number of Jews were prominent. This amply accounts for the Bavarian pro-Nazi enthusiasm and anti-Semitism during the initial stage of the movement. But even this enthusiasm spread mainly among the youth and had little lasting hold upon the older people. Experience in the rest of the Catholic districts, in the Rhine province and Upper Silesia, testifies so unmistakably to the moderating influence of Catholicism that it may be considered as clearly established as so vague a fact, which defies exact measurement, can be. Marxism, again, was a real substitute for religion. Imbued as it was with the values of German idealism, its creed stood on the side of civilisation. The subse-

* V. p. 77.

quent religious substitute of Nazism was devoid of these values and was therefore on the side of barbarism. To the same extent that the disintegration of Christianity had gone farther in Germany than in other countries, the drift towards barbarism was stronger there than elsewhere.

While thus the spiritual ideas of the West were reborn in Germany to a dangerous life of their own, their political lessons were frequently opposed because they came from abroad. This applies in the first place to the ideas of the French Revolution. It has been mentioned that economic and social conditions in Germany had not reached the stage of development which in France had contributed to produce the insurrection against feudalism. This fact, no doubt, justified to a certain extent a counter-revolutionary outlook, which on that account must have commended itself even to the wisest and most detached of statesmen. Such an ideal statesman, however, would have opposed only an over-hasty political progress, but not progress as such. One may, therefore, say that the great reforms which preceded the War of Liberation in Prussia lay more or less in the lines of such wise statesmanship, though no contribution was made to them by the people themselves. And yet the idea of the people's sovereignty should not at that time have been absent from any statesmanship worthy of the name.

Since the foreign progressive ideas were taken up and pursued in Germany by a group of intellectuals, the immature economic conditions wrought more harm than they otherwise might have done, because these intellectuals built on them extreme political theories. Men like Adam Müller, von der Marwitz, and the Bern patrician Ludwig von Haller, instead of striving for the gradual elimination of the feudal relics they found in Prussia, made them the corner-stone of their political systems. Since politics at that time were the business of small circles of educated people who are more directly influenced by elaborate political theories than the broader sections which later became politically important, these systems exercised a strong and lasting effect.[239] They gave the medieval concepts of the German East an enduring form, a form in which they not only outlived their era but, to some extent, the institutions themselves whose reflected images they had been.

For those who desire the preservation of existing conditions the spectre of revolutionary troubles is always a welcome means of deterring those who are anxious for change. Nothing can so easily be used to create prejudice against new ideas as the atrocities elsewhere connected with their realisation. Counter-revolutionaries of all times and places are likely to resort to this method. A considerable time will have to pass in each case before the forces seeking to imitate the revolution and those who are deterred by it have adjusted their respective powers and created a new state of balance. The immediate effect of a revolution in an adjacent country is frequently counter-revolutionary, because those who are interested in the *status quo* are in power and with their power try to subdue those who seek to imitate the revolutionary achievements.

This was the case in England. But this country had for long been a unified nation, and when eventually the forces of revolution could no longer be suppressed a compromise between them and the existing order was effected peacefully and within the framework of existing national institutions. Far different were the effects of the French Revolution in Germany, where they corresponded accurately to the German dissension between East and West. In West and South Germany the revolutionary events set in motion an agitation for parliamentary representation, whilst in Prussia it first inspired reforms from above and later prompted their withdrawal. In some other German States like Mecklenburg and Saxony it brought about no visible change. Thus in Germany this force also severed the national ties, by accentuating in some parts the revolutionary, in others the counter-revolutionary tendencies.

The extent of the effect can hardly be overrated. As a result of the characteristic German immaturity it was largely limited to the intellectual *élite*, but on this it was thorough and shattering. An approval varying from lively sympathy to loud enthusiasm during the first stages of the Revolution was superseded by bitter disillusionment, aversion, and not infrequently an outspoken counter-revolutionary attitude during the Jacobin period.[240] The letter of the Berlin Jewess Henriette Herz, which was written after the flight of the royal couple to Varennes, may be regarded as fairly typical of the general sentiment: [241] " From ardent supporters of the Revolution we became its bitter enemies—and this is a pretty general change. We were far from seeing in the bloody horrors the baptism of a new era, and we would never have purchased it at such a cost. Nor, though our wishes for our fatherland were ardent, would we have desired their fulfilment at the prices paid by the French."

Hegel too—to mention only one out of many—was among the converts.[242] Not only was his original enthusiasm transformed by the terror into intense abhorrence, but this change of mind contributed largely to his glorification of the State. The blood-stained anarchy of the Revolution made the power of the State appear to him more important than the freedom of the people.

It may be argued that the counter-revolutionary effect of the terror in France was not limited to Germany and, therefore, did not affect the course of German history differently from that of other countries. The democratic development of England, for instance, was delayed by it for several decades. The difference is, however, that the political development of England was far ahead of that of Germany. England, when the French Revolution broke out, had already important political institutions to preserve, institutions indeed from which the makers of the French Revolution themselves had derived no small part of their inspiration. Germany, on the other hand, the backward country, stood only on the threshold of modern evolution. Counter-revolution meant for her to continue at a much earlier stage, which was practically medieval. Thus, while the counter-revolutionary feeling caused in England only a temporary delay in an irreversible parliamentary-democratic evolution, in Germany an essentially similar feeling involved the retention of an outlived feudal form of Government, and also further cleavages between the several States following different political courses.

But the most fatal counter-revolutionary consequence was brought about by the fact that the Western ideas came not merely from abroad but from an enemy country. In this respect, too, the German experience of the French Revolution has something in common with the English, but here, as in the other case, the consequences were far more dangerous. For in Germany this period of war also gave birth to the national idea as such, which in the more fortunate island had slowly grown up in the preceding centuries. If the lack of a definite national boundary, of a unified State, of a politically conscious middle-class had stood like evil fairies by the cradle of this German national idea, the hostility generated through the wars against France was an even more sinister godmother. Certain though it is that the feeling of nationality, even if sprung from other sources, has derived part of its strength and justification from

132

armed contests with rival States, its birth from the spirit of military defeat must have truly fateful consequences. But military defeat was the fate of Germany between 1805 and 1807. When this had been followed by the secret preparation of a war of revenge, by the war of revenge itself, and the disappointments of the epoch of Restoration, the memories of the national uprising consisted mainly in hatred of France. This not only left its imprint on the young German nationalism, it could also be easily transferred to the political reforms inspired by French ideas. Henceforth there existed no more suitable means to discredit any progress, including the emancipation of the Jews which had been promulgated in the course of the great reforms, than to describe it as the product of that French influence, freedom from which had just been won in bloody battles.

The impact of the progressive ideas—which emanated likewise from the English and partly also from the American constitutional examples—on a country whose conditions were still backward as compared with the West, finally gave rise to a reactionary movement with some original and significant features. In these features we can see the most characteristic consequences of the above-mentioned West-East collision.

Political reaction is, of course, a phenomenon common to all bodies politic. It is one of the laws of political motion that it takes place largely in a rhythm of action and reaction. But in Germany reaction developed a philosophical outlook which gave it a special significance. In the West, reaction was the outcome of certain interests and ideas which were contained within the framework of Western civilisation. In Germany it meant mainly the repudiation of Western civilisation itself. German reaction found expression in political romanticism. It never completely vanished even in periods of liberal predominance, when Western models were followed. It became the breeding-ground of anti-Semitism. Its most characteristic features re-emerged in a grossly vulgarised form in National Socialism. Political romanticism is the essence of the German resistance to the West.

Romanticism has been described above as a phenomenon of regression which was adopted by the public in order to satisfy needs created by the increasingly heavy strain of life. We have now to consider the special conditions in Germany which favoured this movement. These lay in all those difficulties with which the Western ideas had to struggle on German soil. Romanticism turned to politics under the influence of national frustration mingled with the effect of semi-feudal conditions and interests, of the revolutionary terror in France, and the subsequent wars against her. In reflecting these European tensions, it reflected also the inner-German tension between East and West. In this light it is seen by the German historian of literature Josef Nadler,[243] who attaches decisive importance to the fact that in Germany two entirely different national groups have been welded together, the Roman-Germanic South-West and the German-Slav North-East.[244] " Two strangers by birth, by their historical cradle, by the growth of their thought were joined together to be one couple and destined by fate to grow into one body." [245] In a long process, lasting nearly the whole of the 15th century, the " bodies " of the Slavs east of the Elbe had been Germanised. But only then did the Germanisation of their souls begin. " To become German meant for these new tribes the acceptance of the German culture which had grown before their birth, *i.e.* before the 15th century. . . . This is the meaning, the course, and the significance of that new flowering of German culture which we are wont to call romanticism."[246] Nadler is far from regarding this collision of the two cultures as entirely beneficial. He is fully conscious of the political dangers inherent in it. " As long as the people [the German nation] were content with thinking and writing poetry, a peculiar beauty scintillated from the tension of their inner contrasts. What, then, when these people were called upon to act ? When they began to transform into deeds, in the coarse reality of life, the reflections of their dreams ? " [247]

Thus does Nadler make the inner-German East-West problem responsible for that German philosophy which has been the centre of all difficulties between Germany and the rest of Europe. No matter whether the German inclination to romanticism is explained from the political or from the cultural angle, it resulted in either case from the opposition to something alien. On the first explanation, the alien was the alluring power of the West, which by some circles was considered dangerous and hostile. On the other, it was East Germany's own Slav past whose bewildering after-effects she was anxious to abolish. Romanticism is thus from its beginning no self-confident toying with the past, that rejoices harmlessly over its own peculiarities; rather it is born from opposition and resentment and seeks to outdo the alien in national individuality. This birth from a negation, from the necessity to withstand a powerful adversary—be it without or within—gave the romantic cravings for Germanity from the start a tinge of exaggeration and convulsiveness.[248] Since the romanticists could not rejoice in any present national existence, they looked to the distant past for German glory. In dreams and poems they revived the German Middle Ages with their bold knights and fair ladies. They revelled in memories of the old imperial splendour and the once so mighty Catholic Church. They developed the feeling for scenery, the longing for unspoiled nature, and they delved deep into the fast disappearing mines of folklore, from which they brought to light forgotten treasures.

This resentment against the West and digging into the treasures of the past had an especially important result in the field of law. The Law of Nature which had been a revolutionary force in France was confronted by the theory of Historical Law. The introduction of the Code Napoléon in the territories belonging to the Rhenish Confederation was considered as an immediate challenge.[249] After the War of Liberation ended with the abolition of the French rule, it appeared urgently necessary to eradicate the foreign law. The ideology to justify this eradication was provided by the German philosopher Savigny. He pointed out that the development of the law in any country was determined, not by abstract ideas, but by the national spirit which grew organically with the nation itself, like the language, and which was closely connected with religion, customs, and the entire creative power of the people. In whose interests the rejection of the French law mainly operated may be gathered from the fact that one of the first adversaries of the Code Napoléon, August Wilhelm Rehberg, in his pamphlet published in 1813 attacked primarily the Napoleonic law of property. In attacking the redemption of all ground-rents, the breaking up of landed estates, and the introduction of the principle of " partage forcé " into the law of inheritance, he clearly stood for the privileges of the owners of big estates.[250]

Historical Law which opposed any interference with the organic growth of national law offered an extremely useful weapon to the reactionary movement. Very soon, indeed, adherence to Natural or Historical Law became the badge of opposing parties.[251] The Law of Nature remained the creed of the Liberals, whilst the Conservatives justified their hostility to progress by an appeal to Historical Law.

All this must not be misunderstood as involving any kind of adverse criticism of romanticism and Historical Law. German romanticism was so fertile a source of inspiration in all spheres of art that only with reluctance does one draw into the foreground its unfortunate consequences for the spiritual and political life of the nation. And yet there can hardly be any doubt that the enthusiasm for the Middle Ages greatly stimulated reaction, whilst the discovery of the German " Volkstum " fostered an aggressive nationalism. From both these notions, moreover, it was but one step to anti-Semitism. The economic elements in anti-Semitism were henceforth coloured by the feudal theories of the romanticists, whose natural leaning to economic anti-Semitism was manifest.[252] Where the political and cultural rejection of Jews was to be justified, national exaltation had only to be slightly exaggerated, and a cultural or racial anti-Semitism was reached. Because the Jews, it would then be argued, are irrevocably and definitely excluded from the German past as well as from the German race, they do not belong to the German nation now and cannot do so at any future time. Early history and racial " Volkstum " are the pillars on which the nation is built, yet the Jews have no share in either. What was still more important, reaction and nationalism hampered the progress of democracy and thus became responsible for the absence of the only power which in the crucial post-war period would have been able to prevent a political breakdown—a strong democratic tradition.

It was, moreover, the over-subtle theories of the intellectuals, the logical hair-splitting induced by the lack of contact with reality, which prepared the way for that peculiarly German patent "scientific anti-Semitism". These methods became valuable when, later on, after the Jewish problem in Germany had all but disappeared, people still desired to create one artificially and to prove its existence in pseudo-scientific terms. When the interested circles realised that the subjective definition of the concept " nation ", according to which he who feels himself to be of a nation does in fact belong to it, would leave no doubt as to the nationality of the vast majority of German Jews, they enunciated instead all kinds of " objective " theories of what made a nation, such as history and an arbitrarily defined "Volkstum" or race, in order to exclude the Jews. The over-valuation of the past, instigated by the lack of any ground for pride in the present, was a further danger for the Jews. An assured prospect for the future, the faith in progress, the self-reliant feeling of preparing the way for a new time by new ideas, make for optimism. They permit people to hope for changes and improvements, even if, for the time being, evil practices still prevail. They are inimical to rigid and unalter-able judgments. In the liberal atmosphere of the 19th century the Jews could succeed, because, if they lagged behind the general expectations, they were given the chance to remedy such defects. But to set excessive store by the "natural growth", the "living organism", or the "racial soul", implied the eternal condemnation of the Jew who had grown in different circumstances and came from a different stock.

Especially grave in their bearing on the Jewish problem were the consequences of the attack which the Historical School of Law made against the Law of Nature. It is not necessary here to discuss the respective philosophical and legal merits of these theories, since for our present purpose it is again not the ideas themselves that matter, but the public response they aroused. In this respect the essential fact was that in Germany the Law of Nature had little time to exert its influence before its validity was decisively challenged by the Historical Law. Hardly had the Germans begun to brace themselves for accept-ing the most revolutionary of all modern ideas, that funda-mentally all human beings are free and equal, when they were enticed back to the "welcome bed of ease"[253] of the Historical Law. Thus the great civilising force inherent in the extension of the rule of law to the last inhabitant of the globe was quickly neutralised. Although the Liberals continued to adhere to the Law of Nature, it was degraded to a party doctrine and thus became even less effective outside the party limits than if it had lacked any organised support at all. The Conservative part of the people soon complacently readjusted themselves to the view that law was intrinsically unequal, that it could not be severed from the "Volksgeist", and that arbitrary alterations on the basis of abstract ideas were not admissible. Such an attitude involved serious dangers for a newly emancipated minority. The emancipation of the Jews had been based on the demand for their equal rights. An actual equality between them and their environment existed as yet only in so far as they were fellow human beings, which is a highly abstract kind of equality. But it was precisely to this abstract idea that the emancipators had considered it their duty to pay tribute. The Jews were human beings—were they, however, as yet Germans? No, but they were supposed to become Germans on the basis of the newly acquired rights. Those who denied the right of general principles to determine law, who opposed artificial interferences with its natural evolution, which could only emanate from the " Volksgeist ", could not help being hostile to the emancipation of Jews. As a minority the Jews depended on the abstract and general notion of the Law of Nature. Any limitation of the law was bound to work against their admission. The Historical Law initiated in Germany a tradition of legal exclusiveness which did not make the German public better able or more prepared to accept a minority. When, later, after a comprehensive and successful process of integration into the Gentile society, the Jews were again artificially stamped as an " alien " minority, a strong feeling in the public in favour of the abstract Rights of Man would have been needed to safeguard their rights. But the Rights of Man, together with all the rest of the Western ideas, had by that time long been burnt on the bonfire which the Historical Law had helped to light.254

Mention must finally be made of another group of romantic elements which have proved unfavourable to the Jews and favourable to the development of anti-Semitism. Although they cannot be wholly ascribed to the specific German conditions then prevailing, a certain angry reaction against what was felt to be " French " rationalism and enlightenment played an important part in producing them. This irritation helped to establish the predominance which romanticism assigned to the emotions as against Reason, to obscurity as against clarity, and to the disregard as against the observance of form. At first sight, it is true, the connection of these features with the Jewish problem will not be evident. The romantic Jewesses of the Berlin *salons* felt strongly attracted by the romantic ways and doings, Heine's lyrics are unquestionably permeated with romanticism, and the relations between Bergson's philosophy and romanticism are manifest. All Jews were by no means rationalists, nor were all romanticists Gentile.255 Rather will the connection of the anti-rational attitude with anti-Semitism become clear through the following consideration.

To overcome a social tension as constituted the " genuine " Jewish question, the opposing parties must have some understanding of one another. They must gain an insight into the actual difficulties and then tackle them by common effort. True, it can happen that one of the parties refuses to co-operate and insists on a violent solution of the problem. This was, for instance, the attitude of the thoroughgoing adversaries of emancipation. They were defeated and, later on, became a minority even among the anti-Semites. The vast majority of the anti-Semites were of opinion that in some way or another one had to live with the Jews and to get rid of the objective Jewish problem. This objective problem did gradually lose much of its acuteness, as has been repeatedly pointed out. The Jews integrated themselves into Gentile Society, and the Jewish-Gentile relations became increasingly normal. But this favourable development was not in the interest of all parts of Gentile society. Anti-Jewish feelings which still prevailed among certain Gentile groups—whether they resulted from Jewish competition or from the political activities of some Jews —made it appear undesirable to them that the general tensions between majority and minority should continue to decrease. Because some Jews were disliked by some Gentiles, these Gentiles tried to represent all Jews as harmful to the whole people. It was in this attempt to distort a clash of private interests into a national problem that the romantic tradition rendered valuable service. Such a misrepresentation of a problem is indeed nothing uncommon. Some similar process is involved in the creation of every political ideology. But in the Jewish question it had a special significance.

In the later stages of the Jewish problem the clamour raised by propagandists grew out of all proportion to the social conflict involved. If Conservative politicians called the Social Democrats " fellows without a fatherland " and fought them as the " disturbers of peace and order ", covetous of other people's property, these phrases still had some connection with the most important problem of the epoch—the social question. The Social Democrats, after all, proclaimed themselves to be international and revolutionary. They openly strove for a redistribution of the social product. It was similar with the ideologies which favoured the emancipation of women. Even if its opponents were animated less by the desire to preserve the feminine ideal in all its purity than by the fear of female competition, yet here, too, a major problem affecting half of all human beings was involved. But what was at the bottom of the Jewish problem when the 19th century drew to a close and the 20th opened? A strictly limited complex of facts which were becoming less and less capable of arousing conflicts, and which would have interested only a few people, had it not been for the excessive publicity which these few were able to give it. Where such a disproportion between kernel and shell existed, the ideology had to accomplish a much more difficult task than in the above-mentioned instances of social problems. It had to practise magic as it were, to make very little go a very long way. Here clarity of expression and ordinary intelligible language were out of place. Sentiments, instincts, soul, and dream had to come to their aid, wrapping everything in obscurity and blunting all outlines. Thus, the renunciation of reason, which had once begun as awed humility in the presence of ultimate secrets, was perverted into an instrument of deception and an opiate of thought. While in the West a far-reaching tradition of rational self-education was in the making, while people were striving to establish binding forms and rules, in Germany this initiative was rapidly thwarted by romantic reaction. It was not the creation of romantic ideas itself which was decisive; but the speed and completeness with which romanticism spread among the people was disastrous.

The anti-Semitic literature of all periods abounds in instances of the dangers inherent in this anti-rationalist trend. Two examples, chosen because of the prominence of their authors, may be cited as representative. Wilhelm Stapel, the champion of the theory that in Germany after the first World War there was still an undiminished incompatibility between German and Jewish " Volkstum ", finds himself compelled after a great deal of arguing to resort to the following confession : [256] " Since this is a matter of psychological subtlety, I refuse to shape reality with the razor of concepts. . . . How I act towards the individual Jew and what I concede to him in politics, education, the promotion of culture, etc., is not a matter of reason, not a matter of ' subsumption ' of phenomena under concepts, but a matter of psychical demarcation or attraction. We will never let the sensibility of these instinctive powers be benumbed by general logical expositions." The Nazi so-called " philosopher of culture ", Alfred Rosenberg, betrays even more clearly his hatred for the uncomfortable clarity of reason by saying : [257] " On the subconscious stage man fulfils . . . the commandments of the blood as it were in dreamy sleep. . . . Until civilisation . . . becomes more and more intellectual and gives rise at a later stage not to creative tension, but to dissension. Thus reason and intellect depart from race and species. The individual, severed from the ties of blood and his ancestry, falls a victim to absolute, intellectual phantoms, devoid of imagination. . . . And thus personality, nation, race, and civilisation die from this defilement of blood." The renunciation of Reason is one of the most characteristic features in Nazism. Not only did this facilitate, as will be seen later, its propagandistic success, but it corresponded to the National Socialist need of glossing over real problems and pushing unreal ones into the limelight. If the German people had been less thoroughly trained to mistrust the light of reason and to listen to the " dark voice of the blood ", their power of resistance might have enabled them to make a firmer stand against the vague phrases of an exalted nationalism and anti-Semitism.

The clash of East and West on German soil had, moreover, an important economic consequence. As has been mentioned above, the industrial development began considerably later in Germany than in the West, but it was then extremely quick and thorough.[258] This fact, too, must be considered as a typical consequence of Germany's central position.[259]

The speed with which industrialisation was carried out in Germany had far-reaching effects. Since every fundamental change in the way of life of a community creates a necessity for difficult readjustments which can usually be effected satisfactorily only if the transition from one stage to the other takes place gradually,[260] it follows that the pace and the extent of the change in question determines the degree to which it causes problems of transition. In Germany, indeed, a new equilibrium never was established. A technical level of organisation equalling that of America co-existed with a public consciousness still steeped in pre-capitalist resentments. In many parts of Germany, especially in Prussia, a merchant was never properly recognised in society. The free Hansa towns, and perhaps a centre of commerce like Frankfurt-on-Main, may have formed exceptions to this rule. But the low esteem in which commerce was held was due to the relative strength of the feudal interest still in power, and also to the suddenness of the capitalist emergence which prevented the natural and gradual development of new social standards. Only a thin stratum was in Germany really " capitalistically minded ". Some branches of German industry were pre-eminent in Europe, some of them in the world. Some German cities, or rather certain districts in these cities, were the most progressive of their hemisphere. But side by side with them, a great part of the population lived in ideas belonging to bygone times.[261] To earn money was still not considered a suitable occupation for people of rank. The expression " to make money " would have been frowned upon even in up-to-date circles, and the reluctance to use it should not be taken as accidental. The capitalist system governed ; it governed in some spheres with absolute power and extraordinary success. But in the eyes of the public it had not yet achieved " emancipation ". People did capitalist business, but with a bad conscience.

Thus it came about, for instance, that Germans considered the Western world as degenerate because it tended to think along pacifist lines, and that by contrast they thought of themselves as " youthful " and " heroic ". Respect for the individual human life is indeed the outlook natural to the citizens of a self-confident capitalist society, even though capitalism as such may bring about special conflicts in international affairs.[262] The almost incomprehensible success with which the German youth was persuaded to take the opposite view, to regard the medieval ideals of soldierly glory and heroism as the highest aims of mankind, is partly a pre-capitalist phenomenon. It proves among other things that the psychical adjustment to capitalist economy in Germany lagged far behind her economic development.

The special difficulties under which industrialism took shape in Germany left their marks also on the course of the relations between Jews and Gentiles. In so far as the speed of the economic evolution added generally to the problems of adjustment and accentuated individual and social disorganisation, it must be regarded as one of the sources of those " sham " elements of anti-Semitism which have been dealt with above. As the capitalist process, painful and bewildering at the best, took place in Germany in particularly difficult circumstances, it increased the individual and social maladjustments and the need for all kinds of neurotic, frequently aggressive, compensations resulting therefrom.

But this is not the whole story. As has been previously explained, the relation between Jews and capitalism has always been of a special kind. Through their previous conditions of life the Jews had acquired a special inclination and capacity for capitalism. They were used to a calculative way of thinking and they were not hampered by survivals of the medieval system of trade-corporations. The number of middlemen among them was extremely high. What has been said above about the Jews bearing the brunt of an anti-capitalist hostility * applies with especial force to their position in Germany. The opposition to capitalism, which to a certain degree prevails everywhere, was bound to be especially outspoken where modern business life was regarded with more than normal suspicion. In Germany the Jewish merchant had not only to compete for popular esteem with the peasant, the symbol of productivity, and the artisan graced by ancient tradition, but he had to maintain his position no less arduously against the officer, whom the King's colours distinguished from the rest of mortals, and against the civil servant, the representative of the glorified State. No wonder that in the contest with so many privileged antagonists he was hopelessly worsted. The German prejudice against commercial occupations may have favoured the economic rise of the German Jews, but it largely thwarted their social recognition.

These considerations lead to a point which is of decisive importance for the Jewish question in Germany. As this, too, will be shown to result from Germany's late capitalist development, and thus indirectly from her central position, it will make particularly clear the additional difficulties with which the German Jews had to grapple as compared with their fellows in the Western democracies.

When about the middle of the 19th century the rapid capitalist advance set in in Germany, the figure of the great social problem of the future had already appeared on the political horizon. One year before the only middle-class revolution that took place in Germany, the March Revolution of 1848, the Communist Manifesto by Karl Marx had been published, beginning with the words : " A spectre haunts Europe—the spectre of Communism ". And Marx goes on to expound the view that " in 19th century Germany the bourgeois revolution can only be the immediate precursor of a proletarian

* Cf. pp. 72 and 73.

revolution ". Although this view was mistaken, it still makes us realise how the chances of the proletariat were then assessed by one of its best-informed observers. In the year of the revolution the first proletarian association, " The Workers' Fraternity " (*Arbeiterverbrüderung*), was founded in Germany. This primitive union was strong enough to run its own candidates during the elections for the Frankfurt Parliament.[263] Simultaneously a vigorous trade-union movement set in, which advanced rapidly until it was suppressed by the reaction following the revolutionary events.[264] After the establishment, in 1863, of the General German Workers' Association, which adopted Lassalle's programme demanding State subsidies for workers' co-operatives, there always existed in Germany a proletarian political movement, distinct from the trade unions, which had separated itself from the middle-class parties.

Thus, from the moment when the rising middle-class provided a solid social basis for German Liberalism, it was itself challenged by an independent labour movement. In contrast with the course of events in the Western countries, it was only during the short period when Liberalism was itself an immature movement of intellectuals and petty bourgeois that it represented labour interests as well as those of the middle-class. Thus the long tradition of political solidarity between middle-class and proletariat, which in the West contributed not a little to making Liberalism more radical and the proletarian movement more moderate, did not exist in Germany. To this fact the reactionary turn early taken by German Liberalism must largely be attributed. Although the part played by Bismarck must not be overlooked, it may be doubted whether a political figure even of his stature would have been able so successfully to divide and defeat Liberalism, unless the underlying social conditions had come to his aid. The weakening of German Liberalism under Bismarck was much more than a transitory political phase. It implied the definite elimination of the liberal middle-class as a political force, or the final desertion of the middle-class to the camp of the moderate nationalist reaction. The way for this move had been prepared by the early manifestation of the bourgeois-proletarian class antagonism.

This turn of events became one of the main causes of the anomalous social situation of the Jews in Germany. The Jewish bourgeoisie did not participate in the reactionary movement of German Liberalism. It is true that the overwhelming majority of them also regarded the rising Social Democracy with hostility, and only individual Jews, who were not typical of the Jewish community, joined the workers' party. But the second condition which made it possible for the Gentile bourgeoisie to come to terms with the State Government did not yet obtain among the Jews. Their emancipation was not yet completed. With the introduction of universal and equal suffrage the Gentile middle-class had achieved the most essential aim of their political emancipation and henceforth strove less for the abolition of feudal privileges than for their own unrestricted participation in them. If only they themselves were admitted without discrimination to the high civil service and the officers' corps, they would approve of the privileges attached to these careers and sanction the exclusiveness of both bodies. The emancipation of the Jews, however, was still far from this state of perfection. Their natural political place remained, therefore, the camp of the opposition. They felt that their cause was still best represented by Left-wing Liberalism, by the "Progressive Party". Their middle-class associates, however, had become "National Liberals" or even "Conservatives". Although this separation reflected also the difference in economic interests, particularly in respect to tariffs, between finance and commerce on the one hand and heavy industry on the other, it would not have been as rigid if the specific Jewish point of view had not practically inhibited upright Jews from joining a party of the Right.

This situation has helped the German Jews to preserve a reputation for political moderation which was soon lost to the Gentiles of their class. The fact that their emancipation was not yet complete, a fact which they themselves felt as humiliating, saved them from falling into the crass political errors committed by the Gentile middle-class in Germany. Although it is probable that the majority of the Jews would have kept aloof from nationalist, militarist, and imperialist excesses even without being compelled to do so by their political situation, the high degree to which they identified themselves with their environment would have been a strong temptation to them to follow its example, and not a few of them might have succumbed. If, therefore, a balance is struck of the advantages and disadvantages of the administrative discrimination against the Jews under the imperial regime, it will appear that the stainlessness of their political shield was not too highly purchased by the inconveniences they suffered.

But whatever advantages the anomalous political position of the German Jews may have possessed from a moral point of view, it unquestionably put a grave obstacle in the way of the solution of the Jewish problem. The Jews were not free to give their political allegiance in accordance with their convictions and general interests. The fact that they were Jews continued to play the decisive part in determining their political orientation. Both under the Empire and, after a short interval, under the Weimar Republic, there existed so-called "Jewish parties", that is to say, parties representing the progressive middle-class which received the votes of the overwhelming majority of the Jews. Even so, the Jews formed only a small minority of these parties. But their support was sufficient to preserve the Jewish group character in the political sphere, and it was not surprising that reactionary groups availed themselves of this fact for their purposes of misrepresentation and defamation. Thus Liberalism was vilified or contemptuously dismissed as something merely Jewish. All the infinite difficulties involved in the interweaving of the Jewish problem with party politics originate from this anomaly. It was indeed not limited to Germany, but was likewise to be found in some Eastern countries, such as Austria, Czechoslovakia, and Poland. But there it was a reflection of a "genuine" Jewish question. That it could not be avoided in Germany was less due to the position of the Jews than to that of the Gentile middle-class. This position was, in turn, the result of Germany's situation as a whole and especially of her belated economic development.

These general difficulties have been greatly intensified by another German problem, the problem of Prussia.

The German-Jewish author, Arnold Zweig, in his study of anti-Semitism [265] seeks to account for the corruption of German nationalism by remarking: " This unnatural and un-German hardness, narrowness, rigidity, and self-deification is . . . the true vengeance of the exterminated and suppressed eastern tribes on the German spirit ". This statement comes nearer to the truth than may appear at first sight. The colonial origin of Prussia, where the old Slav settlers were subjugated by the conquering Teutonic knights in an embittered struggle lasting for centuries, has indeed left an indelible mark on German history. The settlement on unproductive soil made it necessary from the beginning to combine vast holdings in one hand.[266]

These became the origin of the great Prussian estates. The power of the individual land-holder thus established, combined with the military tradition, made the Prussian estate owners keen and resourceful opponents, who, in their subsequent struggles against the monarchy, against bureaucracy, and later on against the bourgeoisie, knew how to retain and increase their original power.[267] The maintenance and consolidation of feudal power in Prussia was indeed the essence of what was most " Eastern " in the German tension between East and West. Within the federation of the German Reich, Prussia was economically the most backward country. It was here that the counter-revolutionary theorists * found the medieval system of land-tenure still in full working order. It was here that their theories, which sought to prove the permanent value of these institutions, were most enthusiastically received. It was in Prussia that the ideas of revolutionary France were prevented from affecting the masses of the population, although, in the more sophisticated Berlin, applause for them was not lacking.[268] Nadler's above-mentioned theory of the roots of romanticism points to Prussia as the origin of this movement which contributed so much to the abnormal shaping of German nationalism and the Jewish question. Prussia was the reactionary stronghold and was therefore chiefly responsible for the prevention of the one thing which might have brought about a general political recovery—a democratisation of Germany in the 19th century. The disintegrating consequences of a hurried capitalist development, moreover, were bound to make themselves especially felt in a country whose economy was, to a considerable extent, based on large rural estates. Of the many German difficulties there is indeed hardly one which has not been dangerously accentuated by Prussian peculiarities.

But Prussia, besides aggravating the German problems, provided characteristically Prussian remedies for their solution, which exerted a decisive influence on the whole of Germany. Through their superior efficiency the Prussians helped to mould the German character also in those parts where they encountered—as in South and West Germany—considerable opposition.[269] These Prussian contributions were mainly the building up of an army and a bureaucracy.

The contrasts which existed within the area of the Reich, and which Prussia helped to increase, were no less marked

* Cf. p. 130.

within Prussia herself. The Prussian State was an artificial creation. It had not grown naturally out of a single country or racial group, but had been composed out of diverse elements by inheritance and military conquest. It consisted of many scattered districts and lacked any natural boundary. The religious discussions which played such a fatal rôle in Germany prevailed also within the smaller framework of Prussia. Roughly the North was Protestant, and the West and the extreme East Catholic.[270] Powerful instruments were needed to protect such a heterogeneous land and to knead it into a unified State. Thus the crown was prompted to create such instruments by building up a strong army and an all-embracing bureaucracy.

But these instruments could work satisfactorily only if the monarchical power was virtually unrestricted, since the sovereignty of a free people was the more to be feared the greater the divergences that existed among its members. Just as in Germany the question of civic freedom was overshadowed by that of national unity, so in Prussia it was overshadowed by the need of a stable State. "Everything was ordered from above, initiative on the part of the subjects was frowned upon or forbidden as a disturbance, unconditional obedience was necessary for the functioning of the machine."[271] Moreover, an independent middle-class emerged in this backward Eastern country even later than in the West with its earlier established industries. The aristocratic military caste profited from this situation by making every call for an increased effort on their part an excuse for new political demands. The officers' corps remained—as distinct from Southern Germany—an aristocratic preserve, where the younger sons of the rural nobility found their careers. The bureaucracy obtained compensation for low salaries in a high social position. Its higher sections were to a great extent permeated with members of the aristocracy, and the lower sections were thoroughly militarised by the so-called "Militaeranwaerter" scheme which entitled ex-soldiers to employment in the lower branches of the civil service.

It is not surprising that in a State like Prussia the fateful transition from the 18th to the 19th century was also brought about by reforms "from above". It is reasonable, however, to inquire why such concessions to the spirit of the time were deemed necessary in a country so conspicuously lagging behind the time. The reply to this question has been repeatedly given by historians. It was the imminent war against Napoleon that made an acceleration of domestic reforms appear desirable. Moreover, this "revolution from above" helped to prevent the "damage" which might have been wrought if no concessions had been made to the progressive spirit prevailing even in backward Prussia. By anticipating popular moves, the Government consolidated its authority instead of discrediting it by rigidly adhering to the past. Furthermore, it generally discouraged political activities on the part of the citizens by accustoming them to receive as gifts of the Government even those reforms that elsewhere had been won as the fruits of revolution. The great Prussian reforms thus accentuated certain undesirable features inherent in the Prussian tradition. Just as they had been granted by the authoritarian State, so they were largely withdrawn in the period of Restoration following the victorious termination of the Wars of Liberation, the citizens proving as little capable of withstanding reaction as they had previously been of enforcing their rights. The alliance between the Crown, the army, and the bureaucracy was consolidated anew.[272]

A federal State with so marked and powerful an individuality could only be an obstacle to German unification. The failure of the promising attempts made by the revolution of 1848 and the Parliament of Frankfurt was largely due to Prussia. Only when Prussia had defeated all potential competitors and stood unchallenged at the head of Germany, were the hindrances to German unification removed. When this unification finally came to pass, it was by the grace of Prussia and in the Prussian spirit—in the middle of a victorious war, in the heyday of military power, on the ruins of the defeated Second French Empire. The contribution the people had made to this unification was the blood they had shed on the battlefields.

Bismarck, the founder of this German Reich by the grace of Prussia, was himself a thorough Prussian. "For him", as his biographer Lenz puts it, "'foreign' meant everything that lay outside the black-and-white frontier posts" of Prussia. He sneered at a Prussian aristocrat who protested to him that there was a deep truth hidden in the national idea: "So you too have been bitten by the German dog".[273] In spite of all this, Bismarck was statesman enough to create the German Reich when he deemed that the hour for it had struck. He was far from insisting on an annexation of the South German federal States by Prussia, although a solution of this kind would probably have been to his liking. But it was due to Bismarck's influence that Prussia's predominance was not impaired by the Reich constitution, and that in Prussia through the Three-Class suffrage and the Second Chamber, the Herrenhaus, those forces remained in power that had made Prussia and severely handicapped the Reich.[274]

From what has been said on the Prussian problem it is evident that this was an important addition to those German difficulties which bore upon the Jewish question. Prussia stood for the predominance of aristocrats—while the Jews belonged to the middle-class and championed equal rights; for the tradition of submissiveness—while the Jewish emancipation was inseparable from civic liberty; for militarism—to which the Jews were for many reasons opposed; for the control of a bureaucracy which excluded the Jews, even after their formal emancipation, from its higher careers and whose infringements of liberty they as citizens resented. And, finally, Prussianism meant the retardation of a democratic development which might have counterbalanced the National Socialist assault in the last test of strength.

Yet even more important than these direct consequences of the Prussian spirit were its indirect effects for the Jews. Prussia nourished all the germs which stunted the healthy growth of German nationalism and disposed it to an anti-Semitic degeneration. With so many innate defects, the German national consciousness could not be a wholesome product. Fortunately, however, German nationalism is a product of a kind not likely to arise elsewhere. Certain features of it may indeed appear in other nations, but not the sum total of defects and malformations which, from its emergence, have distinguished German nationalism. Its development was largely determined by Germany's geographical position, together with the economic and social consequences to which this gave rise. Some features may have been due to historical accidents, but the most important trends were conditioned by a few fundamental facts.

Treitschke, whose own fervent nationalism, so far from blinding him to national defects, gave him an exceptionally keen insight into them, ascribes to the German national feeling a number of attributes which show its dangerous points with startling clearness. He speaks of its " arrogance ", of its

" audacious radicalism ", its " idealist rapture " (*Schwärmerei*), its " over-heated enthusiasm ". He goes on to complain of its " morbid bitterness ", its " hazy vagueness " and its " instability ".[275] This passage contains, indeed, an enumeration of nearly all the shortcomings which characterised the relation of the typical German individual to his nation. It need only be added that to a nation so disposed, the sudden success achieved in 1870–71 was bound to bring not health but more complications.[276] The victorious war and the unwonted material prosperity that followed it did not contribute to a national equilibrium. Unity had at last been achieved. But it had come too late and too violently to permit of a steady progress towards normal conditions. Instead, the national vices " arrogance ", " radicalism ", and " over-heated enthusiasm ", continued to flourish with renewed vigour.

Beneath the new patriotism of the German Empire the old problems went on smouldering: the territorial rivalry, outwardly appeased but never entirely settled, which now manifested itself, above all, in the antagonism between Prussia and Bavaria; moreover, there remained the religious dualism and the social question.[277] There were always more and stronger disintegrating factors in Germany than in most other countries, and the communal feeling was younger and weaker. Thus the difficulties which could not be solved were simply shouted down.[278]

A typical attempt to conceal the inner insecurity behind a particularly bold front can be seen in the Pan-German movement. The historian of the Pan-German movement, Mildred S. Wertheimer,[279] describes it rightly as " an organised effort to keep frenzied nationalism at fever heat ". The disease generating the morbid temperature was the national anxiey and mistrust of which there are strange signs everywhere in the Pan-German literature. Everywhere there is indignation against some internal or external powers endangering " Deutschtum ", that conveniently vague notion which could be employed to justify a domestic programme or an imperialist ambition according to choice.[280] The marked self-consciousness of the Pan-German League in all national questions corresponds exactly to its aggressive attitude. No self-confident nation, filled with wholesome national pride, could for a moment listen to warlike tirades of the kind with which the Pan-German literature harassed its readers.[281] Colonies, conquests, living space, defamation of the official German peace policy, and glorification of war—these are the themes which are varied *ad nauseam*.[282] While the Pan-German League thinks in terms of power politics and does not hesitate to demand raw material and export markets,[283] it does not omit to build up a corresponding ideology. It points out that the German people, being a " master-race ", have the right to claim such expansion.[284] And, again, the much misused Darwin is drawn upon to make the "struggle of all against all" into a divine commandment: "God urges us through our conscience to develop the qualities He has implanted in us to their full extent. He wills the struggle of all against all, so that the best, the most efficient, may emerge as victors. The strong is to rule." [285]

The Pan-German movement is the real predecessor of National Socialism. It already enjoins the repudiation of Christianity,[286] though this is still bashfully hidden behind the mask of criticism of a so-called " misunderstood " Christianity. On the other hand, its hostility to humanism and the Rights of Man, which are held to oppose " the indelibly sacred right of the stronger, better, more beautiful " by the " usurped right of everything contemptible, evil, and vulgar ",[287] is outspoken. The Pan-Germans are also determined opponents of democracy ; one needs only to instance the following remark of one of the presidents of the League, Heinrich Class : [288] " If we are victorious [in the future war for which he " yearns "] an elevation of minds will take place, a national Reichstag will be elected. This moment must be used for abolishing the suffrage." But also a lost war would be to the good ; it would lead to fundamental reforms and a dictatorship. Although their demand for raw materials and export markets ought to have made the Pan-Germans above all the representatives of big business,[289] they, like the Nazis, met with their greatest success among the middle- and lower middle-class.[290] The teachers in particular supported it.[291] This feature, too, the Pan-Germans shared with the Nazis.[292]

And yet it would be a mistake to overestimate the similarity between Pan-Germanism and Nazism. Even if all the elements of Pan-Germanism have reappeared in National Socialism, not all elements of National Socialism can be traced back to Pan-Germanism. Nazism is far too complex a phenomenon to be regarded merely as a later reproduction of Pan-Germanism.

Common to both is the fact that they are expressions of the national disease of the German middle and lower-middle class, of the need for a noisy over-compensation of an intrinsic weakness. Indeed, this need manifests itself even more starkly in Pan-Germanism than in Nazism. At the cradle of Nazism there stood, after all, the lost World War and the Peace of Versailles, which was regarded as a humiliation. Such events might have disturbed the equilibrium of a better-balanced nation, although the excessive influence they exercised can be fully explained only by Germany's dangerous pathological condition. But the Pan-German movement came into being during a period of prosperity after a victorious war. That even in such circumstances people should be looking forward to another war as to a deliverance from an intolerable situation, that they should suspect everywhere dangers threatening the German " Volkstum " with ruin,[293] that they should be able to feel themselves a great power only when rattling the sabre— these are all symptoms of a serious malady in the German national consciousness.

The influence of the Pan-German movement on the German people should not be overrated. Mildred Wertheimer [294] goes so far as to maintain that it was in reality negligible. This judgment, however, seems to err in the opposite direction, since through the influence it exerted on teachers, the Pan-German League had a greater effect among the youth than the actual number of its adherents would suggest. It is hardly an exaggeration to say that a not inconsiderable part of German secondary schools before the first World War were avowedly or tacitly under the influence of Pan-German ideas. In this way, people who had originally no sympathy with Pan-Germanism fell unconsciously under the influence of its teachings. The influence of an active, loud-voiced group particularly well represented in academic circles [295] will always extend considerably beyond the sphere of its professed members. Its propaganda tinges the political concepts even of its opponents by dictating to them their line of action. Thus the Pan-Germans must be assumed to bear a large measure of the responsibility for the distortion which the concept " national " has generally undergone among the German public.

The major importance of Pan-Germanism for the purposes of this study is, however, as a symptom of the abnormality of German nationalism. As such it stands in the same category as anti-Semitism. If the Pan-German " disease " must be regarded as one acute manifestation of the morbid dispositions which have been analysed above, pre-war anti-Semitism is another.

Even before the rise of Nazism it was a well-established fact that Germany has played a special rôle in the origin and spread of anti-Semitism.[296] Germany has, in fact, acquired an infamous notoriety for having given birth to the so-called " scientific " anti-Semitism and for having made anti-Semitism into an article of export. This reputation is fully deserved even if it is borne in mind that the existence of an anti-Semitic literature does not of necessity prove a wide anti-Semitic response among the public.

The marked inclination of the German intellectual class towards anti-Semitism, which became especially manifest in the last two decades of the 19th century, originated only to a minor degree from the objective character of the Jewish problem in Germany. The decisive factor in this field, too, was rather the weakness of German national consciousness which made the chance of strengthening it at the cost of an " inner enemy " appear so disastrously attractive. German intellectual anti-Semitism is, like Pan-Germanism, in the first place a morbid symptom of Germany's abnormal national evolution.[297]

There is no need to point out that both symptoms were closely connected with each other. The Pan-German League, it is true, did not introduce the so-called " Aryan-Paragraph ", *i.e.* the ruling by which members of the Jewish race were forbidden to join it, until after the first World War, and not all its presidents were individually anti-Semitic.[298] But its best-known president, Class, was an anti-Semite and used against the Jews all the arguments that the political struggle has made familiar.[299] He once laid his finger on the spot when he pointed out [300] that it was the German lack of resisting power, of instinctive reactions, and of independence which made Jewish influence so dangerous. If instead of saying " made " he had said " caused it to be felt as dangerous " he would have been right. But so far from showing such a balanced judgment, Class did not even content himself with moderate terms like " Jewish influence ". He spoke of the " intellectual leadership of a foreign people ", of " Jewish guidance " from which he feels called upon to " save the soul of the German nation ". For this salvation he looked to " severe laws " of the State.[301] But apart from such propagandist utterances and the individual influence of this or that leader, it would still be true that the origin of the Pan-German idea in the feeling of national inferiority was bound to lead towards anti-Semitism. Since Pan-Germans felt continually haunted by the phantoms of national dangers and, for this reason, needed an assurance of their own strength, notably an enemy over whom to triumph, they were bound, sooner or later, to fall foul of the Jewish minority. They fought with particular energy against the national minorities living in the German borderlands, and they did not hesitate to reckon the Jews among them.[302] Since, however, the Jews were so thoroughly Germanised that such an attitude could not be sufficiently justified by national arguments alone, it was necessary to have recourse to the racial theory.[303] This, although not very helpful where the oppression of the Danes in northern Schleswig was concerned, yielded at least the one criterion needed to exclude Jews from the German nation. The reasons adduced for a display of aggressiveness on the side of the Germans were in no case very convincing. What mattered was to find enemies against whom to direct it.[304]

The German anti-Semitic literature most frequently exhibits the same two features which we have noted above, national insecurity—whether admitted or not—and an absurd exaggeration of Jewish power. Treitschke introduced his famous attack on Jewish radicalism [305] with the remark that Judaism had such a " ruinous and disintegrating effect " because the national consciousness of the Germans was still " immature ". The professor of penal law, Franz Eduard von Liszt, in a response to the question " Are the Jews to become Christians ? ",[306] based his remarks on the text : " We have only just acquired our national unity and are about to consolidate it externally and internally ". He is far from being an outspoken anti-Semite, but pleads, nevertheless, for a repression of Jewish influence on the ground that in the existing circumstances it is a " duty of self-preservation " not to entrust the " protection and promotion of the highest national interests " to the " cosmopolitan-minded " Jews. And to mention a third, if less important, authority, the following passages from *Die weltgeschichtliche Bedeutung des Judentums und seine Zukunft* by the German Gentile Ernst Jörges may be quoted : [307] " At times unconsciously, but at times quite consciously, the German feels that he himself is far from completed in a racial sense. . . . Germany still seeks herself and has not yet found herself. The

German therefore instinctively resents further cross-breeding, especially with alien blood. This is the actual meaning of the German call for racial purity. . . . In the spiritual field too we see the German struggling for centuries for his own national self. And this struggle is not yet concluded. These special conditions explain why the ' völkische ' circles in Germany fanatically deny the Jews admission. He who needs all his strength to make his house fairly habitable for himself, wants no visitors, especially none who add to his trouble." The author is at pains to explain the German-Jewish problem objectively, and he too finds the main difficulty to lie in the national immaturity of the Germans.

A particularly rabid expression of the same point of view is to be found in the work *Die Judenfrage als Frage des Rassencharakters und seiner Schädlichkeit für Existenz und Kultur der Völker* (The Jewish Question as a Question of Racial Character and its Detrimental Effects on the Existence and Culture of the Peoples) by the Berlin economist Eugen Dühring.[308] The value of this book as illustrative of the anti-Semitic mentality is somewhat impaired by the fact that the author was a neurotic. He was blind and showed unmistakable signs of serious nervous disturbances. Moreover, he attributed a check in his career to Jewish machinations, a circumstance which obviously still further upset his mental balance.[309] But in spite of this personal disposition, which to some extent lessens the typical character of Dühring's judgments, he may yet be taken as another example of that collective insecurity to which attention has been drawn. He asks : " Why does the German spirit at present feel so little at home with itself? " and he answers : " Because not only in the religious, but equally in the intellectual field it has . . . forgotten itself and sold itself to Judaism." [310] Here, again, the connection is expressed with a remarkable directness, although the causal relation between the German spirit's not feeling at home and its alleged sale to Judaism has been turned upside down. The German spirit does not feel uneasy because it has sold itself to Judaism, but it believes it has sold itself to Judaism because it feels uneasy with itself.

But Dühring's feeling of national inferiority expresses itself even more clearly in what he calls Germany's " social corruption ". In the introductory chapter of his book, Dühring calls the Jews parasites settling wherever there is corruption and decay. They then direct, he alleges, all their activities towards making these rotten conditions worse still. For such machinations, Dühring continues, the Jews have found ideal conditions in contemporary Germany. He is unsparing in his censures on the depravity of German conditions since the era of Bismarck.[311] Although he does not spare other countries either, he maintains that the urgency of the Jewish question in Germany indicates clearly that here corruption has spread farthest. Dühring's feeling of collective inferiority comes out even more clearly in his absurd exaggeration of Jewish power. He not only considers literature, the Press, all political parties, art, science, the administration of law, and, above all, Christianity,[312] which he opposes with great bitterness, to be under Jewish influence, but he calls Jews and Jewish whoever or whatever he dislikes. He insists that Lessing was of Jewish extraction,[313] he speaks of the "Jew" Nietzsche,[314] and though he cannot do quite the same with Goethe and Schiller, he at least goes so far as to declare them inferior, because they allowed themselves to be influenced by the "Slavo-Jew" Lessing.[315] Not content with talking about "Jewish domination",[316] about "governments under Jewish influence",[317] which we should only expect, he calls the Jewish danger "the shame of the last thousand years".[318] After this *tour de force* the reader will be prepared for practically anything in this line; nevertheless, he may still be surprised to hear from Dühring that also the nationalist [319] and the anti-Semitic movement are under Jewish control.[320] Such utterances may, it is true, belong to that psychological sphere which can be only explained in terms of pathology and should therefore not be taken as typical expression of German thought.

Rather more typical was Paul de Lagarde, the teacher of many generations of Pan-Germans and anti-Semites. Unable to adjust himself to the national conditions of his time, he held violently expansionist ideas. Not content with the Reich as founded by Bismarck, he stood for an extension of German "living space" deep into the Galician, Hungarian, and Russian East. As a matter of course, he demanded a policy of ruthless Germanisation of national minorities, above all in Austria-Hungary.[321] This highly aggressive attitude in foreign and home politics corresponds also in the case of Lagarde with an inner uncertainty of his national feeling, leading to an outrageous fear of foreigners. Lagarde bases his resistance to the liberal ideas of his time primarily on the fact of their originating from foreign countries, notably France.[322] He continuously emphasises the necessity that " Germany should receive at long last a garment fitted to her own body ",[323] and he complains that people indulge in " vague ideas of humanity, before the natural foundations of the nation have been laid ".[324] It is thus only consistent that Lagarde's hypersensibility to "foreign" influence should impel him to savage denunciation of Jews. The Jews are to him foreigners who " hinder the completion of the German people's racial mission ".[325] His fear of their influence leads him to regard world domination as " the aim of this foreign nation ".[326] He came nearer to reality when he explained : " Every Jew who is a nuisance to us is a serious reproach to the genuineness and veracity of our Germanity ".[327] He meant by this that a self-confident German nation would never allow the Jews to become a nuisance by giving them full freedom, while the fact is, of course, that the Jews, however much freedom they were granted, would not have been felt as a nuisance if the Germans had not lacked poise and self-assurance. Two more specifically German features stand out in Lagarde's anti-Semitism, his strong anti-capitalism [328] which makes him condemn the Jews together with capitalist finance,[329] and his anti-denominationalism which, although he remained a Christian, makes him reject the existing churches. He resents the denominational division and concludes from it that it would be unwise to increase the religious dissension by a recognition of the Jews.[330] When it is added that Lagarde's outlook was largely determined by romanticism, it will be sufficiently evident that both his nationalism and his anti-Semitism can be regarded as typical products of the German mentality.

The problem of German inferiority was approached from a somewhat different angle by a man who was German only by adoption, and by birth an Englishman, Houston Stewart Chamberlain. It is very doubtful whether this creator of the most effective anti-Semitic theory, the theory of the racial superiority of the Teutons and the racial inferiority of the Jews, would have arrived at his ideas if he had lived in England. It would rather seem that the German atmosphere of national insecurity and denominational division led him, too, to seek an over-compensation by means of his racial theory. Chamberlain's anxieties apply less to the nation than to the race, because his fundamental preoccupation is with racial and not with national communities. But his racial enthusiasm and his racial fears reflect as much the German swaying between feelings of superiority and inferiority, as the theories of the French Count Gobineau, to whom he owed his inspiration, reflect the apprehensions of the French aristocracy. Chamberlain, like the anti-Semites previously reviewed, sees threats and dangers everywhere. He sees the Teutons walking " on the edge of the precipice " [331] and speaks of their " silent struggle for life and death " [332] against the progressive hybridisation. He foresees that they will perish from their lack of a true, *i.e.* a racial, religion if no help is forthcoming in time.[333] It is a great question whether the same eschatological visions would have come to Chamberlain in the cheerful, self-assured atmosphere of England. And it is certainly impossible that he would have based his fears on the allegedly Teutonic propensity " to set a high price on what is foreign and to set a small store by what is one's own ",[334] on that " modesty " praised by Luther but condemned by him, that " extravagant estimation of the merit of others ".[335] As far as these propensities are Teutonic at all, they are to be found particularly in the Germans. The clearest proof, however, that Chamberlain's racial conception had its roots in German conditions is contained in the passage where he draws the line between what he calls " racial chaos " and "unhybridised Teutonism ". This frontier runs parallel with the boundary between Protestant and Catholic countries in Europe, that is to say, it runs straight across Germany. Chamberlain excludes from the purer Germania all those provinces where the Roman Catholic Church predominates, the Rhine districts and the lands of the Danube together with Spain, Italy, and " Gaul ". " It is still morning", he continues, " and the powers of darkness are ever stretching out their polypus arms, clinging to us with their powers of suction in a hundred places and trying to drag us back into the night."[336] In no other country, indeed, was there an equal opportunity of experiencing an ocular demonstration of this cultural impact of the South-West on the North-East. That Chamberlain should have given it a racial explanation provides still more evidence for the dependence of his racial concepts on typically German experiences.

It is obvious that Chamberlain's exalted racialism was bound to lead him to anti-Semitism. Although he shows in this respect a common sense in which most of his associates are lacking, since he warns against an under-estimation of the Teutons' own strength and an over-estimation of Jewish influence,[337] he still attaches an extraordinary importance to the Jewish problem. He describes it as a problem of race, religion, and spirit, and he tries to prove the harmful effects brought about by Jews in all these spheres. Though he feels himself a Christian, his enmity is also directed against the Christian churches, which " make all men Jews " and thus " inculcate Judaism into German culture ".[338]

Chamberlain's influence on educated circles, especially on academic youth, was extraordinary. Both his teachings and their reception were another example of that " German disease " which had seized more violently on this born English-man than on many born Germans.[339]

Further important evidence in support of the point made here can be found in the elaborate anti-Semitic theory of Wilhelm Stapel, who has been mentioned above in connection with the anti-Semitic hostility to Reason.* Stapel, whose whole argument is intended to prove that the German people is threatened with *Ueberfremdung* (excessive alien influence) by Jewish activities,[340] betrays his national self-mistrust at every turn. And he is one of those who partly admit it : " People who are instinctively sure of their Volkstum will not let them-selves be blinded by foreign Volkstum ",[341] or : " The extent of the bewilderment and the depth of the chasm created when a nation takes over foreign forms of expression, depend on the vitality of that nation. A nation strong in its individuality can grow richer by accepting foreign cultural values. A weak nation can be corrupted by them ! " [342] What Stapel thinks of the strength of German vitality can be judged from his passion-ate complaint about the number of " foreign forms of expres-sion " the German nation has had to endure in the course of its history. He mentions as such influences the Roman-Hellenistic and the Roman-Christian culture, the Roman Law, Humanism, French civilisation, and—during the period of Classicism once again—a rebirth of the ancients. Stapel concludes this enum-eration with the words : " Essentially Germanity has stood its ground, but it has become infinitely rich, multiform, and—vague. Now with the emancipation of the Jews another wave of foreign spirit is coming over us. . . . The genuineness and originality of the German people is endangered."[343] Although Stapel deliberately emphasises this national weakness and describes it as the aim of his book to help the Germans to

* Cf. p. 140.

obtain inner security,[344] he himself is not safe against a some-what undignified self-humiliation and over-estimation of the Jewish opponent. He calls a social boycott against the Jews the "self-defence of a tortured nation against its victorious oppressor",[345] although, for other reasons, he is averse to applying it.

Stapel's anti-Semitism, which evoked no great popular response but had a marked effect on educated Germans, was as much due to the national inferiority complex as were the other brands mentioned before. It was determined by neurotic fear for the "national soul", not by an actual menace emanating from foreign influence. A person who feels the cultural heritages of antiquity, Christianity, and the Renaissance as so many dangers whose pernicious effects Germanity has only just managed to escape, not without the disastrous result, however, of having become richer and more multiform, cannot be re-garded as a competent judge of Jewish influence on the same Germanity. Stapel, moreover, must take great pains to prove that Jewish influence is indeed "foreign" influence. He admits that Jews can identify themselves to a great extent with German "Volkstum", he regards the love of many Jews for Germany as tragic. But he twists the words until the incom-patibility of the two nationalities finally emerges.[346] In this exercise the vagueness of his concepts stands him in good stead. He simply retires into a cloud of uncontrollable emotions which are what they are and defy any clearer description.

Another writer who must be included in this category is the historian of literature Josef Nadler, whose theory of romanticism has been adduced to prove the special difficulties through which the German national development had to struggle.* Nadler's history of literature [347] is an extremely arbitrary yet inspiring work, of great charm. It would be much too crude a judgment merely to dismiss Nadler as an anti-Semite.[348] His attitude to Jews and Judaism is somewhat equivocal. He is not without appreciation for individual Jewish achievements, though he has always shown an inclination to measure their value by the degree of their assimilation to "Aryan" creations and to explain their deficiencies by the Jewish ancestry of the authors.[349] Nadler also recognises certain collective Jewish talents,[350] and eulogises the literary fruits of the German-Jewish symbiosis in Prague.[351] But all this would not have

* Cf. pp. 134 seq.

161

suggested Nadler's inclusion in this chapter, were it not for his strange, fearful over-estimation of the Jewish influence on German intellectual life. For he too is not free from that neurotic German insecurity of which this brand of anti-Semitism is a symptom.

In the introduction to his fourth volume Nadler puts the Jewish problem on the same level as those two processes which, in his view, mainly determined the course of German history. He says : [352] " The first epoch was determined by the Roman-German exchange of blood, the second by the Slav-German. Now a third national process is taking place, which has been in progress for centuries, and it determines the physiognomy of this century : vital processes between the Jewish guest and the German host." Thus, in Nadler's view, the closer relation between Jews and Gentiles, brought about by the emancipation, has made history in the same sense as the contact between Teutons and Romans and that between Germans and Slavs, both of which he regards as fraught with destiny. He goes even further. He believes that in this new contact the oldest and most original German schism re-emerges, the schism between " the Aryan and Semitic orient ", to which he, with his peculiar outlook, attaches enormous importance.[353] In numerous sub-sections of the work, dealing with minor subjects, one finds similar strange over-valuations of the Jewish contributions to German culture, although there major importance is only rarely attributed to them. Nadler characterises the results of the foundation of the Second Empire with these words : By it the citizen has lost his self-respect to the warrior, his future to the worker, and " his spiritual function to the Jew ".[354] He speaks, furthermore, of Jewish education as of a " fundamental question of the Germans ",[355] complains that in the Sudeten country the Jews " control the situation ",[356] that from the Sudeten district they have " ploughed up the Hapsburg monarchy ",[357] that the " popular fermentation induced by the Jews . . . is becoming German destiny ".[358] He calls Koenigsberg a town " where the Jews were leading ",[359] where the Jewish liberals Eduard Simson and Johann Jacoby " had not only full power over a whole swarm of young people ", but from where they also " dominated the up-bringing of the Prussian youth ".[360] He refers to the " new Jewish style " in journalism,[361] and even suggests that the whole German language was transformed by the influx of Jews.[362] It was the

Jews who " set the new fourth estate in motion " [363] and who directed from Paris the vanguard of the Rhineland citizens in their struggle for a constitution.[364] According to Nadler, the Jew Johann Jacoby with his pamphlet " Vier Fragen beantwortet von einem Ostpreussen " (Four Questions Answered by an East-Prussian) exercised an " incalculable influence on the psychological situation of the Germans between 1830 and 1848, comparable only to that exercised by the pamphlet of Abbé Sieyès, " Qu'est-ce que le Tiers État ? " [365] In short—" The Jews rise everywhere ".[366]

It is surprising that Germans themselves have so seldom protested against such a boundless exaggeration of Jewish achievements and belittling of their own.[367] Apart from occasional complaints in the course of political controversy to the effect that this widely held anti-Semitic attitude constituted an insult to the German people, it has not, in general, been seriously resented by that part of the German public which was susceptible to anti-Semitic sentiments. This may be explained as due to the natural inclination of every group to represent itself as the attacked party rather than as the attacker. But that people, so far from feeling ashamed, obviously enjoyed the idea of being dominated and mortally threatened—even of being definitely conquered—by an opponent whose numerical strength was exactly one-hundredth part of their own remains a fact of a totally different nature from those usually found in political arguments. At the root of this feeling there is, no doubt, a widespread neurotic disposition of the Germans. Not only do they lack sufficient self-confidence not to feel perpetually surrounded by dangers, but their self-assurance does not even suffice to make them look down on a minute minority with a natural feeling of superiority. A reader of this anti-Semitic literature cannot escape the impression that its authors dilated, not without a certain pleasure, upon their own weakness. And this may have the following reasons. The misrepresentation of the numerical proportion of the attacking Gentiles and the attacked Jews has a certain psychological effect which comes to the aid of the national inferiority complex. For one thing, the choice of a suitable symbol for an enemy offers a welcome outlet for general aggressiveness, born from national frustration. The struggle against an adversary who is so incomparably weaker, in itself most unfair, is furthermore represented as an honourable contest against odds. And, finally, since the victory itself is determined by the real strength of the opponents, while the triumph is greater the greater the odds are represented to be against it, a struggle of this kind is likely to result in a considerable increase of self-confidence. This psychological effect of a campaign against a weak opponent, who is alleged to wield much greater power than he actually possesses, was certainly not fully realised by many of the anti-Semites who profited from this device. But, whether consciously or unconsciously, both writers and public succumbed to the temptation of developing a kind of psychological automatism for which conditions in Germany were particularly propitious.

German national immaturity made for a continuous oscillation between a feeling of insecurity and its aggressive over-compensation. This lack of balance made it particularly difficult for the Germans to see themselves in a true light. Germans were partly inclined to overvalue everything foreign, and partly to pretend a " dashing " attitude (*Schneidigkeit*), which could not be kept up without a real or alleged foe. In the political field the inferiority complex expressed itself in the feeling of being threatened and surrounded by internal and external enemies. Those, mainly reactionaries, who particularly fostered this feeling, constantly emphasised the necessity not only of preparing for an armed conflict, but also of suppressing political minorities, which were declared to be both strong and inferior. For reasons which have been expounded above, the Jews proved an especially suitable object for such a manœuvre and were therefore frequently chosen as the symbol of an enemy, not because they were actually hated, but because the spread of hatred as such was a psychological need of the German people.

An inner disharmony, a lack of unity, was at the bottom of the intellectual pre-war anti-Semitism in Germany. An artificial homogeneity based on the selection of a common foe was to be substituted for the natural homogeneity based on national feeling which had had no chance of developing before the disintegrating influence of a highly developed industrialism began to shatter it. Moreover, the old national dreams, inspired by vague concepts like " Volkstum " and race, entered into an unholy alliance with Bismarck's " Realpolitik ". The universalistic ideas of a German mission to humanity, which had given an idealistic tinge to the old dreams of German superiority, were discarded or perverted, and what remained was power politics, militarism, and imperialism. The Jews, however, by force of tradition and history, stood on the side of law, civil liberties, and peace. It had not been a mere accident that they received their emancipation as one of the liberties granted as a consequence of the French Revolution. Their existence as free citizens with equal rights was closely connected with the principles of tolerance and of the Rights of Man, and with the will to settle disputes between co-existing groups by means of good will and reason. The fateful transition from the 18th to the 19th century in Germany was accompanied by outstanding philosophical and artistic achievements, which carried the disintegration of the value system farther than elsewhere. But the Jews depended for the establishment of normal relations with the Gentile environment on a more or less well-established moral system. Finally, all the factors which had hampered the German progress towards unity, freedom, and psychical balance had been seriously aggravated by the Prussian problem. Apart from adding to the political and religious disunity, apart from her reactionary leanings, from her attachment to militarism and bureaucracy, Prussia was an obstacle to German unification. And when she finally consented to it, she gave it a form which presented a further difficulty to the integration of the Jews into Gentile society. Immature, incomplete, unstable, uncertain of and dissatisfied with itself—thus German nationalism roved about through the modern world. Now indulging in self-abasement, now posing as the conqueror of the world; now sulkily retiring into a corner, and now frightening Europe with menacing gestures; now pleading for sympathy and now scorning it—thus, fleeing from its own instability, German nationalism encountered the Jewish victim. In the struggle with him it hoped eventually to find itself. Where particularly strong anti-Semitic feeling is encountered in German intellectual circles, and in all those which have partaken of university education, *i.e.* the so-called educated classes, its root lies in this anomaly of the German national consciousness.

Meanwhile the actual Jewish problem, that tension which always and everywhere accompanies the existence of a Jewish minority in a Gentile world, had not ceased to exist. This tension in itself had, it is true, constantly diminished. The German Jews had not only become highly respected citizens, whose achievements were recognised, whose advice was sought, and whose co-operation was appreciated. More than that: people had to a considerable degree ceased to be conscious that there was anything strange or peculiar in their intercourse with Jews. Their relations to them belonged so much to the normal course of daily life that hardly anyone stopped to think about them. Nevertheless, many remained just sufficiently aware of the differences in their Jewish neighbours for false conceptions about them to be possible, provided that such conceptions satisfied psychical needs. And it was here that anti-Semitic propaganda found its mark. It profited from the remaining feeling of difference, from the last vestiges of suspicion against a community that was still distinguishable from the Gentile environment by a few, not very essential, features, and pumped into these feelings all the muddy waters it found in society— personal and collective fears, envy, hatred, arrogance, and cruelty. Anti-Semitic propaganda appealed in the first place to those who were particularly dissatisfied with their fate and sought for an object on which they could lay the blame for their sufferings. In particular, it exploited the " German disease " by identifying anti-Semitism with " true " nationalism from which alone the weakling could draw his individual share of common strength.

Such was the structure of German pre-war anti-Semitism. Only to an infinitely small degree did it still reflect the " genuine " Jewish problem. But what was left of this still sufficed to secure a certain response for anti-Semitic agitation. Where agitators set to work it was only in very rare cases that they aimed at settling what still existed of a Jewish problem in Germany. Normally they pursued much more important political ends behind the screen of anti-Semitism, ends which were largely reactionary, or anti-democratic, or such as served an aggressive foreign policy. The economic situation had changed and the acuteness of the social question indicated that a redistribution of the social product in one way or another would, in the long run, prove inevitable. A resistance to this redistribution could not reckon with any public support if those who were interested in the *status quo* stated openly their designs. They therefore resorted to a political device to cloak their real intentions. They diverted public attention from the actual political and social problems by declaring the Jew the common enemy. Since it was of the utmost importance for them to divert the anti-capitalist feelings of the masses from their real

166

object, capitalism, the popular identification of the Jews with capitalism, was especially opportune. Pernerstorffer's "block-heads" did not die out,* least of all among the lower middle-class which resented "proletarian" Socialism but felt flattered if members of the upper middle-class appealed to them in the name of national solidarity. To this attraction were added the many psychological advantages of anti-Semitism which have been emphasised above. Its vagueness, combined with its alleged "scientific" character, allowed people to associate all kinds of ideas with it and still feel in the possession of an ascertained truth. Its aggressiveness, combined with its alleged service of a high ideal, enabled people to hate with a good conscience and still to feel morally superior. Its reduction of the incomprehensible principles of economics to a formula which could be easily grasped gave people at last the satisfaction, so flattering to the half-educated, of understanding the universe. Anti-Semitism, moreover, promised to provide a panacea for all human ills without serious interference with existing conditions; thus its adherents could feel "progressive" and yet supporters of economic peace, spiritual revolutionaries and yet upholders of law and order. Finally, the attack against a weak minority, alleged to be of overwhelming strength, enabled the ordinary man without running risks to feel himself as heroic Siegfried who fought the dragon.

It is a remarkable proof of the increasing confidence between Jews and Gentiles in Germany that, in spite of so many psychological temptations and of the unfavourable portents of both time and place, the anti-Semitic success there before the first World War was small. Only if this limited success is seen in the light of the present explanations will its full significance for the general problem of the German Jews, and for the most general of Jewish-Gentile relations as a whole, be rightly assessed.

The results so far yielded by this study can be summed up as follows.

(1) During the 19th century and the beginning of the 20th a process of social and moral disintegration took place in the Western world. Life became more complicated, and nearly all sections of the population—though some more than others— were dissatisfied and overstrained. People were inclined to indulge their impulses of self-assertion and aggressiveness,

* Cf. p. 101.

which increasingly rebelled against social restraints, at the cost of part of the conventional morality. In this desire they were assisted by the recasting and lowering of moral standards which was being effected by the intellectual leaders. The combined effect of both processes led to a general indifference towards moral obligations which gradually drifted into moral anarchy.

(2) During the same time those social strata that were most seriously affected by these processes became a relatively larger proportion of the population. During the 19th century these strata were politically emancipated. This emancipation may be termed a " passive " democratisation, with which the " active " democratisation of the masses, that is, their capacity and willingness to undertake the corresponding democratic obligations, did not keep pace. These two lines of development even ran the risk of counteracting each other, since the larger the masses which made actual use of their democratic rights the more numerous among them were those people who repudiated democracy together with other exacting social standards. For it is precisely the politically most indifferent circles—those which are the last to be influenced by political campaigning and which have the least understanding for the democratic form of government as for other complicated institutions—which advocate direct and primitive methods. An exertion by these masses of their latent power is likely to lead to the overthrow and supersession of the political *élites* by those elements of society which are least capable of civilised conduct. If cynical politicians succeed in gaining the ear of these groups by playing on their weariness with democratic responsibilities as with other moral obligations, a crisis of democracy may ensue. This danger is particularly aggravated if big business turns likewise anti-democratic, although for other reasons than the masses, notably because it wants to evade a democratic settlement of the social question.

The process of social integration of the Jews into Gentile society depends for its success on the good will of the environment. The existence of this good will depends essentially on the binding power of the prevailing moral code. The lowering of this code, on the one hand, and the rise to power of those sections among whom the consequent degeneration had proceeded farthest, on the other, seriously endangered the success of the Jewish emancipation.

The two phenomena which we have so far noted characterise

the epoch during which the emancipation and integration of the Jews took place in Central and Western Europe and America, and they are to be found, at least in embryo, in all industrial and democratic countries, although their development may be effectively checked by a strong democratic tradition.

(3) In Germany more than elsewhere unfavourable geographical and historical conditions co-operated to prevent the healthy and normal growth of those forces on which the emancipation and integration of the Jews depended for success. The difficulties due to these causes were accentuated by the problem of Prussia, a country that was artificially created, economically backward, and full of conflicting elements. Prussia's policy led to a delay in German unification and democratisation which aggravated the intrinsic perils of this form of government. It resulted, furthermore, in an aggrandisement of the army and bureaucracy. Both these pillars of government preserved a rigidly exclusive attitude towards the Jews.

The fact that Germany's unification when it did come took place under the auspices of a military conquest, and under the leadership of Prussia, left its mark in a lasting weakness of the German national consciousness and in an inclination towards aggressive over-compensation of this defect. Both characteristics predisposed the German people to seek in anti-Semitism a collective self-assurance and self-exaltation which otherwise were denied to them. German " scientific " anti-Semitism distinctly shows the consequences of such an over-compensation of a national deficiency.

This third phenomenon was confined to the scene of the catastrophe of the German Jews. As a threat to Jewish emancipation it is not a factor that need be reckoned with in other countries, or, at any rate, in anything like the same degree.

(4) The fact that anti-Semitism in Germany was nevertheless very limited before the first World War gains a new significance in the light of these three phenomena. It shows that the " genuine " or " objective " Jewish problem had so largely disappeared that its vestiges could be used only to a minor extent for the necessary rationalisations of " sham " stimuli of anti-Semitism, although these " sham " stimuli were particularly plentiful in the beginning of the 20th century and especially in Germany.

How far were the German Jews prepared to meet the onslaught of anti-Semitism?

The German Jews were a strong, rising community. Their considerable services to the world around them did not prevent them from devoting a remarkable part of their creative power also to their Jewish sphere of life. They were the leading Jewry of the epoch. In their passage from the cultural autonomy of the pre-emancipation period to complete cultural identity with their environment they stood at an especially favourable point. They had approached near enough to their environment for their co-operation to be assured and nearly unquestioned, and for the "genuine" tensions to be abated to a point where they were practically ineffective. On the other hand, Jewish vitality was still strong. Jewish communities flourished, numerous associations preserved a Jewish atmosphere for those who shared their activities, Jewish research continued to attract excellent scholars, and new Jewish ways of life were continuously explored, contested, and re-established both in the religious and Jewish-political sphere. This, so to speak, optimal state of assimilation did not, of course, exist unchallenged. In the big cities, above all in Berlin, where an ever-increasing proportion of German Jewry was concentrated, many trends asserted themselves which led definitely away from Judaism. Also the Jewish birth-rate showed signs of a serious decline, and this symptom of the inability of the German Jews to reproduce themselves was regarded with grave concern by some of their leaders.[367a]

It was one of the characteristics of German Jewry that it utilised the intellectual trends which it absorbed from the Gentile world for effecting a spiritual regeneration of Judaism, which found expression in the Science of Judaism, Jewish religious liberalism, Samson Raphael Hirsch's system of Europeanised orthodoxy, Gabriel Riesser's political fight for Jewish rights, and the Zionist renaissance. Where Jews can react so healthily and so creatively to their environment, the Jewish ethos must still be strong. And where a Jewish ethos still exists in such vigour, disintegrating tendencies are likely to be retarded, if not brought to a standstill. That German Jewry still possessed a stong vitality was demonstrated during the deadly challenge of Hitlerism. Even under this mortal danger it was not only the institutions serving the needs of the moment which attracted the Jewish masses, not only soup kitchens, language classes, and advice bureaus. People also congregated in synagogues and institutes for adult education. If the Jews in Germany had retained, as at first they believed they would, a possibility of continuing to live in Germany, they would have answered even this dreadful challenge by a re-assertion of their Judaism. Nobody knows what fruits would have come forth, because the hope was destroyed before it could mature.

This short outline of Jewish life in Germany stands in strange contrast to the contents of the preceding chapters. It shows that Jewish life could unfold itself hopefully at a time and in a place where external dangers were accumulating on the horizon. Hardly ever is Jewish life a life without danger, the individual Jewish life rarely, and the collective Jewish life never. But all the dangers, both the general and the particular, were unable to impair seriously the activities of the Jewish community in Germany. Only when they were disastrously multiplied by a fatal concurrence of untoward circumstances did they acquire destructive power.

IV

THE CATASTROPHE

IT WILL have become clear from the previous chapters that National Socialism, the political movement that brought about the catastrophe of the German Jews, did not suddenly spring into existence, but was the outcome of certain trends in the social development. But it will be equally clear that these trends, for all their potential dangers, would not have culminated in a catastrophe of this magnitude had they not been fatefully accentuated by the German post-war crisis. It is the aim of this chapter to explain the effect of this crisis on each of the tendencies described above.

When the stormy waves of military defeat and its consequences swept over Germany in 1918, the dykes which should have protected the social structure showed many dangerous fissures. The rising floods penetrated into these fissures, and more than one dyke burst. Emergency dams were erected, but they lacked solid foundations. Thus the waters broke in and the German nation was submerged. The body which declared itself, in 1933, to be the German people was in reality only a morbidly degenerate part of it. Its members quickly disappeared again from the political scene. But before doing so they had handed over authority to a clique of adventurers who did not let it slip from their hands. The floods receded at last. But by a ruthless exercise of their power over life and death, the new potentates utterly destroyed all chance of healthy life arising out of the devastation. From the ruins of the old society they built a stronghold. This contained workshops, military barracks, and torture chambers—all of them equipped with the latest technical devices.

Even if the dykes protecting the German people against the roaring flood had been sound and solid, they would not have been able to withstand the danger without difficulty A military defeat like that inflicted in 1918, along with the cessions of territory and the economic burden of the reparations which followed, was a grave test for the powers of endurance of the German nation. Yet even in these extremely difficult conditions there were some hopeful beginnings which made it seem possible that the worst might be averted. After the defeat of 1871, France had also showed signs of disintegration, and the anti-Semitic episodes connected with the names of Boulanger and Dreyfus even invite comparison with the National Socialist movement. But in the end the forces of resistance in France proved sufficiently strong to prevent a catastrophe. Perhaps in Germany, too, a recovery might have been possible after the devastating flood—if only the dykes had not collapsed so completely.

But there was, to begin with, the havoc wrought by the epoch. Sombart described capitalism even in the stages of its normal development as a " witches' sabbath ", and a capitalist hell reigned in Germany after the first World War. Money lost its value. The savings of the lower and middle-classes disappeared. Unemployment, the constant concomitant of the business cycle, increased to an unheard-of extent. On the other hand, thanks to the influx of foreign loans after 1924, commerce and industry was concentrated into large combines. The contrast between rich and poor grew more marked. The absurdity of a situation in which the technical capacity of an Americanised industry could not be used to give work to idle hands, bread to the starving, and clothes to the shivering was so manifest that it inevitably led to a distrust of the whole system. Since capitalism had never succeeded in making itself popular, and in Germany less than elsewhere, its apparent failure was not felt as an unwelcome disillusionment, destroying a beloved idol, but as the realisation of a long-expected doom. An expressly anti-capitalist attitude was adopted by circles which had so far felt no conscious hostility to capitalism. As long as their choice had been between " capitalist middle-class " against " socialist proletarians ", innumerable independent or half-independent shopkeepers and black-coated employees had been prevented by their anti-proletarian prejudices from joining the socialist ranks. But now it was just these people whose lives were thrown into such disorder by the capitalist disintegration that their adherence to the system was seriously challenged. The proletarian anti-capitalist feeling continued to be catered for by the parties of the proletarian Left. But the anti-capitalist feeling of the petty bourgeoisie looked long in vain for political shelter to this or that old or new party, until eventually the political vacuum was filled by National Socialism.

There were good reasons why this class could not find a resting-place at some earlier stage. It has previously been suggested that the lower middle-class might have developed an ideology which, besides giving it self-confidence and hope, imposed on it the obligation to live up to a certain moral code. This chance had now been missed. The sense of insecurity, hopelessness, and disillusionment was so great that it made any serious intellectual or moral effort impossible. It was only the most immediate economic interests, combined with scarcely veiled instincts of hatred, envy, and revenge, that determined the political attitude of these vacillating petty-bourgeois voters. Thus they were drawn irresistibly from the intellectual and idealistic " Democratic Party ", which they had at first supported and which they should have continued to support, to the old parties of the Right, which attracted them by their fervent nationalism and their hostility to Socialism. From there they sank farther into the " Economic Party " whose very name indicated that by now economic interests were considered to be all that mattered and that any idealistic burden was deliberately avoided. But if the " Economic Party " did not impose any positive moral obligations on its followers, it still restrained the release of amoral and anti-social impulses. It was, for instance, not anti-Semitic. Thus its appeal to the masses was not primitive enough, and it had finally to give way to the still more primitive appeal of the Nazis. The mental and physical exhaustion had proceeded too far for a collective effort for the maintenance of social values to be still possible. The remaining energy did not even suffice for the negative function of keeping in check the passions of hatred and aggressiveness or directing them solely against the ordinary political opponent. It was therefore no wonder that the Nazi incitement to indulge unrestrictedly these anti-social impulses was felt to be irresistibly tempting.

The part played by the first World War in shattering the moral codes of all the warring nations is by now generally recognised. It must, nevertheless, be pointed out that this crisis was bound to have especially far-reaching effects in Germany. In that country not only had religion been still further discredited—partly because the appalling horrors of the war stood in too marked a contrast to its teaching, partly

174

because the Church had violated the commandment of love by its participation in the propaganda of hatred—but the secular supports of a civilised *Weltanschauung* had also been destroyed. Although from a moral point of view the principles of German life during the imperial era had been questionable enough if compared with the fundamental ideas of Western civilisation, yet the soldierly spirit, civil obedience, and loyalty to Kaiser and Reich had at least been solid pillars on which to base the life of the community. They had helped to develop a high sense of duty and an exemplary love of order—in a word, the conventional ideas and traditions of German society. All these principles of civilised conduct had disappeared with the Empire. An enormous earthquake caused the ground to tremble under the feet of every individual. Not only did God seem to have deserted His believers, not only did the parson's voice sound hollow, but the dream of a mighty Fatherland had dissolved in nothing, the imperial splendour lay in ruins, and the once trusted politicians had been exposed as liars. Even the captains of industry had been deprived of their halo of omnipotence, which had made them at once admired and dreaded. People demanded workers' councils, and on the horizon there loomed the economic twilight of the gods— socialisation.

Between 1918 and 1933 events followed each other abruptly —revolutionary disintegration, strikes, radicalism, the murder of men who until yesterday had represented the Reich, left no idol still standing for the little man in Germany. The period has been too often described for a more detailed account to be required here. All that needs to be said is that, owing to the German post-war crisis, all the threads that have been seen running through German pre-war history grew into ropes. But not ropes which could support and bind together, but such as, lashed by the tempest, pulled the disintegrating social structure of the German nation wholly asunder.

One such thread had been the anti-capitalist resentment. It now became a spirit of destructive fury in the lower middle-class, directed against any existing economy whatever. An-other thread had been the moral and intellectual fatigue originating from the arduous struggle for life. This had grown into the scourge of a general unfettering of primitive impulses. A third thread had been the disparagement of moral standards, brought about by intellectuals and politicians. This had grown into a complete moral chaos which left the individual without guidance for the most common actions of daily life, no less than for dealing with the ultimate questions of life and death.

The dangers inherent in the half-education of the time, at once so inadequate and so arrogant, were likewise bound to multiply in this crucial period. The claim to self-determination had grown more insistent not only because of the progress of popular education, but also because the experience of war and the genuinely democratic State of Weimar had contributed to make people eager to exercise their political rights. Simultaneously the economic and political position had become more bewildering than ever. Only those who witnessed the wild passion for argument which raged at that time in meeting-halls, at beer tables, in family circles, and chance crowds gathering at street corners, can form an idea of the overmastering need which was felt by all and sundry to obtain themselves, and help others to gain, a clear conception of the world around them which had got so hopelessly out of joint. The strength of this desire was only surpassed by the inadequacy of the means employed in satisfying it. Only very few found the necessary time and energy for reading comprehensive treatises, and not much larger was the number of those eager people who derived their information from serious articles and lectures. The ferment created by the general revolution had ceased to affect merely this or that political decision. It had stirred up the lowest human instincts and it was these that gave the key to action. People, however, who considered themselves educated required that decisions dictated by their instincts should be cloaked by seemingly rational arguments, so that they could be accepted by their "scientific" conscience. The problem, therefore, was to find an ideology which could pose as scholarly while being in reality in close conformity with the instinctive desires. If something of this kind could be evolved, preferably a few slogans with a strong emotional appeal and with vague allusions to a profound philosophical background, then there was every prospect of its enthusiastic acceptance. And then all the passions aroused by the impulses which were promised satisfaction by the propaganda symbols would provide further conviction of the truth which these symbols were alleged to embody.[368] In this way another of the trends previously mentioned was aggravated in the post-war period: the claim of the half-educated to understand the world and to share in its direction led to a psychological condition in which people became hopelessly susceptible to propaganda, if only this combined gratification of instincts with a seemingly scientific character.[369]

The consequences of another trend, the dependence of politics on economic interests, need only be briefly touched here, because it is obvious that the economic disorganisation of the post-war crisis could not fail to aggravate this tendency also. During the time of inflation and deflation the economic position of the individual not only influenced his political outlook indirectly, but governed it almost absolutely. Choice of party depended almost entirely on whether one was the owner or the tenant of his house, whether a civil servant or a business man. The economic position of most people was so completely undermined, their resources so utterly exhausted that the question of the economic policy which he was to support could easily resolve itself into one of life and death for him. The factors which in normal times counteracted the predominance of economic considerations were almost completely lacking. True, there were individuals who made fortunes and even a period of more general recovery, from 1924 to 1929. But these did not suffice to create a feeling of real security. The period of prosperity was much too short to efface the memory of the past depression, and was fraught with dismal apprehensions as to a recurrence of another time of distress. The fact that this short and precarious economic recuperation was nevertheless unmistakably reflected in a decline in Nazi votes was not due to a loosening of the economic trammels on political thought. The voters who at that time abandoned the Nazi Party did so not because they rose above their economic interests, but because their despair and inability to think became less marked, so that they began again to look for a representation of their interests where they were more likely to find it.

While tracing the development of each of the previously described tendencies after the first World War, we must not omit to consider the socialist workers' movement. What happened to Marxist Socialism, which had so successfully combined the appeal to the instincts with respect for moral standards, under the impact of that destructive crisis? In dealing with this question we must first make a distinction between the Social Democratic Party and the rest of the proletarian parties, which during the post-war years split off from Social Democracy and partly—like the Independent Social Democratic Party in 1922 —joined it again. These equally professed their allegiance to Marxism as they interpreted it. But in the matter of sense of responsibility and acknowledgment of moral standards they differed very considerably from the pre-war Social Democratic outlook. They made greater or smaller concessions to the general feeling of intellectual and moral weariness. Their methods of influencing the masses kept midway between the tactics of guidance and enlightenment, still retained by the Social Democratic Party, and those of incitement and mass hypnotism, carried to extreme length by Nazi propaganda. At times there was not much difference between the methods employed by the Communists and the Nazis, except that the Communist propaganda served in the last resort a clear and rational programme. The radicalism of this programme and the way in which it was presented also appealed mainly to the instincts, and indeed primarily to the same instincts as did the Nazi Party. An exception was, however, its attitude towards anti-Semitism, which was renounced by the Communists because it was incompatible with their principles. But the part played by anti-Semitism in the Nazi movement was by no means left unfilled by Communist propaganda. Only there were other scapegoats—the bourgeois, the Nazis, the " Social Fascists " as the Communists called the Social Democrats— which fulfilled part of the functions reserved by the Nazis for the Jews. As the Communist agitation, in spite of all its eagerness to obtain mass responses, kept within the frame of a consistent party programme, it chose the objects for its aggression in conformity with its genuine political objectives. It is a regrettable manifestation of the laws prevailing in mass psychology that this remaining sense of political responsibility was of no avail to the Communists. It was not by chance that in the competition between the two radical wings the less scrupulous was victorious. The total lack of a serious programme in the Nazi Party, the distinct nihilism which characterised it, was not the least factor which gave it a propagandistic superiority over a party definitely bound to a proletarian-socialist doctrine.

The followers of both parties were less clearly separated from each other than might have been expected from the antagonism of their ideologies. Apart from the solid party nucleus on each side, the adherents of both fluctuated largely

178

from one to the other. This is a further proof that at a time of emotional mass appeals the actual political issues play only minor parts.

The emergence of socialist splinter parties was the price the socialist workers' movement had to pay to the aroused mass instincts.* Apart from this the Social Democratic Party weathered the storm remarkably well. Although it had to struggle against a multitude of adverse factors, any one of which might have sufficed to undermine its influence on the voters, it was able in the last tolerably free election of 1933 still to retain as many as 120 seats among the 566 members of the Reichstag. And yet it had not only been left behind by the extremists Right and Left because of its moderation, but it was likewise seriously hampered by its parliamentarian policy of compromise up to the end of the Brüning Cabinet in 1932. The Social Democratic Party, which in 1918 had promised a Socialist Republic to its followers, had gradually lost all revolutionary *élan* and had drawn back to a line of cautious reform. It represented in the Weimar Republic the actual " conservative " element, while the parties of the Right tried to draw the political carriage backwards and the Communists to push the revolution onwards. But what it meant for the party to be " conservative ", or at best to progress slowly, while the spread of economic and social confusion seemed categorically to demand energetic measures ; what it meant further to be forced to a defensive attitude when the workers whom it represented were full of revolutionary expectations—all this can easily be imagined.

This situation was, of course, bound to react unfavourably on the fortunes of the Social Democratic Party. Despite its still considerable strength, the growth of the radical wings was a sign that its structure had changed. In consequence of its " conservatism " it became more and more a party of those who had something to lose, of the skilled workers, the trade unionists, and the older age-groups.[370] But even considering this change, the loyalty of large parts of the German working-class to the Social Democracy remains a hopeful sign. It shows that even at a time when the masses were on the move as never before and when all conditions favoured the success of an unscrupulous appeal to the instincts, a moderate and responsible

* Cf. what has been said on p. 114 about certain syndicalistic tendencies during the same period.

179

policy was still able to retain a high degree of popularity.

This fact seems to contradict the proposition laid down above that in certain unfavourable circumstances the masses are bound to abandon any exacting moral standards and to fall a prey to whatever propaganda most flatters their primitive instincts. The Social Democratic example shows that this tendency can be counteracted by wise political education and a solid political tradition. Even while admitting the most depressing conclusions of mass psychology—depressing in the sense in which any insight into the frailty of the higher human faculties such as intellect and morality is depressing—one can infer from the facts given above that the attempt to educate the masses can arouse in them moral and intellectual powers if only the more natural impulses are not entirely neglected. It was the ability to combine the two processes in the right proportions which during the years of extreme crisis maintained the popularity of German Social Democracy and made it a strong fortress against the propaganda of hatred and revenge so highly favoured by the general conditions of the time.

We have now to examine what happened to another of the trends previously mentioned, the tendency towards " total democratisation ".* The Weimar Constitution had considerably enlarged the franchise. All men and women over the age of 20 had the right to vote. The abolition of Second Chambers in the Reich as well as in the territorial States, the abandonment of all property qualifications, a thorough-going system of proportional representation, the transfer of surplus votes to so-called Reich Lists—all these regulations rendered possible an almost photographic picture of the people's will in Parliament. But this was only the legal basis for the " total democracy " we have described above. Even under so thoroughly democratic an electoral law, this extreme phase of democratic development was not bound to come into being as long as the people were not determined to make their potential rights effective. This determination, however, increased in proportion as politics became the concern of all strata of the population. As a result of war, defeat, revolution, and economic breakdown people felt to a degree hitherto unknown that every political decision had an immediate bearing on their welfare. Confident, as the result of their half-education, that they could see through any obscurity, they made up their minds, in spite of all

* Cf. p. 116.

their bewilderment, actively to assert their political influence. The men faced a political scene which had entirely changed. The women were almost completely unprepared for the use of the political power put into their hands. The youth was even less trained for politics, but had brought home from the battle-fields that recklessness and self-confidence of immaturity which is the worst enemy of sound judgment in difficult issues. " Total " democracy thus came into being in Germany in particularly unfavourable circumstances. Symbols and slogans which demanded the minimum control of primitive urges were in such conditions bound to gain unprecedented success.

The idea of democracy itself has been described above as one of the first victims of radical democratisation. As might have been expected, the anti-democratic outlook spread rapidly in post-war Germany. Big business felt seriously threatened by the increasing power of organised labour. This had become manifest not only in labour's complete political emancipation, but also in certain attempts at socialisation, and, above all, in the Works Councils Law (*Betriebsrätegesetz*), and the important functions conferred on the trade unions.[371] The radical tendencies of the workers which displayed themselves in the growth of the Independent Labour Party and the Communist Party made a second more violent phase of the revolution appear possible. This development further undermined the never very strong loyalty of industry and big business to democracy. In its Weimar form especially, democracy protected too many labour interests to attract strong capitalist sympathies.[372]

In this crucial period only one thing could have prevented a democratic failure—a strong democratic tradition. Only if democracy had been an accepted and unquestioned way of life of long standing would it have been able to stand the extraordinary test of this post-war crisis. In fact, however, German democracy had only just been established as the consequence of a military defeat. Since it was contrary to all the accustomed ideas, a flood of resentments surged against it. The bitterest of these was due to the feeling which in other shapes had previously played such a disastrous rôle in German history, that the Weimar Republic had been created according to Western models and was therefore an imitation of the national enemy. This itself was a sufficiently powerful argument against democracy in a nation that had never attained sufficient self-confidence to be able to accept foreign gifts without losing its poise. And the argument was further emphasised by those who tried to profit from this German weakness for their own ends. Thus hostility to democracy spread among those who should have been its natural supporters. When the earthquake of Nazi propaganda shattered the political foundations of the Weimar Republic, these had already been largely undermined by the anti-democratic outlook of the people.

It is understandable that under the impression of such an experience as the defeat of 1918 a growth so naturally frail as German nationalism was bound to deteriorate hopelessly. It could not stand the blow. Under the weight of its impact it degenerated into an acute state of hysteria or paranoia or whatever psychiatric term may most suitably be applied to it.

The revolution of 1918 and the removal of the formerly privileged groups from the leading positions in the State showed the way in which the feelings of guilt, generated by the national humiliation, might have been adequately purged. The flight of the Kaiser provided a subject which could be used with perfect safety for gratifying the aggressive impulses. But the Germans were not accustomed to think in terms of political liberty. They did not feel any profound satisfaction at being finally delivered from semi-autocracy and feudalism. For that reason attacks against those now deprived of their privileges, but always trying to reassert them, had but little attraction. German history had for so long been dominated by the striving for national unity and grandeur, liberty had for so long been a primarily nationalist concept, that the interest in civil liberties had become emaciated. Only the political Left laid the blame for the national breakdown fairly and squarely on the former rulers. It is not surprising that the extreme Right did not condescend to self-accusation. That, however, the moderate parties between Right and Left and, still more, the politically indifferent masses, should have increasingly rallied to the Right rather than to the Left is a fact of most ominous significance. Among the causes to which such conduct must be attributed, the hypertrophic, and at that time hypersensitive, national consciousness is one of the most important. This led people to look for a scapegoat from " outside " rather than to blame part of the people for the national catastrophe, because in this part they felt themselves to be attacked.

Instead of fixing the responsibility for the defeat on the old governing class and thus carrying out an inner catharsis both in the political and psychological field, the majority attempted to exculpate the whole nation. Indeed, after a short time, the further step was taken of altogether denying the defeat. The more difficult it was to perform this feat, the more ample was applause in store for the magicians who accomplished it.[373]

But not only did the national feeling of the Germans lack that inner balance which alone would have enabled them to recover from the shock of the national defeat. The situation was further aggravated by all the other unfavourable conditions which have been described above. Internal national conflicts which had largely lost their importance in peace-time were again rendered acute by the national misfortune. The Separatist Movement instigated in the Rhineland during the first post-war years was as much a symptom of territorial dissension as was the tension between Bavaria and Prussia, which characterised the whole Weimar period. In both these phenomena there was likewise involved another of the great German conflicts, the denominational disunion. This was always latent and could be made use of whenever a Catholic land wanted to assert itself against a Protestant one, and vice versa. Owing to the intermixture of the two denominations in Germany, this conflict made itself felt within the individual States as well. The Catholics had only just won full emancipation. They were now admitted on equal terms with Protestants to the civil service, whereas they had previously suffered from discrimination. With the overcrowding of all occupations and especially of the higher professions, which resulted from the demobilisation and the discharge of most of the former members of the professional army, this new group of Catholic competitors became the cause of additional frictions. And, apart from such political difficulties, German nationalism continued to show fateful signs of its parentage in the romantic spirit.

Before going more closely into this matter it seems necessary to insert a few remarks on the much discussed question whether National Socialism has any place in the history of ideas. After numerous attempts inside and outside Germany to trace the ideological genealogy of Nazism, in which in varying order Luther, the romantics, Darwin, Nietzsche, the German idealist philosophers headed by Hegel, as well as Frederick the Great and Bismarck, have figured as its spiritual ancestors, this question has gradually tended to be answered in the negative. The opinion has become prevalent that Nazism presents a fairly indiscriminate combination of ideological elements which would be too highly honoured by any attempt to prove their relationship with exalted models of the past.[374] This, on the whole, is the view taken in this study. If it ascribes importance to the part which romanticism and the gradual shaping of the German notion of nationalism played in the rise of Nazism, this does not indicate a transmission of ideas in the ordinary sense.

A transmission of this kind cannot be assumed because, to begin with, Nazism is no consistent system of ideas. In spite of the immense emphasis placed on the idea of leadership, Nazism differs from other political movements in so far as it was only to a very limited degree shaped by the intellectual powers of its leader or leaders. The creation of Nazism did not consist in the conception and popularisation of a new idea, but in the articulation and symbolisation of spontaneous mass desires, which were given a superficial consistency by the help of vague and meaningless phrases. More than any modern social movement Nazism is a spontaneous, not an ideological, movement.

This fundamental characteristic does not exclude the fact that Hitler and his leading clique had at times a fairly clear vision of their political aims. The connection, however, between this vision and what was presented to the people as National Socialism was, as far as it existed at all, a very loose one. Hitler desired personal power, he meant to prepare for a war of revenge. He also intended to make a return for the money received from the industrialists by disbanding the trade unions. But it is obvious that in his propaganda he could not reveal these intentions, or could, at best, make only veiled allusions to them. What he said was what the people liked to hear. It consisted of a loosely combined, inconsistent conglomeration of ideas and suggestions each of which was intended to satisfy some one of the most common mass desires.

It is thus in the way in which these desires took shape and in the means by which they were satisfied that the influence of German educational tradition becomes discernible. This tradition—largely diluted and distorted, it is true—had penetrated to all sections of the population. The masses had at least gone through elementary schools and had breathed the

German educational atmosphere. The previously discussed law of ideological "gravitation" had operated upon them. That is to say, out of the cultural material presented to them they had imbibed only the comparatively crude, easily understandable, elements which appealed to their instincts. Fundamentally, this process goes on in all countries. But what distinguished the education of the German masses from that of their neighbours who were thoroughly permeated with Western civilisation was the character of the teaching which was doled out to them.

German school education is generally considered comparatively satisfactory, as far as the instilling of knowledge is concerned. But we are concerned here rather with the so-called *Gesinnungsfächer* (ideological subjects), *i.e.*, above all, the teaching of German and History, in which what may be called the spiritual atmosphere was the most important element. Even after allowing for all the dilution and distortion of original spiritual concepts in the course of school-teaching, it makes a great difference whether children and juveniles are brought up in an atmosphere of Christianity or whether religious instruction is only just another subject which has been somewhat artificially fitted into the syllabus alongside of the other lessons. The children's minds will be very differently affected according as the whole tone of the school inculcates helpfulness towards the weak and unhappy or recognises the right of the strongest, as it is exercised in the playground, as the true guide in life also. Where the natural love of one's country is deepened by the pride in the country's accomplishments on behalf of human freedom and justice, it will have a better moral effect than where it rests on the claim that the country is inhabited by a master race, destined to dominate the world. A decisive difference will finally be found to exist between an education which sets a premium on clear thinking, readiness to shoulder responsibility, civic pride, and the will to progress, and one which glorifies "profound instincts" that can "only with difficulty be expressed in words" but are "never wrong", which makes the first virtue an unconditional obedience that neither questions nor doubts, and which preaches the cult of the State and the medieval social order adorning them with all the products of a rapturous phantasy. Far as one may be from the illusion that the Western teachers have ever really succeeded in educating their pupils to their ideals, the constant endeavour to approximate to them is nevertheless an educational factor of primary importance. The neglect of this leaves a gap in the education of youth which cannot be filled. If the attempt to teach people neighbourly love, humanitarian responsibility, clarity of thought, and civic courage is abandoned from the beginning, then those inhibitions which are so necessary in later life to counteract the inevitable downward " gravitation " have not even been implanted in youth.

Mass desires will never soar to spiritual heights, because for one thing they must represent the lowest " common denominator " on which masses are agreed. Mass desires of bewildered and desperate people will have an even more degraded " common denominator ". Mass desires of unhappy people, however, whose tendencies towards aggression, power, and mental laziness had not been effectively checked, even in their youth, can least of all be expected to come up to reasonable moral and intellectual standards. In so far as the German spiritual heritage had failed to check these tendencies or had even encouraged them, it shares in the responsibility for the emergence of Nazism. Its contribution lay in the psychological concessions it made to the human instincts. The Germans, indeed, believed that they dealt very strictly with themselves when they glorified the fulfilment of duty, heroism, and devotion to the State. But in reality, by such doctrines as by many of the " easier " norms their philosophers had provided, they delivered man from far heavier burdens : from personal responsibility, self-discipline, and spiritual freedom—to mention only three burdens which are rarely considered as such, but which are among the first things of which man will become tired when his strength begins to fail him.

We spoke above of " the fateful consequences of the birth of German nationalism from the romantic spirit ". This is not to be understood as implying that National Socialism was a late descendant of romanticism, in the sense in which, e.g., the German Youth Movement can be regarded as its legitimate heir. The relations between Nazism and romanticism were in fact very indirect ; they were mainly to be seen in the way in which romanticism had accustomed the German people to certain habits of thinking and feeling which, in turn, prepared them for the later conception and reception of Nazism. Or, in other words : romanticism counteracted certain Western habits of thinking and feeling which would have increased the resistance both to the conception and the reception of Nazism. The resistance would have had to display both of these facets because of the interdependence, peculiar to National Socialism, between the conception of mass desires and the reception of the slogans which were designed to satisfy them. The Nazi propaganda, being primarily an endeavour to make mass desires articulate, it can be said that the first conception of Nazism lay in the mass desires themselves. But the way in which the propagandists gave expression to the mass desires aimed in turn at mass effect. By means of the symbols and slogans the masses were to be given the feeling that they were understood, they were to feel that their secret longings had been put into words. The re-action of the masses to the words and signs by which their own desires were expressed is what is called the reception of Nazism. This too was facilitated by the fact that the slogans and symbols originated in the same seed-ground of romanticism. Leaders and led joined hands the more easily because the barriers of intellectual and moral standards which should have separated them had previously been pulled down.

All the characteristics of romanticism mentioned in earlier chapters left their imprint on Nazism during the period in which it rose to power. The substitution of various alternatives for rationalism and enlightenment* the justification of vio-lence,† the historical theory of law,‡ the glorification of the Middle Ages,§ the exaltation of the emotions‖—all these motives re-emerge in a grossly vulgarised form in Nazi propa-ganda. Not that Nazism took any one of the original ideas seriously. Although individual Nazis believed in individual ideas, the movement as a whole dealt with them as mere expedients. The confusion of thought prevailing with regard to a re-establishment of the corporative or " Estate " idea of the Middle Ages, e.g., has been described by Dr. Franz Neumann.[375] The movement had also no consistent theory of law. The theories expounded by Carl Schmitt [376] were attempts at a subsequent justification of Nazism and were entirely irrelevant for its effect on the masses. Nazism could certainly not claim to have adopted the Historical Theory of Law. But the early repudia-tion by Historical Law of the universal obligations imposed by Natural Law had contributed to prepare the minds of those who had a special interest in understanding by law primarily a national matter. Much more, no doubt, was needed to make

* Cf. p. 84.   † Cf. p. 89.   ‡ Cf. p. 135.   § Cf. p. 135.   ‖ Cf. p. 138.

187

the Germans swallow such a phrase as " Right is what is useful to the German people ". They were eventually able to do so because of the innate repugnance to Western ideas inspired by their misguided nationalism.[377]

A no less fatal part in the post-war era was played by most of the tendencies which may be regarded as specially Prussian. The Weimar Constitution had abolished the last of the feudal prerogatives and had tried to substitute the freest self-determination of the people for the old spirit of submission. Militarism was also supposed to have been discarded. What remained of the pillars of old Prussia was only the bureaucracy, and even its most objectionable features were to be eliminated by the democratisation of the civil service. Thus Weimar *de jure* abolished the old Prussia, and a new historical epoch, delivered from the old burdens, might have set in. But in reality the power of the old institutions did not vanish with their legal abolition. In the first place, this did not succeed in bringing about their actual removal. A state of suspense was created in which the previously ruling classes became the stronghold of reaction and discontent. Reaction and discontent, however, were far from confined to these actually deposed classes. Since their dethronement coincided with a time of dire need, they became the symbol of lost happiness even for those who formerly had often sighed under their oppression. Imperial power, military bands, and everything connected with " Prussian discipline " became during the post-war era the symbols of the " good old times ". Their disappearance incited suspicion and hatred against the " bad, new times ".

The authoritarian State had exercised its functions too long for its influence to be obliterated by a legislative act. The German middle-class had lived through their decisive age of development without democratic education. Their political maturity had been artificially delayed, and they were now unwilling and unable to shoulder its burden. The psychologist Suttie [378] describes the psychological condition of children who have too suddenly been dismissed from the loving atmosphere of the nursery and left to themselves. As the typical reaction to this experience he regards the formation of gangs which proclaim the ideal of manliness and strongly resent everything " feminine " and " girlish ". Force, violence, cunning, and even crime exert powerful attraction on these children. Every trick is admired, even if it has a criminal touch, every swindle is considered "clever", and there is an inclination to all kinds of secret plotting. Suttie is of opinion that this behaviour originates in reality in the suppressed longing for the lost paradise of childhood. He calls it "a revenge upon, and a repudiation of, the 'weaning' mother, on the defensive principle of the 'sour grapes'". There is here an obvious analogy not only with the psychological condition of the Storm Troopers and the inner Nazi circle, but also with the moral indifference of broad sections of the lower middle-class at the time of their release from the paternalism of the authoritarian State. The comparison also goes a long way to explain the apparent contradiction between the "manliness" on which the Nazis prided themselves and the femininity of their attitude to their leader. The first characteristic corresponded to the defiance of the children who had been released against their will from tutelage, the second to their actual wish to be restored to the previous state. The masses that became responsible for the rise of Nazism swayed indeed between these extremes. This, too, was a revenge of old Prussia beyond her grave, which had been dug by the official constitution.

It would, however, be incorrect to assume that all the characteristics of Prussia and Germany had a weakening effect on their resistance against the demoralising effects of the post-war crisis. Germany's love of order, e.g., and her proverbial obedience to bureaucracy produced results not entirely unfavourable in this situation. It was, however, their less estimable features which were taken over by National Socialism.

National Socialism, as has been pointed out at the beginning of this study, cannot be fully understood if it is seen simply as an exhibition of human depravity, or even if it is attributed solely to a disruptive economic crisis. Still less can the catastrophe of the Jews be understood if it is regarded as the logical outcome of German pre-war anti-Semitism in the form in which this had gained notoriety through some of its intellectual standard-bearers. Only if all the sequences of cause and effect over a long period are viewed together can one succeed in understanding why the economic crisis resulted in precisely those phenomena which made up National Socialism. Only to a very limited extent did the crisis produce new national characteristics in the Germans. Rather did it work on the existing characteristics in such a way as to intensify those which were the least desirable. The sum total of these undesirable traits, which exist everywhere but were more widespread in Germany than in other countries, was the ladder by which Nazism ascended to power.

It would be wrong to minimise the importance of Nazism by regarding its ultimate success as due merely to its seizure of power by political intrigues and the quasi *coup d'état* of the Reichstag fire. True, political accidents did co-operate towards the final outcome. But it is not this final outcome that should attract the main attention of the student of the catastrophe of European Jewry. What matters is to understand how under a free democratic constitution a party like that of the Nazis won mass support. Even if, as might easily have happened, the Nazi Party had disintegrated and disappeared after its decline during the autumn of 1932, the phenomenon of its attractiveness for the masses would have lost nothing of its dangerous significance. There would then be no less need of examining how this danger arose. And a second aspect of the main problem should be made quite clear. Even if the last wholesale expulsion and extermination of European Jews should have exceeded the original intentions even of Nazi leaders; even if, as will be shown later, anti-Semitism played only a minor part in the decision of the voters for Nazism; even if, to put it briefly, anti-Semitism in Germany was much less strong than it would appear from the Nazi success and its terrible consequences, it was still an issue of extreme seriousness. Even if all necessary qualifications are made, anti-Semitism remains with Nazism one of the focal problems of contemporary German history. And, lastly, there is a third point bearing upon the nature of this enquiry. A strict line is to be drawn between Nazism during the so-called period of struggle, before the accession to power, and Nazism after this accession. With the moment of the accession to power a comprehensive change came about in the relations of the Nazi Party to the people who had helped it to gain power. No single word was spoken or written after the 30th January 1933 which gives any direct indication of the feeling of the masses. Only indirectly and with great caution can conclusions on public opinion be drawn from governmental actions, propagandistic utterances, or even from personal experiences after that time. What in the period after Hitler's appointment as Chancellor figures as Nazism has only the name in common with Nazism before this time. The Nazi Party had then ceased to be a people's movement marshalling

190

the whole nation for or against itself; it had become a co-agulated organisation, enlarged by the influx of opportunists, which in none of its utterances any longer expressed the natural reactions of the masses. This fact is not altered by the more or less ingenious attempts of the Nazi propagandists to maintain the appearance of continuing to represent popular feeling. The analysis of Nazism which follows will deal only with the first stage of the movement.

In the description given above of the general and local phenomena of disintegration, an interdependence between social and spiritual factors has in each case been pointed out. It has been assumed that whether or not there is a connection between social conditions and the genesis of ideas, there is at any rate a connection between social conditions and the *effect* of ideas. Not only has the general character of the social conditions an important influence on whether and to what extent an idea produces any effect at all, but a special kind of connection is also to be found between the number and condi-tions of life of people affected by an idea, on the one hand, and the way in which they accept the idea on the other. With the movements that preceded Nazism the primary thing was the idea, the secondary the response of the public. Nazism, taken as a whole, is in contrast not an independent spiritual concep-tion. Here, the primary thing was the leanings of the public, the secondary the ideological concoction.

This must not, however, be misunderstood to mean that the masses dictated the actual content of the ideology they wanted to embrace. This would have gone far beyond their capacity to express a united will, not to mention their reasoning powers. What the masses contributed to the Nazi propaganda slogans, which virtually constituted the whole of Nazism during the fight for power, was solely their inarticulate primitive impulses. The masses did not ask for anti-Semitism, they wanted to hate. They did not ask for the racial doctrine, they wanted to feel superior. They did not ask for the legend of the " stab in the back ", they desired to rid themselves of what they felt to be a national humiliation. They did not demand the leader principle, but they wanted once more to obey instead of taking their own decisions. To find the most effective means of satis-fying each of these desires—in this and in this alone consisted the intellectual achievement of the Nazi ideologists.

Nazism thus completely reversed the logical order between

spontaneous and ideological elements in a social movement. Lacking as it did any consistent system of ideas, it nevertheless satisfied the mass desires in a way which pretended to follow a definite idea and derived from this sham idea a higher authority. And the extremely effective way in which Nazism gratified the mass desires incited the same kind of desires also in those elements of the population which had not previously harboured them. The prospect of experiencing such a pleasant gratification of one's desires as was held out by the Nazi symbols made the desires contagious. Or, to put it more simply, the double attraction of an unrestricted gratification of primitive impulses and the conviction of serving a great cause induced more and more people to join the Nazi movement.

In the light of this close connection between the existence of mass desires and their gratification, the question whether within the Nazi movement the masses were actors or instruments diminishes in importance. They were, in fact, both at the same time. It is precisely this combination of action and reaction of the masses which characterises National Socialism. The late Professor Emil Lederer suggested that the masses were mainly the creators of the movement. To controvert this view, Dr. Franz Neumann [379] argues that in that case " Social imperialism would be not a device to ensnare the masses but an articulation of the spontaneous longing of the masses. Racism would not be the concern of small groups alone, but would be deeply imbedded in the masses. Leadership adoration would be a genuine semi-religious phenomenon and not merely a device to prevent insight into the operation of the social-economic mechanism "—implying that all this is impossible. In fact, it was quite possible, almost necessary for the masses to be both the creators and the victims of the movement. In each of Dr. Neumann's examples the alternatives support each other and are even interdependent. Precisely because " social imperialism " was " the articulation of the spontaneous longing of the masses " it was such an extremely suitable " device to ensnare the masses ". Because " racism "—or rather some of its constituent elements—was " deeply imbedded in the masses " it could develop from a " concern of small groups " into the pseudo-scientific basis of a mass doctrine. And because " leadership adoration " is " a genuine semi-religious phenomenon " it could successfully be used " to prevent insight into the operation of the social-economic mechanism ". In course of time, however, the relative import-ance of the two alternatives somewhat altered. While in the early stages of the movement its spontaneous character was more pronounced, the ideological elements became rigid after they had been formulated, and they were more and more used as propagandistic slogans. This process was completed with the seizure of power. With this event the propaganda phrases were definitely severed from the mass desires and became pure shibboleths. But at that time, as has already been pointed out, the entire relation between masses and Nazism entered upon a fundamentally new phase.[380]

What, then, were the most prevalent mass desires during that post-war period, and in what way did the Nazis attempt to satisfy them? For the time being, this satisfaction could only be a theoretical one—a circumstance which makes the success even more remarkable. The masses demanded work and bread. The Nazis could not give these, at least not during the first few years. Only slowly did the party machinery become capable of granting practical aid to its followers. The prospect of work and bread was also held out by the other parties. There must have been, then, something in Nazi propaganda which inspired the masses with special confidence. The bulk of those who filled the party meetings could not expect a job or a rise from their new party allegiance. Many of them had even to put up with certain disadvantages in case their adherence to Nazism became known. In spite of this they flocked to it in growing numbers. What drove them to do this?

Nazism contained an incomparable and unsurpassable combination of all those psychological elements which the masses needed in the situation which has been described above. Hitler emptied Pandora's box on to them. He could not immediately give bread to the starving and wages to the unemployed. But he absolved the weary, the desperate, and the down-trodden from the heaviest burdens of their souls. He allowed them to rest, to gather hope, and to feel superior. He released them from the loads of reason, responsibility, and morality. He led them back into the regressive paradise of irresponsibility and implicit faith. He let them relax into a pre-civilised, pre-social, infantile stage. He allowed them to hate and believe, to strike out and obey, to march and feel as the masters of the world.

As has already been pointed out, the increasing complication of life in general, and of life in Germany in particular, resulted in a gradual lowering of the barriers of conscience, which was supposed to keep the primitive impulses under control. With frustration reaching an unprecedented intensity during the post-war crisis, the urgency of the most elementary human needs came to a head—no matter whether they demanded direct satisfaction, like hunger, or indirect, like the instinct of aggressiveness when " displaced " from its legitimate object. The power to check them, however, was almost entirely paralysed. It is the essence of Nazism that, in its way, it restored a situation which had thus become untenable.

The reception of Nazism was enthusiastic because it reduced the conscience to silence. Nazism allowed, or rather ordered, the removal of all inhibitions which civilisation had placed in the way of the elementary urges. It became thus " a magnificent festival for the ego which might then once again feel satisfied with itself ".[381] The Nazi mass meetings, particularly the annual party rallies with their frenzy of banners, colours, lights, music, and military splendour, had indeed the character of enormous mass festivals. By extinguishing individuality they relieved man from his vexation. In hours of mass ecstasy the conscience was silent. But people could not celebrate festivals all the time. Nazi propaganda therefore devised other means for easing the burden of conscience throughout the new everyday life it was about to create.

There is still another point in Freud's psychology which helps towards an understanding of the enthusiastic reception of Nazism. Freud states that in the mental development of man primitive stages are superseded by higher ones, but they nevertheless survive as potential causes of regression. " The earlier mental state . . . may at any time again become the mode of expression of the forces in the mind, and that exclusively, as though all later developments had been annulled, undone. . . . The primitive stages can always be re-established ; the primitive mind is, in the fullest meaning of the word, imperishable." [382] Since every step leading to the later stages is reached at the cost of a painful renunciation of impulses and can only be sustained in the same way, there exists a latent tendency, particularly in difficult times, to sink back to an earlier stage of development. This tendency was ministered to by Nazism. Nazism removed the remaining moral supports, weakened and overworked as they were. And not only did it make regression possible, but it spread and deepened the need for it, because it provided the regressive state with many morbid sensations which exerted continuously a dangerous attraction on the onlookers.

People were seized by an immense weariness of thinking and accepting responsibility. They had watched the progress of the war at first with intense excitement, later on with diminishing interest. But all the time they had been satisfied that their judgment with regard to Germany's military situation was correct. The defeat, among other things, meant to them an enormous loss of confidence in their own capacity to judge and to take the right decisions. The political and economic disorders of the post-war time, which they entirely failed to understand, were not calculated to restore their self-confidence. Clear thinking, logical argument, and the willingness to shoulder responsibility had always belonged to the " difficult " concomitants of civilisation. Its implicit demands had always been satisfied only insufficiently and under strain, and their authority had been undermined in Germany more than anywhere else. Now the situation had come to a head, and people despaired of reason altogether, thus turning their backs on one of the most characteristic human functions.

Nazism did not fail to work on these resentments. It availed itself of them to remove the last vestiges of preparedness to think and accept responsibility, for which it furnished an attractive substitute, the Nazi dogma. This relieved its believers once and for all from the burden of mental independence. It gave them mental security and ease. By an adroit mixture of suggestion and compulsion its propaganda removed all doubts from the people's mind. Thinking became not merely unnecessary, it was not even allowed. And in its place was given the longed-for repose of faith.[383]

It is, however, characteristic of the satisfactions provided by Nazism that they all overstepped the mark set by the original mass desires, in disregard of the fact that after a desire has been fulfilled a reaction will usually set in in the individual which, in certain conditions, may even lead to the emergence of contrary wishes. Nazism was anxious to maintain the original state of the masses, during which they had been driven almost entirely by instincts, because its primitive system of mass domination would have been impaired by a reawakening of the higher human faculties. It is at this point that the view of

Dr. Neumann that the masses were the victims of Nazism becomes more correct than that of Professor Lederer, that they were its creators. Gradually the slogans which, in the first stage, were solely destined to make the general desires articulate, are transformed into mere shibboleths. As such—apart from serving the interests of certain wire-pullers—they are misused to prevent the desires from becoming silent. The intermixture of both aims and the hardly noticeable transition from one stage into another was one of the main propagandistic accomplishments of the movement. It ensured not only the primary success of Nazism, but enabled it to retain a lasting hold on the masses. If the masses had been allowed to regain some kind of independent thought and thus to shake off the intoxication of their passions, they would not yet have been in the right mood for definitively surrendering their political power. Before the spectacle could be staged of a nation voluntarily choosing to submit to despotism, the nation, or at least a considerable part of it, had first to be reduced to a pre-social and pre-human stage of existence.

In order to prevent from the beginning any recovery by the masses of their critical faculty, Hitler surrounded his doctrine with a great number of attributes copied from the Catholic Church, which he hated and secretly admired.[384] He stressed its dogmatic character, its intolerance, its duty to destroy rivals. Hitler himself was not ashamed of posing as Christ;[385] the reverence amounting to deification with which he was adored by his lieutenants and followers was an indispensable element of his pseudo-religion. In its endeavour completely to silence reason by a few articles of faith, Nazism was greatly assisted by the old romantic tradition of mistrusting the critical faculty and of indulging in an excess of emotion. Hitler paid tribute to this inclination primarily in his speeches, but *Mein Kampf* also contains many passages to the same effect. It was Alfred Rosenberg, however, who went to the furthest lengths in the use of words which have no real meaning or which senselessly intermingle concepts.[386] The support which Rosenberg found among the intellectual youth in particular would not have been explicable without their romantic grounding.

The pseudo-religion which Hitler presented to the masses gratified their primitive needs for quiet, lack of responsibility, and an authority to obey. But it gave them merely the external symbols of religion, not the inner values. The only positive aim which Nazism offered to the masses was the reconstruction of a powerful German Reich. The so-called " Socialism of Action " itself consisted actually only of the fight against proletarian Socialism, which had been branded " Marxism ", and in some vague ideas about economic peace. A new faith could hardly be expected to emanate from it. The ideas of the Leader and of the totalitarian State were not new. They had only been transferred from the religious to the political sphere. National fanaticism—which, in contrast to Rauschning,[387] we are inclined to take seriously as an article of faith among the Nazis—was a poor basis on which to build a whole religious system. True, the national feeling at that time ran perhaps higher than ever before, and an appeal to national pride and defiance could count on a resounding success. But since even the national dogma as presented by Nazism was bound to lack precision, since a detailed description of the future national greatness and its implications could not be given, there still remained a marked lack of religious content.

This lack had of necessity to be concealed, and the methods of irrational propaganda accomplished this very successfully. By its original symbols, by its uniforms, songs, and badges, by its catch-phrases which sounded so imposing and inspiring, Nazism made politics attractive even to those who had never taken any interest in them. People could now be " political " without undergoing the pain of reasoning. Could a movement be wrong that acted so vigorously, so fanatically, and so victoriously? How difficult had it often been to find one's way in the maze of political arguments. Every one of them seemed to be right when it was heard or read, but there was also much to be said for the precise opposite. Nazism did not argue. It marched. And its marching columns trampled down all doubts.

But as not every individual could at every moment be under the direct influence of the propagandist high pressure, as trouble and need continued to prevail and might have revived the old habit of thinking, nearly forgotten but still potentially dangerous, religious fervour had to be further inflamed by the addition of an effective anti-symbol to the mysteries of Nazism. Only few good religions, and certainly not a bad one, can do without a devil. A figure must be created which can be taken to task for all remaining evils, whose responsibility is unquestionable. This personification was bound to become the more horrible the less real blessing could be expected from the new religion.

The pseudo-religious, anti-rational character of Nazism is then to be regarded as the first point making for its dependence on anti-Semitism. Where thinking was no longer needed or, rather, no longer allowed, where criticism had to be avoided by all means, and a dim religious haze had to conceal the deficiency in real religion, a common enemy was the appropriate remedy.[388] Apart from his general features which have been extensively shown to single him out for attack, the Jew was particularly suitable as an anti-symbol for a creed based on authority and the renunciation of reason. The Jew was considered as intelligent, indeed as the typical intellectual. He was made out to be hostile to authority, a disintegrator and critic. In Hitler's repugnance to " objectivity ", which he uses as a term of abuse,[389] his fear of clear thinking and criticism can be discerned, and one feels tempted to attribute this fear to a personal experience which he had in Vienna when arguing with a Jew. " Indeed," he says,[390] " I found it extremely difficult myself to be a match for the dialectical perfidy of that race." That in Hitler's language " dialectical perfidy " may well stand for " dialectical superiority " hardly needs to be pointed out. The later adoption by the Nazis of the general rule that " Jews are not admitted " may with a certain amount of probability be traced back to such early impressions. The Nazi dogma was too shaky and too easily upset to be exposed to critical probing. Thus the Jew, in whom, among other things, reason seemed to be personified, was defamed. Things were much easier both for the weary people themselves and for those who sought their suffrages when the masses, like the animal and primeval man, surrendered to the " iron logic of nature ". To rise above nature by means of a specifically human faculty like reason, or even to try to dominate nature, was Jewish impudence.[391]

But the masses were not only weary of thinking and taking their own decisions. They were weary of civilisation as a whole. The disappointments and frustrations of the war and post-war period had considerably enhanced their aggressiveness. To a larger extent than in normal times, people were in need of an object for their latent hatred and of a scapegoat on whom to blame their own feelings of guilt. For the reasons which have been mentioned they did not direct their hostility in the first place against the representatives of the old regime, who, on the contrary, regained some measure of popularity. Another outlet was thus urgently required. If, as Freud maintains, aggressiveness is *the* anti-social impulse which civilisation tries with all available means to suppress or else to satisfy in a harmless manner, the increasing political extremism of all shades during these crucial years indicated that the controlling powers of civilisation were being gradually overborne. But the battle was not lost until Nazism opened wide the sluices of aggressiveness. It did not only give free rein to the hatred which had been pent up, it also instigated more hatred by all available means. For hatred was the one thing needed for waging total war on the existing society.

This consideration helps to throw a clearer light on the anti-Christian attitude of Nazism. Maurice Samuel in his inspiring book, *The Great Hatred*,[392] has suggested that anti-Semitism is really hatred of Christianity. Since, however, people did not dare to attack openly a strong and venerated faith like Christianity, they pretended to attack the Jews while aiming really at the parent religion of Christianity. A similar opinion is expressed by Freud in *Moses and Monotheism*.[393] This view appears to be supported by the fact that there obviously exists a close relation between modern anti-Semitism and an anti-Christian outlook. When, after the emancipation of the Jews, the anti-Semitic problem entered its modern phase, Christianity changed with amazing rapidity from the side of the attacker to the side of the attacked. The number of anti-Christian anti-Semites or of anti-Semites who, while professing themselves Christians have severely criticised the existing Christianity, has been conspicuously great of late.[394] For the explanation of this fact it is, however, not necessary to go back to the deeper religious relationship between Judaism and Christianity. The same connection as between modern anti-Semitism and an anti-Christian attitude exists also between anti-Semitism and anti-humanitarianism, and anti-Semitism and an anti-social attitude in the most general sense. The common element in all these "anti" views is their resistance on behalf of the elementary impulses to the restraints of civilisation. No additional religious explanation is needed to make it clear that this resistance must, in the sphere of ideas, turn against Christianity as its most formidable enemy. If the mood of repugnance against civilisation is exploited for political purposes it may be directed against any symbol suitable as a target for aggressiveness. It may be used to attack the Negro, or the Freemason, or the Liberal, or the Jew, or any other scapegoat, not because any of them is held responsible for Christianity, but because they are at hand, and exposed, and weak.

The interconnection between hatred against Judaism and Christianity and humanitarianism in Nazism is indeed striking. Hitler himself, although avoiding open attacks on Christianity [395] and sometimes even speaking appreciatively of it—in reference, however, rather to its religious shape than to its ethical content—expressed a determined anti-humanitarian attitude.[396] The same applies to Rosenberg. Rosenberg puts the Christian commandment of love on the same level with sympathy, humanism, the Rights of Man, and democracy. To Rosenberg every feeling of social responsibility is a rebellion against nature, according to whose laws the strong is bound to prevail and the weak to perish.[397] He displays the same indignation against the legal equality of all citizens,[398] against the emancipation of women, against any kind of political and cultural universalism,[399] and—the Jews. He goes so far as to say that concepts like humanity, freedom, and liberalism are only different names for the one Jewish God.[400] In contrast to these ideals of a progressive civilisation, Rosenberg professes over and over again his faith in the ideas of heroism, honour, and duty, the latter two notions being of secondary importance and only interpretations of the " heroic ". Rosenberg's philosophy is poor. It stands for a " fallen " Nietzscheism and is based on Chamberlain's racial theory. In order to expound an allegedly " new morality ", which amounts actually to a boundless moral anarchy, he appeals to the authority of Leibniz.[401] Rosenberg is one of those who consciously trace themselves back to romanticism, although he feels himself called upon to revise romantic ideas along racial lines.[402] It is typical of Rosenberg, the so-called philosopher of the movement, that in one way or another he has debased every one of the ideas from which his philosophy took its origin. The main characteristics of his entire ideology is that he absolves its followers from the demands of reason and social morality and gives them the right to indulge their regressive wishes without restraint.[403]

It would have been dangerous to abandon social responsibility and substitute for it the cult of the heroic man, responsible solely to himself, if simultaneously an outlet had not been offered for the thus unfettered aggressiveness. Society had, after all, to be kept in working order. Nazism therefore reintroduced part of the decried social responsibility in the limited and less exacting form of in-group morality towards the " people's community ". The definition of the " people's community " as a racial entity, an enlarged horde as it were, sufficiently adapted this concept to primeval urges. It appealed to the gregarious instinct. One of its main supports was, moreover, the people's narcissistic love of their own kith and kin, which was made even more attractive by an ample glorification of it. But even this limited in-group morality involved some renunciation of aggressiveness, and it became the more desirable to present the embittered masses with another suitable gift from Pandora's box.

This gift was anti-Semitism, the official rehabilitation of hatred. Its importance as such cannot be easily overrated. Rarely since the emergence of modern society have hatred and brutality been so extolled.[404] Rarely have they been so frankly, so ingeniously, and so continuously provoked and directed against a living object. ⌈The aggressiveness which had been swollen to bursting point by the extraordinary sufferings of the people, and had been kept in check with ever-increasing difficulty, at length found relief.⌋ Now at last they felt understood and definitely emancipated from the " difficult " love of their neighbours for the sake of mankind.

It is a fact that can hardly be over-estimated that even under the spur of this provocative propaganda the passions of the German people remained in general so restrained—Rosenberg would probably have said " weakened by Christianity "—that only in rare cases did the Nazi preaching of hatred result in spontaneous acts of atrocity. Those who under its immediate influence began to regard the Jew as the source of all their vexations, only rarely resorted to direct physical assaults. But even so, the vehement hatred, authoritatively allowed and even encouraged, was not lacking in the malevolent effect on the primitive impulses which it incited and justified. ⌈The mere feeling of knowing at long last whom to hold responsible for all hardship, of being able to vent one's anger in talks with like-minded neighbours, and of finding more and more proofs in writing, speeches, and pictures, that in indulging this rage one was in the comforting company of all " enlightened " fellow-citizens—this was in itself a great relief.

The examination of the first two gifts from Pandora's box

teaches two lessons. (1) The secret of the Nazi success lay in providing relief for the primitive urges and peace for the conscience. Hitler, knowing and despising the masses, realised what the masses most wanted. In their weariness and insecurity they wanted to be relieved from freedom and responsibility. He gave them a pseudo-religious authority. In the midst of their frustrations they wanted to be relieved from love of their neighbours. He permitted them to hate and to inveigh. The old parties, bound as they were by the tradition of civilisation—if only in its German form—had to keep their attacks within reasonable limits and thus to restrain the violence of their propaganda. Nazism offered in contrast the attraction of unrestricted outbreaks of abuse and spite. Words which had been previously banned, even from the bar-room, suddenly became habitual political jargon. Daily scuffles provided the opportunity to show " a German man's courage ". It was precisely this deliberate descent to the lowest level of demagogy and the endeavour to lower it constantly still further which made Nazism prevail over its political competitors. (2) The form in which Nazism provided the gratification of the various passions was of its own choice. The masses merely clamoured for someone to exercise authority over them. That authority was cloaked in the specific Nazi garb and adorned with specific Nazi symbols and anti-symbols was the contribution of the leaders, especially of Hitler. The wish of the masses was only to hate and abuse. The choice of the Jew as an object was a secondary, almost accidental contribution of the party leaders. Italian Fascism, which was so closely related to Nazism in its primitive anti-rational methods, chose Liberalism and the Freemasons. The Austrian semi-Fascism of Dollfuss and Schuschnigg was officially satisfied with the fight against its real opponents, the " Austro-Marxists "—although the genuine Jewish question was far more acute in Austria than in Germany, anti-Semitism among the population was widespread, and the high proportion of Jews among the Social Democratic leaders might have encouraged an official anti-Semitic outlook. In Germany also there were temporary and even permanent anti-symbols beside the Jew. There was the " ignominious treaty of Versailles ", the " enemy alliance " (*Feindbund*), the " Catholic orders ", the " November criminals ", etc. But public attention could not be focused too intensely on the former enemies, the Catholic Church or the socialist and communist workers, because this would have involved political action as yet beyond the strength of the party. Anti-Semitism could, however, be safely pursued. And, moreover, the violent personal anti-Semitism of Hitler, which cannot be explained here, played a sinister part in the selection of this propagandistic device.

People in post-war Germany, however, were not only morally and intellectually exhausted. Their self-esteem had also been badly wounded by the defeat and impoverishment. The need for self-assertion, which is, according to Professor Morris Ginsberg, " a characteristic of the whole make-up of personality rather than a special instinct ",[404a] was extraordinarily strong. To meet this need Hitler offered the inestimable gifts of racial nationalism and the legend of the stab-in-the-back—gifts, not in the sense that they were entirely new, but that they were presented to the masses with an unequalled propagandistic force.

In this ideological competition the republican parties proved no match for their opponents. They took the military defeat for granted and sought to make the German people accept it. Since, however, the previously ruling classes to whom they attributed the responsibility for it proved an inappropriate scapegoat on grounds mentioned above, the sense of humiliation and guilt continued to weigh on a considerable part of the nation. The building up of a free democracy, the readmission to the comity of nations—these boons were to a people like the German entirely insufficient compensations for the acute privations. It is not impossible that these difficulties might have been partly overcome if the republican leaders had made up their minds to abandon appeals to reason in favour of irrational propaganda in order to influence masses in a state of crisis. This is, to a certain extent, borne out by the successes achieved by the Social Democratic Party after the introduction—hesitating and late though it was—of the emotional propaganda of the " Three Arrows " and the " Iron Front ". By these devices the Social Democratic Party, which had for a considerable time been slowly but as it seemed inevitably losing supporters, suddenly won two seats in the elections for the Hessian Diet, in the spring of 1932. This was a recovery of great significance in an apparently desperate situation. Similarly the number of Social Democratic votes increased wherever the propaganda was based on the new symbols. The increase was even proportionate to the length of time during which the new propaganda methods had been applied.[405]   But even if the old party tradition had been abandoned earlier in favour of concessions to the anti-rational mood of the time, it must still be assumed that the political aims of the party would have worked as a handicap when compared with those offered by the Nazis.

Never could a programme of democratic reconstruction and adjustment to the European order have prevailed against the racial doctrine and the legend of the stab-in-the-back.   Belief in these gave the masses precisely what they desired, a restoration of their self-esteem, without having to undergo the difficult and unpleasant process of self-criticism and self-purification. They could eradicate the defeat from their consciousness and feel once again as victors.   Immutable, supreme laws of nature had placed them at the head of creation, as Nordic noblemen. A temporary reverse could not invalidate their destiny of world domination.   No reader of the party literature on this subject can have any doubts as to the flattering effect this kind of argument must have had on people suffering from weakened self-respect.   This was precisely the reason why the Nazis introduced these elements into their ideological medley.   The theoretical basis of the alleged racial superiority of the Germans was a secondary matter.   Such a basis, of course, had to be found because the Nazis, eager to secure as broad a response as possible, did not want to lose potential followers who attached importance to theories,   Therefore Hans F. K. Günther was chosen to be the racial theorist of the German nation.   Yet even Günther's division of the European races into a Nordic, Westic, Ostic, or East Baltic, and Dinaric race was much too complicated for propagandistic use.   Nazism, therefore, did violence not only to Günther's theories but to the whole racial science by resorting to the scientifically untenable notion of an "Aryan race" which was henceforth applied to the whole German people.   Other nations were arbitrarily included or excluded in accordance with political expediency.[406]   The necessary simplification had now been achieved.   But even so, the Nazis were reluctant to dispense with the term "Germanic" which had been well known throughout Germany since Chamberlain. On the other hand, the fact could not be ignored that the Germanic ideal, which corresponds roughly with Günther's Nordic type, was pretty rare in Germany.   Nazi speakers, therefore, had recourse to the vagueness so characteristic of Nazism, and used now the one and now the other word without troubling about consistency.

Thus Hitler in *Mein Kampf* [407] launches out into a glorification of the " Aryan "—incidentally without making even an attempt to prove his statements. Rosenberg speaks now of the " Nordic " soul [408] and now of " Germanic " heroism ; [409] and he adds a further element of vagueness by speaking of " nordicised " blood (*vernordetes Blut*) [410] or " germanically conditioned " blood (*germanisch bedingtes Blut*) [411]. The Nazi propagandist of racism, Johannes Leers, speaks of the " Indo-Germanic race " and adds in brackets " Aryan-Nordic " in order to exhaust every possibility.[412] In the endeavour to attribute as far as possible all human accomplishments to Nordic Aryans, historical truth is frequently disregarded. The very foundation of Nazi racism indeed, the assumption that psychical traits are strictly dependent on physical characteristics, is abandoned if it involves the loss of a desirable figure to the Nordic race or the inclusion of an abhorred one in its ranks.[413]

There is thus no end of contradictions and vagueness in the " völkische " racism. The actual aim is to empty the concept of any intelligible content, so that all that remains is something dark and mysterious, precisely that mystic quality of the blood which cannot be comprehended but only " sensed ". For all those, moreover, who set a high value on " science ", it was dignified by a pseudo-scholarly halo. In this way once again the tastes and wants of broad sections of the German people were catered for, and a wide response was secured.

As for the legend of the stab-in-the-back, its purpose obviously was to achieve the exculpation of the German people at the cost of a fictitious bearer of the guilt. The figure chosen to be held responsible for the defeat had to be so closely related to the events of the war that it could be made to appear guilty. It had, on the other hand, to stand out so distinctly from the rest of the Germans that with a little artificial colouring it could be opposed to the German people. Such terms as " Marxists " and " November criminals " fulfilled the first, but not the second, condition. Only by identifying them both in the habitually vague manner with Jews was the second condition likewise fulfilled. Now the whole German nation was exculpated, its guilt having been passed on to the " foreigner ".

True, the Jews known to the individual Gentiles were no longer foreigners. But these Jews were not those who had stabbed the victorious army in the back. These well-known Jewish neighbours had certainly fought and suffered like the Gentiles, they could then not be meant. Those who were meant belonged to the mysterious Jewish power which had plotted the war and deliberately lost it,[414] which sought the ruin of the German people and of which Germany had therefore to rid herself. With great subtlety, although without actually putting the difference into words, the propaganda distinguished between the living Jewish people and the fictitious picture of " the Jew ". The few distinct features which were still noticeable in the Jews of the present, and which might therefore be used for the purpose of arousing suspicion in bewildered minds, were enormously exaggerated so as to yield some basic lines for the picture of " the Jew ". The rest of the picture was filled in according to taste, with the devilish grimaces visualised by an over-excited fantasy. The separation of the living Jews from the Jewish symbol was made sufficiently clear to obviate constant comparison of both. It was a common feature of Nazi anti-Semitism that most people affected by it made mental reservations with respect to their Jewish acquaintances who so conspicuously differed from the frightful spectre which was supposed to represent them.* Thus the legend of the stab-in-the-back relieved innumerable Germans from the nightmare of the military defeat. Only one who knows the military pride of the German will be able to gauge the pressure of this nightmare, and assess rightly the value of this other gift from Pandora's box.

Neither could the racial doctrine fulfil its purpose of restoring the injured self-respect of the German people if the Nordic, or Aryan, or Teuton it extolled could not visibly distinguish himself from another type, outside of and beneath his own racial community. This need was the greater since the racial heterogeneity of the German nation was obvious and had been revealed anew by Günther. Something had already been achieved by using the terms Nordic, Aryan, and Teutonic so loosely that the wide differences in the valuation of the several German types, amounting to a defamation of a large part of the population, was glossed over.[415] But Rosenberg, *e.g.*, joined with Günther in the degradation of the

* Cf., however, the possibility pointed out on p. 56.

" Alpine " or " Eastern " race. He characterised this racial type, which is spread all over the German-speaking countries and can be found, above all, in Central Germany, Franconia, Baden, Alsace, and parts of the German East, with the following words : ". . . democracy in the political field, lack of spiritual interests, timid pacifism combined with businesslike shrewdness and ruthlessness in pursuing commercial undertakings that promise gain—these are the terrible signs of Alpine exuberances throughout European life".[416] This character sketch recalls the catalogue of qualities usually strung off to describe the Jews. But it would have been impossible to use an essential part of the German people as an anti-type. On the contrary, since among the German population there existed a not inconsiderable proportion to whom the above description was alleged to apply, and since the racial doctrine was meant to be used for strengthening the self-esteem of the whole nation, the necessity to oppose this whole to another anti-type became more urgent.

How great were the contradictions and how forcibly they demanded an apparent solution is shown, among other things, also by these two utterances of Hitler. In *Mein Kampf* he repeats Günther's and Rosenberg's racial theories in substance, and admits : " Unfortunately the German national being is not based on a uniform racial type ". Like Günther he enumerates the individual racial types and describes at length the favourable and unfavourable consequences of this lack of racial unity.[417] In one of his speeches, however, he defies his better knowledge by twisting the facts in the following way : " In Germany where everyone who is a German at all has the same blood, has the same eyes and speaks the same language, here there can be no class, here can be only a single people and beyond this nothing else ".[418] In order to reconcile such glaring contradictions there existed only one means. The whole German people—Nordics, Easterners, Westerners, and Alpines —had to be welded together by being contrasted with one anti-type, the Jews.

In the light of these difficulties it might appear that the racial theory was a needlessly complicated substitute for a pure nationalism without racial differentiation. It might be presumed that a merely national self-exaltation would have produced the same effect without implying an internal dissension, which in turn had to be bridged over by anti-Semitism.

There existed, indeed, some national movements of not inconsiderable moment in pre-war Germany which kept aloof from anti-Semitism. As examples may be mentioned sections of the " Wandervögel " and of the " Freideutsche Jugend ", the official attitude of the Verein für das Deutschtum im Ausland, the Navy Association (Flottenverein), and similar patriotic associations. The German Jews did not lack the national and cultural loyalty to their country which made participation in such movements possible, although most of them disapproved of their imperialist sentiments. Indeed, if the attempt to restore the shattered nerves of the German nation after the defeat had had no ulterior motives, the stimulus of a national pride based on cultural achievements would have been completely sufficient. It might have been accomplished with all kinds of emotional appeals, and even the inevitable anti-symbol need not have been missing. For the " Wandervögel " also had given preference to the German woods against the southern palms and praised the creative power of the German language over the beautiful clarity of the French, without any aggressive intention and often even in an expressly pacifist mood.

But it was precisely this ulterior motive which mattered most. The object was to satisfy mass desires on as low a level as possible, so that by means of the state of regression a new despotism could be erected. Nazism sought to make people not self-confident, but overbearing, to give them not mental balance, but self-exaltation, to inspire them not with self-respect in combination with respect for others, but with submissiveness to the Leader combined with aggression towards the " enemy ". For creating such a state of mind a national feeling based primarily on cultural achievements was unsuited. It seemed more promising to fall back on more primitive notions, borrowed actually from zoology. That these were vague and incomprehensible made them even more expedient. Thus in this sphere, too, the listener would not be disturbed by logical objections, but could rapturously hearken to the " murmur of the blood ".[419] Above all, however, Nazism would not be fighting a distant opponent, but one present in the immediate neighbourhood. In this way the desire for self-assertion was fulfilled with the help of the crudest implements. To Burckhardt [420] the misery of everything earthly is revealed by the fact " that even the individual thinks he can achieve the full consciousness of his value only by comparing himself with others and making the other feel this according to the prevailing circumstances ". He continues very significantly : " The State, law, religion, and custom take great pains to bridle this inclination of the individual, that is to say, to repress it into his inner self. It is then regarded as ridiculous, repulsive, danger-ous, and criminal for the individual to indulge it openly." Nazism held out the alluring prospect that under its sway " the State, law, religion, and custom " would suddenly cease to bridle the tendency towards demonstrative superciliousness. It even encouraged it and promised to it complete satisfaction. It need hardly be emphasised that such a promise meant a " festival for the ego " which could now indulge its desire without feeling " ridiculous, repulsive, dangerous, and criminal ".

This end would never have been so thoroughly achieved if merely the national spirit had been strengthened and the German nation had been contrasted with other nations in language not more violent than political consideration would have allowed. Jew-baiting offered a much more advantageous instrument. But Jew-baiting could be based much more easily on the racial doctrine, since—considering the extent of Jewish integration—nationalism would have had to be very arbitrarily distorted before it could be used to justify the ousting of the Jews from the German nation. If such a distortion was attempted as, e.g., in Gustav Stapel's *Volkstum*, such an artificial product was not suited to be expressed in crude propagandistic slogans. The racial theory, on the other hand, was a service-able instrument. The average recognisability of the Jewish type was only just sufficient to make it possible to talk of a " foreign " Jewish race. That there was actually no other sense in the entire racial phraseology but to profit from this difference of type in order to create a useful anti-type becomes apparent from the *Instructions on History Teaching* by Rödiger, who says : [421] " There is no Aryan race. We describe as Aryan the Indo-Germans to which group the Germans, Slavs, Persians, Indians, and the ancient Romans belong. . . . We need here to make clear the idea of what is Aryan. Children know that it means : ' Non-Jewish '."

So much for the choice of the racial idea by the Nazi leaders. As far as its reception by the German public is concerned this was favoured by practically every national peculiarity. There was first of all the habit, resulting from the arid intellectualism of German thought, of being guided less by concrete reality than by abstract notions. There was, furthermore, the tendency towards transcending any limit of which Arndt has been mentioned as an example and which was due to the lack of natural boundaries and to the retarded foundation of a national State. Moreover, there was added the early abandonment of Christian universalism, the resentment against the secular idea of Humanity as having emanated from the " hostile " West, and the too hasty substitution for it of romantic nationalism, with its harking back to the Middle Ages and its concept of congenital characteristics, both unchangeable and imperishable. If mention is made lastly of the rejection of Natural Right, the Rights of Man, and Reason, of the continuous necessity to replace the deficient national homogeneity by artificial means, and of other secondary factors, enumerated in the course of this study, it will be quite evident that the German people were well prepared to accept the racial interpretation of the national concept. On these grounds, part of the educated classes had been captivated by the ideas of Houston Stewart Chamberlain in spite of the absence of any special need of self-assertion, such as prevailed after the first World War. Though the historical succession of ideas has little or no bearing on the psychological reaction of the amorphous masses, it cannot be neglected in explaining the growth of racism, which found special response in educated circles. Here, indeed, the intellectual tradition operated with full force. And this intellectual tradition did much to promote the acceptance of a theory whose scientific value was so entirely doubtful.

We see, then, that the German people had been rendered susceptible by psychological as well as by historical and ideological factors to a collective consciousness, favouring at the same time a haughty exclusiveness and the gratification of the most elementary instincts. The racial principle combined many attractions.

It has been shown above that Nazism proceeded in three ways both towards a satisfaction of mass desires and towards securing mass adherence. Every one of these ways led the movement at the same time towards including anti-Semitism among its ideological elements, because in all three cases it was only the introduction of the Jewish symbol which gave to the propagandist devices their finishing touches. In none of the three instances was there an immediate connection of the mass desires with anti-Semitism. But the desires were exceedingly vehement and the Nazi wish to satisfy them was unrestrained by any considerations of reason or morality. The success, therefore, was enormous. It would have been the same if it had proved feasible to choose another group or idea as anti-symbol, as the object of aggression, and as the bearer of collective guilt. If, e.g., the Catholics had been a weak minority and not one-third of the German population, they might have been selected as scapegoats without difficulty. From the hostile publicity which propaganda gave to the Freemasons in Fascist Italy, to the Kulaks in Soviet Russia after the Bolshevik Revolution, and to the Trotskyists there under Stalin, it would be rash to infer that there was any strong previously existing hostility on the part of the masses towards these groups. Even where this kind of propaganda has some foundation in actual social conditions, as was the case in Soviet Russia, it is carried to such lengths that it creates tensions out of all proportion to the defects which it attacks. It would be conceivable that during a serious period of crisis and internal disruption in England a ruthless propaganda, unchecked by suitable counter-measures, would be able to work up the Scottish or the Roman Catholic question into urgent problems—even if allowance is made for the fact that resistance to unjustified accusations would be stronger in England than it has been in Germany. And yet such a propagandistic success would not justify the conclusion that the Scottish and Roman Catholic problems are to-day pregnant with serious conflicts. It would be equally inadmissible to deny that they generate some kind of antagonism, precisely as it has never been denied that the Jewish problem still gave rise to some lingering tensions. It is of decisive importance to disentangle as carefully as possible these different factors contributing to the Nazi success, which was in itself an extraordinarily complex phenomenon.

Before attempting to assign its various elements to their respective causes, two further facts involved in the complex of Nazi ideology and propaganda must be analysed. Both seem to contradict the fundamental thesis that the secret of the Nazi success was its liberation of primitive impulses. The first of these facts is the organisation of Nazi units on military lines. It might be argued that marching and shooting and constant drill in all weathers by no means pampered these impulses but exacted definite self-sacrifices on behalf of ideals—however misconceived these may have been. Despite a certain super-ficial plausibility in this argument, it does not justify a more favourable view of the Nazi bands, such as Storm Troops (S.A.), Protective Squads (S.S.), Hitler Youth, and their branches. It should rather be considered that not all impulses are of necessity anti-social. According to Professor Ginsberg, it is a " fundamental drive to go outside of ourselves, and to enter into relationship with others ". " It is not necessarily a desire to co-operate in the service of common ends," Professor Ginsberg continues, " nor is it as such benevolent. Rather is it the need of some kind of response from others, and the tendency to respond to them." [422] If an individual indulges this need, he cannot indeed be praised because for the sake of an ideal he represses his urges. It was thus not a sacrifice of urges but rather their indulgence which made the young people flock into the Nazi bands. This, of course, applies only to the early period of the movement during which these formations were being built up. There is little doubt that the voluntary enlistment in them gave place gradually to severe coercion and that, in later years, notably after the seizure of power, the service had totally ceased to satisfy instinctive desires. But by that time other factors had come into being which kept together the military groups. The point made here is solely that, in the period in which the Nazi Party set out on its victorious march throughout Germany, not only the onlookers but also the party soldiers themselves found satisfaction for their regressive desires when they marched through the streets in uniforms and with banners, singing and playing.

The wish to " enter into relationship with others " was in Germany combined with a strong love of militarism, which had been painfully thwarted by the defeat and the peace treaty. It is manifest that the quasi-military gangs which were created by Nazism derived a great deal of their attraction from their power to compensate for the loss of the traditional military display. Attention has been drawn to this point so frequently that it needs no more than a passing reference. But mention should also be made of other psychological factors which favoured the rally of young people in soldierly formations. The urge to seek adventure, exercise,[423] risks, to flee from discipline, school and home life exists in every young generation. While in non-militarist nations it is likely to lead to an emphasis on sport and games, it could in Germany be easily exploited for the so-called

" military sport ". Rauschning [424] points to the connection that exists between the utterly purposeless wanderlust of the German youth movement and the marching mania (*Marschier-wut*) of the Nazis. He sees in both the " simple urge to move one's feet in order to get the better of the inner revolutionary unrest ".[425] The psychology of the gang has been referred to above * in explanation of the psychological condition of numerous Germans who had been too suddenly dismissed from the cosy guardianship of the old authoritarian government. While in this more general connection it could only serve as an analogy, it applies directly to the mentality of the Nazi bands. Youthful defiance, forced " manliness ", anti-feminism, and the craze for everything dashing and daring were character-istic of these organisations. If the age-groups originally described by Suttie are younger than the ones from which S.A. and S.S. were recruited, it should not be forgotten that, as a result of the deliberately generated general backwardness, there prevailed an infantilism which considerably raised the age of those susceptible to the gang ideal. In consequence of this prolonged childishness the actual need to play continued likewise longer than in normal times, and this, too, found its gratification in the Hitler bands.[426] It must, finally, not be overlooked that the cadres of these militarist associations be-came the playground of all those elements which through the war had been thrown out of their ordinary tracks and could not find their way back into social life. It was these people who became the leaders of the groups in question. The degree of their maladjustments varied from transitory difficulties to out-right criminal propensities. When courage and sacrifices were demanded, these individuals were certainly not among the last to respond. But courage and sacrifices for a cause which made such far-reaching concessions to asocial urges cannot be regarded as a real moral achievement. It is precisely this frequent combination of gang-morality and an asocial attitude in the Nazi movement which should serve as a warning not to esteem its pseudo-moral qualities too highly.

These few remarks may suffice to make it clear that the high-sounding watchwords on duty and idealism with which the military formations of Nazism used to plume themselves were largely undeserved, since with these kinds of activities the party also satisfied another set of desires. How this way of

* Cf. p. 188.

213

satisfaction led also in a direct line towards anti-Semitism should be briefly pointed out for the sake of completeness. The followers of the Nazi bands, being entirely bent on physical culture and aggression, needed the stimulus of a visible and near opponent as much as did the Nazi ideology itself. It was only natural, therefore, that their leaders should hound them on against the Jews as their primary target. Only in rare cases, it is true, did these members of the Nazi gangs commit violent assaults against Jews—a peculiarity of the whole Nazi movement which, in consideration of the permanent Jew-baiting, appears paradoxical and can only be rightly assessed in the light of all the circumstances bearing on the problem. But it seemed nevertheless profitable to make use of the Jewish bogy. For those opponents who were really dangerous, and with whom actual fighting continually took place, viz. the socialists and communists, were thought to be much more effectively defamed when they were called " Jewish Marxists ". The claim to be fighting in reality " foreign " people and the victims of " foreign " ideas was intended to justify the slogan of the " people's community ". This would have been reduced to absurdity if an open war had been waged against practically the entire working class.

We now come to that element in Nazism, the idealist character of which seems to be established almost beyond doubt. It may be emphasised beforehand that our anslysis of it will have one object only, to unveil the secret of the Nazi success in such a way as to bring to light as distinctly as possible the part which anti-Semitism played in it. We are not concerned here to expose the evils of Nazism as such, these having been fully established in the eyes of all the world. It is the aim of this study to make clear that Nazism owes its successes not to its political programme, a very prominent item in which was anti-Semitism, but to its ruthlessly applied method of gratifying the passions of the weary and desperate masses. Its success, it will be shown, was in direct proportion to the completeness with which it managed to bring about this gratification. If, therefore, it should turn out that Nazism in some of its demands opposed the feelings of the masses, that it exacted from them sacrifices of their instinctive needs and still obtained their applause, our explanation of the essence of Nazism would be challenged. If such an idealistic strain in Nazism should have existed, then it would have to be treated with more respect, and especially anti-Semitism would gain in importance.

It is on this account that the seemingly strongest idealist component of Nazism, viz. its demand for heroic self-sacrifice, ultimately for the sacrifice of life itself for Führer and Fatherland, demands our closer attention. Even severe critics of Nazism [427] usually do not deny to it the credit of having been capable of inspiring courage and self-denial; that is to say, strong moral powers. This appreciation is not even diminished by a healthy abomination of the Nazi aims. The Nazi literature is indeed full of appeals for self-denial and readiness for sacrifice, and there is no lack of intimations that in the case of war the supreme sacrifice of life itself would be demanded. Why did this note in the propaganda not prove a deterrent? If it is true that in these post-war years the German people were tired and desperate, that they were craving to get rid of the inhibitions of civilisation and of social responsibility—why, then, did so many of them follow a call which demanded the ultimate sacrifice of life itself?

It must be frankly admitted that a not inconsiderable group of young people responded to the call from genuine self-denying idealism. All that is best in nationalism, in that strangely complex feeling the pure ingredients of which are so easily misused, was included as much in the Nazi phraseology as were the lowest urges. But the proportion of this idealism among the motives which made people follow the Nazi appeal was far less than might appear at first sight, if by idealism is understood, as it has been hitherto, the devotion to an idea under renunciation of primitive impulses.[428]

To begin with, the Nazi technique of propaganda put the people to whom it appealed, especially in its mass meetings, into a state of mind where self-denial had lost its terrors. Hitler repeatedly compared the masses to a woman who longed to submit to the " ruthless force and brutality " of a strong man.[429] Unfortunately his mass psychological insight must be treated with all respect. His success was to no small extent due to this and the use he made of it. In this respect, moreover, his view is shared not only by Le Bon [430] but also by Freud, who speaks of the thirst of the masses for submission and of their desire to "be dominated by unrestricted force".[431] In this rapturous state of feminine masochism, whose orgastic character every eye-witness will confirm, death for the worshipped leader was no longer feared by a large part of the

215

audience.[432] Those captivated by the mass frenzy even longed for the complete extinction of their own selves.

This partial reduction of the " idealist devotion to Führer and Fatherland " to a sexually conditioned devotion to the Führer largely diminishes its moral value in a strict sense. But there are other factors which, when properly assessed, point in the same direction. The appeal to sacrifice lives and limbs for the Fatherland is usually combined with expressions of national exaltation, preferably such as emphasise the necessity of collective self-preservation.[433] When Hitler, by appealing to the most elemental feeling in human nature, to the wish for survival, has made sure of a wide response, he adds that " the conservation of the species always presupposes that the individual is ready to sacrifice himself ".[434] He thus induces the listener or reader to accept unknowingly, at a moment when he is unrestrictedly indulging his instinct of self-preservation, his own death sentence. The listener or reader probably distinguishes between individual and collective self-preservation only in so far as he feels the collective kind to be allowed and required beyond any doubt, so that he plunges himself and his urge to live only too willingly into the whole. This frequent connection produces eventually a " conditioned reflex ". The " hero's death " becomes a necessary component of the pleasant notion of the preservation of the species and thus loses part of its horror. That, apart from such subtle methods of persuasion, much trouble was taken to diminish the natural fear of death by all kinds of tricks is, among other things, shown by the fact that Nazis were even prepared to enter for this purpose into an alliance with their dreaded enemy, religion. Professor Ziegler states in an outline of military training of the youth : [435] " Military readiness implies always preparedness for death. A religion which really succeeds in reducing or removing the natural horror of suffering and death facilitates the military will." But contempt is thrown on the world of the " liberal bourgeois ". This must be left behind, " for the bourgeois world is a world without death ".[436]

There remains, finally, another fact which makes the heroic enthusiasm of many Nazis compatible with the low moral value attributed to the movement in this study. A certain need for self-sacrifice is part of the elementary human social urges. The opposition between civilisation and barbarism is not fully identical with the opposition between good and evil and between social and anti-social. This fact constitutes one of the problems of mass psychology.* Le Bon [437] has to give two different definitions of the concept of morality in order to answer the difficult question whether masses are always immoral. If by morality is understood, he argues, the "constant respect for certain social conventions and the permanent repression of selfish impulses", the masses are obviously always immoral. If, however, morality is understood to include "the transitory display of certain qualities such as abnegation, self-sacrifice, disinterestedness, devotion", then it must be admitted that "crowds may exhibit a very lofty morality".[438] Thus Le Bon, too, who has a very unfavourable opinion of the psychology of the masses,[439] is perplexed by the heroism frequently displayed by masses, and which he can neither deny nor decry. The problem admits of solution if the figure of the Hero is seen as the opposite of the "Civis" on whom, as the word indicates, civilisation is based. The hero is neither immoral, nor evil, nor selfish, but he is primitive. In a thoroughly civilised society the capability of suffering and inflicting hardship, which is one of the main characteristics of the hero, has in ordinary times been largely reduced in importance. When this capability regains importance, as during a war, such a state of affairs is called with much justification a relapse into barbarism. It is therefore not surprising that a movement which owes its existence to the regression from civilisation to barbarism, and which made it one of its principal aims to uphold this regressive state, exhibited also the valuable features of regression. Those who were instigated by the Nazi propaganda to warlike enthusiasm were not elevated over their primitive selves but gave them free play, exactly as those who felt happy because they no longer had to think, to decide, and to love their neighbours. But some of the primitive leanings which were indulged by "heroic" persons are of a kind which civilisation should not suppress but encourage and use for purposes of welfare and peace.

From this examination of Nazi "self-denial" it will be understood that to admit its existence involves no contradiction with what has been said about the release of primitive impulses effected by Nazism. A difference exists only between the nature of the urges which were released in each case. As a matter of course, these were assorted differently in the young

* Cf. p. 212.

217

and vigorous from what they were in the older and wearied. It was the incomparable propagandistic achievement of Nazism that it catered for all these groups with the same consummate skill. It allowed the elementary human nature, which had been incessantly but still insufficiently repressed by civilisation, to burst the worn-out barriers and to submerge ideas and institutions which it had taken thousands of laborious years to wrest from its grasp.

But Nazi agitation was not only directed to the darker layers of the human mind. It offered no smaller attractions to the more alert consciousness of people who cared to listen. Nazism by no means neglected the appeal also to economic egoism which, as pointed out above, had grown even more compelling under the pressure of economic disaster. This appeal was indeed no monopoly of Nazism ; what was distinctive was the way in which it was made. Since the Nazi orators were not bound to any political programme but were guided by the sole motive of securing as large a following as possible, they pretended to represent the interests of precisely that circle of listeners which happened to attend their meeting. This unlimited opportunism of the Nazi propaganda is so well known that it is hardly necessary to adduce any examples. The party programme of 25th February 1920, which had been declared unchangeable on 22nd May 1926, consisted of a number of more or less vague points containing promises for all walks of life. Such points as might have scared certain sections of the population, as " breakage of the serfdom of interest ", the communalisation of department stores, and the agrarian reform, were interpreted as being directed solely against the Jews. A distinction was made between " creative " and " rapacious ", *i.e.* Jewish, capital, and it was explained that the " serfdom of interest " concerned only the latter. In an " authentic interpretation " of point 17 of the party programme, which demanded the expropriation of rural property without compensation, Hitler stated on 13th April 1928 that this meant only the expropriation of the " Jewish real estate speculating corporations ".[440] The anti-Jewish meaning of the fight against the department stores was fairly obvious, in view of the Jewish predominance in this branch.[441]

Vagueness in programmatic and other written statements, unrestricted promises in speeches, which counted on the bad memory of their hearers, and the use of language so obscure

218

and involved that it could be made to mean anything—these were the means by which Nazi propaganda appealed to the interests of its public. Professor Melchior Palyi [442] rightly points out that the irrational symbols of Nazism were able to exert so wide an effect on the mass emotions not least because the masses believed that these symbols were the expression of the political aims they visualised more or less clearly. Only few followers, and among them predominantly women and youngsters, were driven so far by their ecstasy as to neglect entirely economic considerations. The overwhelming majority hoped, as a matter of course, to improve their conditions in a very real way and were, as far as these motives were concerned, perfectly "rational". Up to a certain degree they were also "rational" in their resolve to try for once this "new" party, since all the others had "failed". In spite of this, however, the emotional attraction of the Nazi symbols was again more powerful than those inspired by them would have been willing to admit. The overwhelming force of Nazism lay really in its combination of rational promises and an irrational propaganda which induced the masses to believe in them, entirely vague and contradictory though they were. If people had approached these contradictions with rational criticism, they would have been repelled by them. But precisely this power of criticism, which had been increasingly weakened for so long, was effectively silenced by the pseudo-religious colouring of the agitation. Thus people responded to the deliberately vague allusions by associating their own longings with them, and they felt that these were being understood and fulfilled.

It was furthermore an especially well-tried device of Nazism to deprive certain words of their established sense and to change their meaning completely. This happened, above all, to the word which, in the course of German history, had more than once suffered such a distortion, to the word "freedom". Nazism reckoned on the one hand with supreme mastership on the "Fear of Freedom" [443] of tired masses, and proceeded to release them from it by imposing a new authority. But it knew, on the other hand, that the word "freedom" does not lose its inspiring force even with people who are just about to plunge headlong into a new serfdom. For this reason Nazism was not content with killing freedom itself, it distorted the word also. Once again it was used to designate not individual liberty from governmental infringements but collective liberty from an exterior enemy. In the Nazi vocabulary freedom meant almost exclusively " freedom from the fetters of Versailles ".[444] The word " democracy" fared similarly. Here, too, Nazism did not rely entirely on the weariness of democracy and the success of the propaganda of defamation. In order to make sure of the widest possible success also among those parts of the population where there still existed sympathies for the democratic idea, the Nazi State was declared to be the real people's State and the Leader principle the truly democratic.[445] The same confusion of well-known terms can be seen at work when Hitler says in a speech : [446] " The true German 'People's State' . . . will then for the first time be the German Republic, even if an emperor or a king should stand at its head ".[447]

In this misuse of language Nazi propagandists profited largely, as has been repeatedly mentioned, from the German tendency to use vague and ambiguous terms as well as from their tendency to substitute emotion for reason. But even though they probably thus obtained greater success than would have been possible among people who were used to more precise language, this method was still not sufficiently infallible. Besides using ill-defined terms, they therefore had recourse to a crude mixture of concepts so obscure that it could be used to explain anything which could not be otherwise explained. And the Jewish myth was useful for this function too.

Here its purpose was, of course, not to satisfy mass desires, but rather the political designs of the leaders themselves. The people, to say the least, were not interested in the obscuring of political problems. They were, on the contrary, interested in their being tackled and solved. The leaders, on the other hand, had a vital interest in concealment, since to gain mass adherence it was essential to inculcate the belief that unity in all questions of principle prevailed throughout the nation. By choosing to establish this sham unity through an alleged Jewish world conspiracy, they applied a pure propaganda device which no longer had anything to do with the original mass desires.

Hitler was of opinion that the following three matters constituted the great problems of German home politics : the social question, the religious question, and the question of national unification.[448] How did he and his lieutenants deal with these questions ?

The attitude of Nazism to the social problem is well known.

Its existence was denied. The antagonism between capitalists and workers which was alleged to constitute it was attributed to "Jewish-Marxist instigation". The people's community was substituted for the class struggle, the term "Socialism" was usurped by the Nazis, and what had hitherto been known as Socialism was named "Marxism". Capital, in which the workers had been used to see their main enemy, was re-named "rapacious capital", stock exchange, or simply Jewish capital. To win over the socialist workers themselves they were offered general absolution as soon as they subscribed to the dogma that they had been the victims of Jewish-Marxist seduction.[449] And the parties of the Right, in order that they might become worthy of an alliance in the eyes of those who regarded them as compromised, had to undergo a similar purification. Their previous sins were washed away *en masse* as having been the consequence of their " systematic hybridisation " by Jews.[450] Thus all conflicting interests creating a social question were reconciled at the cost of the Jews.[451]

The importance of this Nazi attempt to establish economic peace was very considerable. Although it had little effect on the socialistically trained proletariat, it succeeded in winning the adherence of the lower middle-class which was at once anti-capitalistic and anti-proletarian. It secured, moreover, financial help from big business. The industrialists, it is true, were not interested in anti-Semitism as such. One among many proofs of this is the fact that Hitler, in his great address to the industrialists in Düsseldorf of the 27th January 1932, mentioned neither the word Jew nor anti-Semitism. The only anti-symbol he used was that of Bolshevism.[452] It cannot, however, be doubted that his audience was by that time well aware of the harsh anti-Semitic note Nazi propaganda used to strike everywhere else. Their dislike of any clamorous anti-Semitism, of which Hitler's omission to mention it on this occasion would have been an indubitable proof, if it had not been a well-established fact before, would appear strangely to contradict their backing of the Nazi Party ; but there is an easy solution to this seeming inconsistency. The industrialists accepted anti-Semitism as a tactical device because they realised that it presented the best propaganda platform on which to build an ideology of economic harmony ; and this ideology, in the name of which they wanted to destroy the trade unions, was precisely the point that mattered to the industrialists. The alliance between big business and lower middle-class under the cover of an all-embracing ideology is the main characteristic of Fascism and Nazism. While in Italy it was effected primarily in the name of nationalism and anti-liberalism, in Germany anti-Semitism was chosen to fulfil this fundamental function also.

The religious dualism, in which Hitler saw the second great obstacle in the way towards German unification, he was not able to deny.[453] Before he considered the time mature for a frontal assault against Christianity, he attempted for the time being to mitigate the denominational antagonism.[454] As a means to this end he recommended both denominations to unite on the basis of anti-Semitism.[455] Such a common platform would indeed not only have eliminated much of the religious conflict, but it would also have considerably weakened Christianity itself and thus dealt a blow at Hitler's most powerful adversary. He did not define his attitude to the denominational question more precisely. On the contrary, he warned against the interference in this matter of those immature minds who might think they could do " what even a Bismarck failed to do " .[456] He who would try to do such a thing, Hitler continued, "is acting as a champion of Jewish interests, whether consciously or unconsciously does not matter. For it is in the interests of the Jews to-day that the energies of the patriotic movement should be squandered in a religious conflict." In this way the second of the three great German problems is likewise settled by reference to the Jewish myth. He who touches upon it defends Jewish interests, therefore every true German is bound in duty to pass over it in silence. While intending a radical solution in the future, Hitler judged that the proclamation of a taboo on it on such grounds would serve his purpose for the time being.

With regard to the third problem, Hitler's attitude had to be chosen especially carefully, because he himself intended to build the Third Reich on strictly unitary lines. The masses, however, particularly in Bavaria, where he started his agitation, inclined to a particularist outlook. In virtue of its regressive tendency, Nazism was bound to encourage particularist views as being more natural than centralist views which belong to a more artificial stage of civilisation.[457] It actually did so by arousing the pride of every " Gau " in the beauty of its individual scenery and folk-lore, by encouraging dialects, traditional dress, folk-songs and folk-dances, and by intimating in local propaganda that every " Gau " was superior to every other from a cultural point of view. While this harmless cultural particularism was greatly encouraged, the political centralism was for the time being put as far into the background as possible. Where it had to be mentioned at all, the never-failing Jewish myth was used as a lightning-rod for any unpleasant associations. Hitler first of all laid the responsibility for the traditional friction between Prussia and Bavaria at the door of the Jews.[458] Speaking of the post-revolutionary period during which, as a result of the national disintegration, the internal conflict had been greatly intensified, he declared in so many words :[459] " The controversy over federation and unification, so cunningly propagandized by the Jews in 1919–20 and onwards . . ." Had Hitler been honest, he would have been bound to praise the progress towards centralisation which had been brought about by the Weimar Republic. To acknowledge, however, even a partial success on the part of the Republic was out of the question. He shrewdly got over the difficulty by stigmatising the centralising process initiated by the Weimar Constitution as " Jewish " and by opposing to it his own idea of centralisation, which, however, he did not care to set forth in detail.[460] He furthermore sought to draw a distinction between Prussia and Berlin. He encouraged sympathies for Prussia while making Berlin the target of Bavarian particularist resentment. Berlin, in turn, he identified with " the Jews ".[461] In this way the conflict between unitary and federal ideas was, in the end, also settled at the cost of the Jews.[462]

The same device was applied in foreign policy. Here Hitler's usual theme was that Germany would be able to live in peace and harmony with the whole world if the Jewish influence abroad did not counteract her endeavours to do so.[463] Hitler sought an alliance with Great Britain. But being aware of the opposition which existed there against his policy, he attributed this hostile feeling to the Jews. Thus he thought he might still claim that " the better kind of solid statesmanship "[464] was in harmony with him. But in this connection the Jewish myth was made to render him even more amazing services. Two conditions imposed by the Treaty of Versailles had been the cession of the former German colonies and the destruction of the German fleet. Both these stipulations were usually vehemently attacked with the rest of the "dictated peace" by nationalist propagandists. Hitler knew the public feeling. He realised that many people, although of themselves they would hardly have regarded these two questions as vital, had nevertheless become accustomed, from their general resentment and the instigation of the Right-wing Press, to advocate the restoration of the colonial possessions and of a protecting fleet. Hitler realised, on the other hand, that these two questions were likely to arouse divergences of opinion between Germany and Britain. He sought, therefore, to shelve them without, however, hurting the public feeling. For this purpose he resorted again to the device of laying the blame on the Jews. He insisted that the propaganda for colonies and the fleet emanated from the "Jewish Press" for whose alleged indifference in national questions he could otherwise not find enough words of abuse. The Jews, he said, were responsible for the fact that "many of our good German simpletons . . . babble about a restoration of German sea-power and protest against the robbery of our colonies ".465

With regard to the question of the Upper Adige, Hitler used similar manœuvres. The suppression of the German-speaking population of South Tyrol by Italian Fascism was another matter which exercised German public opinion to a certain extent. Only a small part of those who blamed the ruthless policy of forcibly Italianising the 250,000 odd Germans in these formerly Austrian provinces desired a revision of frontiers. What they advocated was the grant of reasonable minority rights, such as had actually existed up to 1924. The whole language used by the Nazis in dealing with questions of nationality made it appear a matter of course that they would fall into line with this widespread feeling, and this expectation was particularly strong among the German inhabitants of Upper Adige themselves. But Hitler's plans for political alliances included not only Great Britain but also Italy, and so this conflict too had to be glossed over. He therefore employed the same outworn device: "Often", he writes in *Mein Kampf*,466 "one becomes really depressed on seeing how the Jewish wire-pullers succeeded in concentrating the attention of the people on things which are only of secondary importance to-day. . . . In this connection I have to think of the Wooden Horse in the riding of which the Jew showed extraordinary skill during these years. I mean South Tyrol."

Hitler, indeed, did not hesitate to denounce even strictly patriotic causes as of " Jewish make " if these were in opposition to his wider aims.

That in the Nazi vocabulary the terms Bolshevism and Jewry were all but identical is a well-known fact. That, however, the frictions between Imperial Germany and Tsarist Russia were also due to Jewish machinations is a less well-known claim of Nazi propaganda.[467] With the same monotony the Jews are made responsible for the German-French [468] and the German-American [469] dissension, as well as for the tensions between Germany and the Far East.[470]

Anti-Semitism was thus called on to fulfil three functions within the framework of Nazi propaganda. It was to furnish or illustrate the symbols which served to satisfy primitive impulses. It was to make possible the opportunist appeal to different groups of interests. And it was to serve in concealing real political problems, so that, in spite of them, a unity of interests could be pretended to exist. It was thus given a central position by the Nazi propagandists, of whose competence in their own line there can be no question. The question then arises : Why did the Nazis choose anti-Semitism as the central piece of their propaganda ? And further : How did the German people, especially the Nazi followers, respond ?

The obvious way which suggests itself of answering the first question is to point to the anti-Semitic outlook of the broad masses and to regard Nazi anti-Semitism as one of the typical ways in which Nazism tried to fulfil mass desires. This would be fully in accord with the emphasis which, in the course of this study, has been laid on precisely this propagandistic device of Nazism. Nevertheless, such an answer would be wrong. It is not corroborated but refuted by what has been said about the favourite trick of Nazi propaganda. It is important in this connection to draw the right conclusion from the election of March 1933, in which nearly 44 per cent of the voters supported the violently anti-Semitic Nazi Party. It was precisely this electoral success which enabled the Nazi Party to consolidate its power and carry through its anti-Semitic measures. On a superficial view, these facts might seem to indicate that 44 per cent of the German people approved of the expulsion and elimination of the German Jews. But such a view would involve two mistakes. First, the 44 per cent of the voters cannot be regarded as having all had a violently anti-Semitic outlook. And secondly, even the genuine anti-Semites among them, and very probably even members of the inner party circle, did not visualise at the time of the election the radical measures which were later carried out. The first of these considerations throws a different light on the connection between anti-Semitism and the electoral success of the Nazis. The success is a fact, and so is the anti-Semitic propaganda. Must then the success be attributed to anti-Semitism ?

This question cannot be answered by a simple Yes or No. One can only consider which is supported by the greater weight of probability. In reviewing above the factors which moulded German public opinion, we showed how through the concurrence of causes arising from the epoch, the scene, and the immediately preceding events the broad masses of the German nation lost their willingness and capacity to judge for themselves even with the average competence otherwise prevailing in a mass society. They longed to be led back into a regressive paradise of primitive urges, where they would be compelled neither to think nor to be good, where they could feel irresponsible and the masters of the world. They had, moreover, to a greater extent than elsewhere, fallen out with the capitalist system of economy, which had proved even less capable in Germany than in other countries of winning popular sympathy. Not only were the masses in post-war Germany completely devoted to their own personal self-interest, as is the case everywhere under the sway of capitalist competition, but they had been driven by the complete economic disorganisation, by poverty, and unemployment into a more extreme economic egoism and hatred against competitors. The capitalist circles, in turn, felt threatened by the labour organisations and sought to subdue their influence. The hypersensitive national consciousness of the Germans, which had for long shown a tendency towards morbid degeneration, had by now completely lost its balance and swayed uneasily between feelings of inferiority and arrogant self-assertion. People had ceased to understand the world. They had been deceived by all the forces they had trusted. The existing democratic system, which even in normal times depends for its working on patience, understanding, and good-will, met, on the contrary, with impatience, misunderstanding, and ill-will, and seemed, therefore, in no way able to cope with the accumulating difficulties. The old curse which had weighed heavily on Germany from the

Roman period onwards, that progress came from the enemy and was therefore resented, was again renewed in this democracy and furnished a cheap and effective slogan against it. All this had rendered people utterly distrustful of everything offered to them in the way of usual party politics. Their state of profound disillusionment made them demand something completely out of the ordinary—no matter what its implications were—which they were no longer able to visualise. " It cannot go on like this ", ran their most popular saying. " Everything must change."

Such was the situation which the Nazis found when they started their main campaign of propaganda. Their lust for power, their moral indifference, and Hitler's cynical estimate of human weakness induced them to exploit to the full every possibility inherent in this collective psychological breakdown. Only by disentangling the several elements of Nazi propaganda, each of which was calculated to turn to the fullest account this mixture of misery, despair, apathy, and hunger for life, is it possible to understand this striking propagandistic success.[471]

It is no accident that in this enumeration of the factors which shaped public opinion anti-Semitism did not figure. This does not, of course, mean that people were not anti-Semitically inclined. There was so much frustration, resentment, anxiety, and hostility that no anti-movement could fail to thrive. But if, going back to the distinction made earlier in this study, it is asked to what extent the genuine Jewish question contributed to the anti-Semitism of this period, the answer must be that only small relics of a real group-tension existed. These relics, it is true, had undergone a slight accentuation as a result of the full emancipation brought about under the Weimar Republic, and of the immigration to central Germany from the eastern districts ceded to Poland, and from Poland herself.[472] But however seriously we regard the problems of adjustment thus created in the political, occupational, and local spheres, we cannot for a moment suppose that under their impact the Jewish question in Germany would have given reason for anxiety in normal times. Rather it may be assumed with a high degree of probability that while at first there would have been a natural tendency on the part of a previously under-privileged group to make the fullest possible use of every advantage conferred by emancipation, this would soon have passed over into a new state of balance. The fact is that concurrently with the entry of Jews into Parliament and the higher civil service, hitherto closed to them, and with their even larger concentration in Berlin, the Jewish middle-class as a whole lost a great deal of their property, and the proportion of employees among the Jews increased, particularly in industry. That is to say, their economic normalisation at least matched the growth of new tensions in other spheres.[473]

The situation was aggravated by the fact that both the old and the new tensions belonged to those spheres in which hostile reactions are likely to be aroused, such as commerce and finance, the big cities, and political extremism. This condition, as has previously been shown, is one of the main reasons why the comparatively harmless group antagonism between Jews and Gentiles can particularly easily be worked up into group hatred, entirely out of proportion to the actual social problem. If it is further considered that in these danger zones the Jews acted generally with an efficiency resulting from the operation of the " Law of Challenge and Response "* and that a residue of seemingly incompatible contradictions, which admitted of all kinds of malignant explanations, adhered to their way of life even in most recent times, it will be readily seen that the problem was capable of being distorted almost beyond recognition.

The Jews came to the fore as representatives of the State at a time when the State was in itself the object of violent attacks. It was, on the whole, unfortunate for the harmony of Jewish-Gentile relations that further progress towards full emancipation was made by the Jews at a time when the whole of the German nation had suffered from a terrible set-back. That the Jews suffered as much as the rest from the consequences of the defeat was obscured by the fact that their legal status had improved at the time of national disaster. The same, indeed, applied to workers and women, and the fight against the new rights of the workers was partly instigated by the same kind of resentment. But in this field the real social problem by far overshadowed such minor considerations. How little the group-tension between men and women is suitable as a channel for general resentments is illustrated among other things by the fact that the coincidence of the full emancipation of women and the national defeat almost entirely escaped the public notice. It was primarily the Jewish case in which the genuine

* Cf. p. 42.

tension was multiplied by " sham " motives. Hitler and his staff of propagandists did their best to canalise as many of these " sham " grievances as possible into the residual antagonism, where they became not only harmless but eminently useful to them. By thus encouraging the masses to work off their discontents and give rein to their instincts they held out an attraction with which no one of the competing parties could rival.

The process which was here carried out on many millions of people by means of a gigantic propagandistic effort is known to psychology as displacement. Where the aggressiveness generated by frustration is not allowed to operate against the person who has been the cause of the frustration, a substitute is chosen as an object for attack by way of displacement. It has already been pointed out that " out-groups " are particularly suitable objects for this displacement. The usefulness of this process for the Nazi movement was twofold. The diversion of aggression to a field where it became harmless from the Nazi point of view, made it, first of all, possible to satisfy the aggressive drive as such, and in this way to compete successfully with other less aggressive parties. The hatred for the Jews which was thus generated furthermore enhanced the effect of the Jewish myth, which was of such supreme importance for the other purposes described above, each of which aimed at gaining the widest possible mass support for the party. This extreme usefulness of the Jewish scapegoat provides, then, the answer to the first of the questions asked above, why the Nazis chose to make anti-Semitism the nucleus of their propaganda. It must be added that Hitler was personally a fervent anti-Semite. The ruthlessness with which the anti-Semitic programme of the Nazi Party, and beyond it the deportation and destruction of the German Jews, were carried out is no doubt largely due to his individual attitude. But Hitler was not only an anti-Semite, he was also a vegetarian and a teetotaller, yet he was wise enough not to burden his political programme by such unpopular demands. His personal anti-Semitism, however, he transferred deliberately into his policy because he knew its advantages.

But do not these advantages imply that latent anti-Semitism was very strong among the people and that it was for this reason that the anti-Semitic slogans met with such a resounding success ? This conclusion seems obvious, yet it does not do justice to all the factors involved. It is contradicted, to begin with, by the parallelism between the ups and downs of the economic crisis and the numbers of anti-Semitic votes in the general elections up to 1933. Between May and December 1924, when, as a consequence of the Dawes Agreement, an economic recovery took place, the number of anti-Semitic mandates receded from 40 (Deutsch-Völkische Freiheitspartei) to 14 (N.S.D.A.P.). Between 1928 and 1930, *i.e.* with the coming of the world economic crisis, the proportion of anti-Semitic voters increased for the first time from 3·5 per cent (2·6 for the N.S.D.A.P. and 0·9 for the D.V.F.P.) to 18·3 per cent, and thenceforth mounted steadily with the growing extent of the crisis. When, during the autumn of 1932, the first indications of an economic revival made themselves felt, the Nazi Party lost two million votes. Its share in the ballot decreased from 37·4 per cent to 33·1 per cent. The significance of this first symptom of decline was incomparably greater than is suggested by mere figures, since it came after what had been widely held to be an irresistible rise. While the number of the anti-Semitic votes thus fluctuated, the Jewish question had remained constant. As far as the problem of Jews in the representation of the State is concerned, one might even say that it had lost in acuteness. For in 1930, the year of the first striking success of the Nazis, the Minister of Finance, Hilferding, the last of the six Jewish Ministers of the Weimar Republic—among 250 Gentiles—had left the cabinet. If, therefore, the Nazi success reflected so faithfully the economic crisis but not the development of the actual Jewish question, this may be taken as indicating that people looked to Nazism primarily for a way out of the crisis. It does not prove that people were not affected by anti-Semitic propaganda, but it does suggest that anti-Semitism was not the consideration by which they were chiefly influenced. It was neither the " Jewish " capitalists, nor the " Jewish " Marxists, nor the " Jewish " Republic, nor the " Jewish " scandals, and it was certainly not the " Jewish " " cultural Bolshevism " which drove people to despair and thus to Nazism. But it was, according to their respective group situations, capitalism or Marxism, the Republic, corruption, or some radical eccentricities in which people were inclined to see the causes of their discontents. Since some Jews among a majority of Gentiles were connected with all these phenomena, a small number of them in leading positions, a general identification of the so-called sphere of disturbance and " the " Jews were just sufficiently plausible to make people, in the conditions which have been described, succumb to the allurement of such an " explanation ".

It must be assumed that a fairly large proportion of those who, driven by economic distress and attracted by the specific qualities of Nazi propaganda, followed the party call were subsequently converted to anti-Semitism. There can be no doubt that under the propagandistic high pressure of the years 1930 to 1933 an increasingly large number of Germans professed to be anti-Semites. True, a small proportion of the party members remained at all times opposed to the anti-Semitic doctrines, considering them unessential and being held to the party by more " essential " aims. Apart from these there existed a larger group of party followers who remained indifferent to the Jewish question, but were at any rate not repelled by the vehement anti-Semitism. A probably still larger group among the adherents of Nazism were clearly attracted by anti-Semitism. The distinctions between these three types, especially between the last two, were, of course, not rigid. All these statements, indeed, for obvious reasons cannot be regarded as exact. They are based on estimates derived from wide personal experience during the critical years, and were continually corroborated by other evidence. When all allowance has been made, they may be described as not unduly optimistic.

In spite of all these qualifications of the anti-Semitic outlook of party followers, the crucial fact remains that at the time of the Nazi rise to power anti-Semitic feeling ran extremely high in Germany. Even if we suppose that only the last of the three groups of Nazis mentioned above was in favour of the policy of persecution of Jews as carried out by the Nazi Government, we should have to conclude that the integration of the Jewish group into Gentile society in Germany has proved to be a failure. A failure in the sense that after more than a century of intercourse between Jews and Gentiles the tension between both groups still proved intolerable for a considerable part of the Gentile majority.

In order, however, rightly to assess the part played by anti-Semitism with those Nazis for whom it formed a positive attraction, a balance must be struck between all the reasons which have been previously shown to underlie the Nazi success. Here it is necessary to recall all the factors which contributed to make the post-war Germans what they were. It should be remembered how time and place co-operated to prevent them from a healthy progress towards a higher civilisation, so that they increasingly succumbed to the temptation to accept only the easiest, most direct political maxims, and how among these maxims an exclusive, aggressive, and primitive nationalism began to be ever more dominant. It must be further realised how the tendency to " gravitation " in the moral and intellectual sphere was aggravated under the influence of the economic and social disorganisation of the post-war period and how the controls of the individual conscience as well as those of civilisation as a whole broke down under the impact. When it is finally realised that every element of this situation was exploited to the full by a propaganda as ruthless as it was efficient, then it will be seen that the decisive factor of the Nazi success was this. In an excessively complicated situation Nazism offered to a society in full disintegration a political diet whose disastrous effects this society was no longer able to realise. People felt that it contained titbits for every palate. The titbits were, so to speak, coated with anti-Semitism. This covering gave them consistency and finish. But it was not the covering for the sake of which they were greedily swallowed. It was the boundless psychical starvation on the one hand and the excellent taste of the morsels on the other which secured their acceptance. The wrapping in which the new security, the new self-assurance, the exculpation, the permission to hate was served might equally well have had another colour and another spice. The food itself would not, for that reason, have been less enthusiastically received.

The conclusiveness of this analogy is confirmed by the following consideration. If those people who, under the influence of anti-Semitic propaganda would have described themselves as anti-Semites, had been moved by outright hatred of the Jews, their practical aggression against them would have been excessive after the Jews had been openly abandoned to the people's fury. Violence would not then have been limited to the organised activities of Nazi gangs, but would have become endemic in the whole people and seriously endangered the life of every Jew in Germany. This, however, did not happen. Even during the years in which the party increased by leaps and bounds, spontaneous terrorist assaults on Jews were extremely rare. The defilements of Jewish cemeteries which occurred more frequently could in most cases be traced to the instigation of inner party circles.[474] In spite of the ardent endeavours of the same party circles, the boycott against Jewish shopkeepers and professional men before the seizure of power was negligible, although this would have been an inconspicuous and safe way of demonstrating one's anti-Jewish feeling. From this all but complete lack of practical anti-Semitic reactions at a time when the behaviour of the public was still a correct index to its sentiments, it can only be inferred that the overwhelming majority of the people did not feel their relations to the Jewish minority as unbearable. The obvious contrast between the attraction of the anti-Semitic slogans and the people's neglect to implement them can rather be explained as follows.

Under the influence of mass meetings and an incessant propaganda people were led to accept certain symbols because these helped them to imbibe the doctrines which promised release to their rebelling impulses. Such acceptance, however, did not mean that they were converted to an anti-Semitism which would have survived a rational examination or which could be made a basis of rational action. In other words, even those people who in this time of crisis declared themselves to be convinced anti-Semites did not by this profession turn against the living Jewish individuals whom they knew as their neighbours, but against the " Jew ", that uncanny and mysterious image which propaganda had succeeded in presenting as the source of all their distress.[475]

Thus Nazi anti-Semitism testifies far less to the existence of a Jewish problem in Germany than to a multitude of other German problems which urgently needed a solution and for which a large number of people could be persuaded to hold the Jews responsible. These people did not realise the difference. They would even have strongly opposed such an explanation of their anti-Semitic outlook. They clung to the symptom of their neurosis as if they had known how much mental relief it afforded them. And so much indeed was real about it that they did not wish the Jews well. They would also, after consideration, have expressed the wish to see them eliminated from the civil service and their proportion in certain branches of trade, in the Press, theatre, and the liberal professions diminished. In the majority of such demands the competitive motive was manifest, although an endeavour was made to cloak it in more general expressions like the aversion to " Jewish control ", " excessive alien influence " (*Ueberfremdung*), etc. Individual hotheads gave freer vent to their anti-Semitic fantasies, but, on the whole, demands going beyond this were not popular outside the fanaticised S.A. and related groups. The idea that a considerable number of the anti-Semites of that time would have approved of the expulsion and physical annihilation of their Jewish fellow citizens, with whom they were acquainted, is against the opinion of all contemporary observers. The general attitude of the people at the time when the anti-Jewish measures were gradually carried out gives a further indication of the degree of their anti-Semitic feelings.[476] Nearly all observations agree that the average German citizen had already in the first years of the Nazi regime begun to express disapproval of the severe anti-Jewish measures. His criticism, however, was not infrequently accompanied by remarks to the effect that he too regarded a certain reduction of the Jewish influence as desirable. The comparative rarity of anti-Semitic outrages even at a time when the fear of punishment had already been largely diminished through the partiality of the courts, the obstinacy with which Gentiles clung to their Jewish business friends in spite of all incitements to boycott them, the numerous proofs of personal confidence which—with many opposite experiences— fell to the lot of every individual Jew after 1933—all these facts are of great significance if they are seen against the background which has been here described.

The attitude of the German people towards anti-Semitism may be summed up as follows :

(1) Such anti-Semitism as existed in Germany during the relatively normal years before the first World War was only to a small extent the result of a real tension between Jews and Gentiles. Even at that time it was far more an expression of a national self-mistrust for which people tried to compensate themselves at the cost of a minority with predominantly liberal ideas.

(2) As a consequence of the first World War and the ensuing crisis, certain social and political developments favouring the emergence of Nazism reached a climax. The anti-Semitism preached by the Nazis did not play a decisive part in winning adherents for the movement.

(3) With the flood of Nazi propaganda, anti-Semitic feeling increased. It seized upon people primarily because of the

234

psychological satisfaction which this anti-symbol offered to their regressive needs for aggression, self-glorification, irresponsibility, and authoritarianism. That this anti-symbol was personified by the Jews was more or less accidental.

(4) The symbolic anti-Semitism thus instigated was directed less against the living Jews than against the mythical Jew. Only in exceptional cases did the excited masses commit spontaneous acts of violence against Jews.

(5) Persons who under the influence of crisis and propaganda professed to be anti-Semites did not desire or expect anti-Jewish measures comparable with those taken by the Nazi Government. They approved of a limitation of Jewish influence, but thought neither of the expulsion, nor the deportation, nor the destruction of the Jews.

These points provide an answer not only to the question to what extent anti-Semitism contributed to, and profited by, the Nazi success, but also to the question whether it is possible to infer from the catastrophe of the German Jews a breakdown of the relations between Jews and Gentiles in Germany. It has been shown that the actual relations between Jews and Gentiles were but slightly responsible for anti-Semitism, that anti-Semitism was only partially responsible for Nazism, and that anti-Semitism, as it came to be embodied in the Nazi movement, does not account for the catastrophe of the Jews.

Each of the three steps of the argument that the Jewish-Gentile relations in Germany were responsible for the catastrophe of the Jews has thus been separately examined and found to be unconvincing. The apparent causal connection between the two phenomena has thereby been all but completely severed. And, so far as the idea of the " Bankruptcy of Emancipation " has drawn its support from the catastrophe of the Jews in Germany, it has lost its foundation.

CONCLUSION

THE END OF THIS INVESTIGATION has been reached and there remains the task of summarising its results.

During the period of emancipation a gradual integration of the German Jews into German-Gentile society proceeded, generally speaking, steadily if not without disturbances and temporary set-backs. The entire scope of the process can be gathered from a comparison of the social and cultural conditions of the German Jews in 1812 and in 1912. From an internally largely homogeneous group differing in nearly every respect from its environment, the Jews had become an internally largely heterogeneous group which in every respect was very similar to its environment. Only some comparatively unimportant characteristics in the religious, ethnical, and political field, as well as in the matter of local and occupational distribution, constituted what was still distinguishable in the Jewish group.

By looking for the gist of the Jewish problem not in the legal sphere, *i.e.* in the gradual conferment of formal rights, but in the social sphere, *i.e.* in the process of social adaptation, the anti-Semitic protests, which were intermittently raised by certain Gentile circles, gain a new significance. They must be regarded as the inevitable reactions to a complicated and relatively new social process, not as the early symptoms of an irreconcilable hatred which eventually culminated in Nazism. Even these movements achieved noticeable success only in times of economic crises, when general dissatisfaction was exceptionally widespread. After the critical situation had been overcome, they usually lost all political importance. This dependence of anti-Semitism on the trade cycle is one of the factors indicating the loose connection between anti-Semitism and the Jewish question proper.

Beneath the social surface which was temporarily agitated by anti-Semitic movements, a more profound social process took place, parallel to the Gentile-Jewish integration. It consisted of the progressive normalisation of the relations between Jews and Gentiles. The Gentiles became increasingly indifferent to the fact that Jews lived in their midst, if and when their Jew-consciousness was not artificially enhanced.

These not unfavourable prospects for the disappearance of the real Jewish question and of what may be called normal German anti-Semitism were, however, to some extent counteracted by unfavourable tendencies in other spheres. These tendencies were connected with the general trends of social evolution during the era of capitalism, and with the special difficulties of German history during the same period. The general standard of political integrity sank, on the one hand owing to the fact that the moral energy of all classes was gradually sapped in the course of an increasingly difficult struggle for life, and on the other owing to the admission of those groups to political co-operation which were particularly affected by this development and least able to withstand its fateful consequences. Simple, direct slogans with an effective appeal to the lower instincts, like the " struggle for life ", the " right of the strongest ", " my country—right or wrong ", and the like, which were coined by intellectual and political leaders, won popularity, their acceptance satisfying the desire to excuse a crudely egoist behaviour by allegedly idealist motives and thus to preserve a good conscience. Latent aggressiveness became stronger and bolder and could be used by political leaders whenever they considered it opportune to " displace " it on to the Jewish scapegoat.

The general lowering of moral standards and the access to power of the classes which were least able to resist it, was in Germany complicated by a number of special conditions. Nearly all of them can be traced back to the central position of Germany in Europe. The continuous antagonism between the Western ideas and tendencies of progress and the Eastern ideas and tendencies of reaction on German soil led to a number of disastrous consequences. Of these the most fateful were the long postponement of national unification and democratisation. The extraordinarily long period of national frustration and the fact that unification eventually took place in an atmosphere of military victory and under Prussian guidance resulted in a permanent insecurity of German national consciousness. This insecurity in turn led to the constant reinterpretation of the national idea, which was usually given the sense of aggressive intolerance both towards foreign nations and internal subgroups, such as national minorities and the Jews.

These tendencies portended certain dangers to the success of Jewish emancipation in Germany. Although Jews and

Gentiles were continually drawing nearer, the mutual relations were challenged by the rise of an amoral economic egoism and of nationalist aggressiveness. But these dangers, although they must not be overlooked in an examination of the roots of National Socialism, should also not be overrated. The relations between Jews and Gentiles in Germany would never have given rise to anti-Semitic feelings of the violence shown in the Nazi movement if the social disorganisation which followed the first World War had not immensely strengthened the disintegrating factors and paralysed the forces making for peace and order. One of the decisive factors was that democracy, which in such grave circumstances would have been able to work satisfactorily only if it had been supported by strong moral reserves accumulated in a long era of democratic tradition, failed utterly.

Nazism does not owe its origin to anti-Semitism, but the anti-Semitism of this post-war period was a concomitant of the Nazi success. In spite of the many factors which favoured the acceptance of anti-Semitism by the German people, those anti-Semitic symbols, which were accepted under the influence of a turbulent mass emotion, bore little resemblance to real Jew-hatred, understood as the cool and lasting conviction that the Jewish question must be radically settled at the cost of the Jews. Even the irrational anti-Semitism which the Nazis did succeed in arousing failed to sink into people's minds to any considerable degree. Only with hesitation was it translated into action. The small number of spontaneous acts of violence against Jews before, and even after, the Nazi seizure of power, as well as the laxity with which the boycott was generally carried out unless the instructions were strictly enforced, indicate the extent to which people were affected by organised Jew-baiting. All these statements must not be taken absolutely, but relatively to the vehemence of such an active Jew-hatred as might have been expected as the result of the acute general frustration, the extraordinary efficiency of propaganda, and the diminishing fear of punishment.

Jewish emancipation in Germany has been undone. Does this mean that it was a failure? Has the way of life of German Jews which was initiated by their emancipation broken down on account of its intrinsic deficiencies? This is the crucial question which was raised at the beginning of this study. It hangs as a menace over the lives of Jews everywhere, because an erroneous answer would conjure up new dangers for them.

On the strength of our previous investigations we may venture to answer the question emphatically in the negative. The way of life of the Jews in Germany, which can be briefly characterised as combining identification with their environment with the will to remain Jews and to retain the values of Judaism, has not been reduced to an absurdity. It has been shown that not only must the causes of the German-Jewish catastrophe not be sought in the Jewish way of life, but that this way of life was itself a powerful source of resistance to the approaching catastrophe. A conspicuous discrepancy existed between the anti-Semitic fury displayed at Nazi mass meetings and the reluctance with which the more extreme anti-Jewish measures were generally obeyed. This contradiction can only be explained if a difference is assumed to have existed between the mass feelings excited by an elaborate propaganda and the feeling of those people whose mentality was still approximately normal. This state of normality implied an ordinary standard of neighbourliness towards the Jews; and its derangement in a number of individuals who should have been immune against such a thing can only be accounted for by the extent of the social and psychical disorganisation at the time of the Nazi flood. The social upheaval which was required to tear the fabric of Jewish-Gentile relationship even partly asunder shows how closely—in spite of all impediments—this fabric had been woven. Jewish emancipation is on the same footing as the emancipation of the workers and of women, and as democracy itself. If the conclusion is drawn that recent events in Germany have compromised its underlying idea beyond rehabilitation, then the idea of workers' and women's emancipation and of democracy itself would have been equally shown as untenable.

The question remains whether these events have a lesson for Jews in other countries. We have seen that certain factors which contributed to bring about the catastrophe in Germany exist everywhere. The chronic frustrations and anxieties arising from the struggle for life and the disposition of large sections of the population to be swayed in their political activities by emotional rather than by rational motives are such ever-present menaces. Many of the specific features of the Jewish group which single it out for attack are found throughout the globe. But although in Germany these menaces were powerful and the agencies for countering them particularly weak, although an extraordinary crisis intensified the dangers and all but destroyed the counter-agents, although a propaganda of unparalleled violence attempted to fan the flames of Jew-hatred to white-heat, the relations between Jews and Gentiles stood the strain remarkably well. If circumstances had not driven people into despair and so into the hands of the Nazis with overwhelming force, if political intrigues had not come to the aid of the Nazis just as they were beginning to lose ground, if, lastly, Hitler had not been possessed with a frenzy which was absolutely demoniacal—expulsion and destruction would never have befallen the Jews. The rights of the Jews might have been temporarily restricted by administrative measures. The status of the Jews might have been reduced roughly to what it had been under the Kaiser. But if on that fatal 30th of January 1933 the connection between trade cycle and spontaneous anti-Semitism had not been irreparably severed, because no spontaneous reaction of the people was subsequently possible—a second full emancipation of the Jews would have taken place sooner or later with economic and political recovery.

In view of the utterly exceptional character of the events in Germany during the post-war years, the balance we have struck need not appear too unfavourable. It teaches Jews everywhere not to disregard the fact that they live as minorities and that they are exposed to all the dangers of minority status, particularly to the peril of being used as a scapegoat for any political or social failure of the larger community. They should take this fact to heart, even if they personally are hardly aware any longer of belonging to the Jewish group. They should learn to see themselves not only with their own eyes but also with the eyes of their social environment. If in consequence they feel compelled against their will to impose certain restrictions on themselves beyond those imposed on all law-abiding citizens, they should consider this irksome necessity a concession to human imperfection. It is the price the Jews have to pay for their status as a permanent minority, and it will remain the lot of the majority of Jews no matter how prosperous the future of the State of Israel may be. Only in rare cases would the neglect of such self-imposed restrictions entail any harm for society as a whole. On the contrary, an increased consciousness of their status as a minority might easily dissuade some Jews who might be of value to the community from putting their forces at the disposal of the whole as unreservedly as they might otherwise do. The argument for such restrictions is rather that even generally useful gifts, presented by a minority to a majority, may sometimes fail to benefit the majority and may be disastrous to the minority, especially when, in times of crisis, group antagonism distorts the judgment. By becoming more clearly aware of the nature of latent aggressiveness being diverted to sub-groups, Jews and Gentiles will be able to counteract more effectively the ensuing dangers. By studying more closely the nature of prejudices, sweeping generalisations and scapegoats, and by applying new educational methods, people may become more critical of themselves. If Jew-consciousness is replaced by prejudice-consciousness there will be less chance of the device of a scapegoat being used with such disastrous success as it obtained in Germany.

But still more favourable lessons can be derived from the German example. In few other countries is the national consciousness as immature as it is in Germany. In few other countries does a person feel justified in thinking of himself as " nationally minded " only if he persecutes every other shade of opinion as " non national " with all the hatred of which he is capable. Since to be a " good German " was tantamount to being reactionary, and since the brand " un-German " was stamped on every movement serving progress, peace, and freedom, the traditional outlook of the majority of Jewish citizens in Germany was in permanent danger of being thus stigmatised. But in countries where people are not so prone to misuse the word " national " as the designation of a reactionary party, a formidable obstacle is removed from the political path of the Jews. Where democracy has taken root and people have been educated by it and for it, their power of resisting its inherent dangers has been strengthened. Persons who are used to think and judge for themselves on political matters succumb less easily to the seductive influence of slogans and symbols than those who have only just been released from the tutelage of an authoritarian State and find themselves confronted by a confusing mass of problems. Those who for decades have learned to carry the obligations of freedom will not break down under its burden. Those for whom tolerance of people of different origin is a matter of daily routine are more likely to steer clear of aggressive intolerance against a group of such people. Those who have not been taught to flee from the light of facts into the shades of pseudo-scientific theories will not be so easily carried away by a torrent of bombastic words

241

presenting themselves in the guise of science. People, finally, who have not been so hopelessly overpowered by a desire to seek compensation in hatred and self-exaltation for a life of misery will not sink so deep into the abyss of their primitive nature. The Jews being everywhere a minority depend for their existence on an advanced state of civilisation in their environment. The deadly force in Nazism that brought about their ruin was directed primarily not against them but against civilisation itself.

It is beyond our power, as it is beyond the power of any human being without the gift of prophecy, to state categorically that the German example cannot and will not be repeated elsewhere. But it can be said with confidence that the German example *need* not be repeated, nay, that its repetition is improbable. Professor A. J. Toynbee in discussing the proposition that the rise and fall of cultural entities move in predestined cycles and that, consequently, the end of Western culture is imminent,[477] proves that no compulsory power exists which makes such a course inevitable. And he derives from this proof the following comforting reflections : " Yet, even in our forlorn and melancholy plight our deliverance from the incubus of the predestinarian creed should put us in better heart ; for, if this creed is non-proven, then even in Life-in-Death there is still Hope-against-Hope. The Goddess with whom we have to do battle is not Saeva Necessitas with her lethal armoury, but only Probability whom mortal valour wielding mortal weapons may one day drive ignominiously off the field. . . ." The conclusions to which this study has led us are even more cheering. The goddess with whom we have to do battle is not even Probability but Possibility. The confidence that one day this will be victoriously overcome thus appears even more solidly founded.

The catastrophe of the German Jews has been the conclusion of one of mankind's great tragedies. If, according to the laws of the classical tragedy, the guilt of the hero is to be established, it may conceivably be found in the too unreserved devotion of the German Jews to their German country. The force that drew many of the best from both communities towards each other was something more than an accident of birth. It was a fateful attraction, the strength of which is revealed abundantly by the extremes of love and hate to which it gave rise. We, however, at the end of this study, do not feel called upon to sit in judgment over the unhappy victim. We think of his former grandeur, of his accomplishments and his dignity. If guilt is to be determined, then it must rest inexpiably on those who requited his love and his labours with the terrors of the raving beast.

No poet has yet come forward to give a worthy form to the tragedy of German Jewry. It will be a tragedy embracing many themes, love and hatred, will-power and endurance, the genius of the few and the righteous toil of the many. It will be a tragedy for which world history itself will provide the background and in which all human passions—national, individual, and group passions—will perform as actors. Perhaps this study has advanced some of the preliminary material. We wait for the poet who will lend it his vision and his words.

NOTES

(For details concerning places and years of publication, cf. Bibliography.)
The sign § indicates that an originally German quotation has been translated by the writer of this study.

INTRODUCTION : FAILURE OF EMANCIPATION?

1. *The Jewish Year Book*, 5709-10. Ed. Albert M. Hyamson, London, 1949.

2. Only a few examples may be mentioned: Herbert von Beckerath, *In Defence of the West*; *Constructive Democracy, A Symposium*; *Democracy in Transition*, by a Group of Social Scientists in the Ohio State University; *Dictatorship in the Modern World*, ed. by Guy Stanton Ford; J. S. Fulton and C. R. Morris, *In Defence of Democracy*; A. D. Lindsay, *The Essentials of Democracy*, and *I Believe in Democracy*; Walter Lippman, *The Good Society*; Charles E. Merriam, *The New Democracy and the New Despotism*; John Middleton Murry, *The Defence of Democracy*; *New Governments in Europe, The Trend toward Dictatorship*, preface by Raymond Leslie Buell.

3. Ernst Frankenstein, *Justice for My People*; Ludwig Lewisohn, *Israel* and *the Answer*; Milton Steinberg, *The Making of the Modern Jew*, pp. 144, 232, 235; George Sacks, *The Intelligent Man's Guide to Jew-Baiting*, p. 162; a Gentile view: A. J. Toynbee, *A Study of History*, ii, 252, footnote; the feeling of " Defeatism " is reported by Jessie Bernard, " Biculturality : A Study in Social Schizophrenia ", in *Jews in a Gentile World*, p. 282; I. O. Hertzler, " The Sociology of Anti-Semitism through History ", in *Jews in a Gentile World*, p. 63. One voice speaking against the " Failure of Emancipation " is that of M. Polanyi, " Jewish Problems " in *The Political Quarterly*, xiv, 40.

I

ANTI-SEMITISM : A SPECIAL CASE OF GROUP TENSION

4. The number of Jews in Germany amounted in 1820 to 270,000 or 1·9 per cent of the total population. In 1925 it amounted to 564,379 or 0·9 of the total population. Cf. Jakob Lestschinsky, *Das wirtschaftliche Schicksal des deutschen Judentums*, p. 50.

5. This is not to deny that the Jews in Germany carried out to a remarkable extent what Julian Morgenstern, in *Assimilation, Isolation or Reform? Contemporary Jewish Record*, calls " active assimilation ", viz. " the process . . . of assimilating without being assimilated ". The difference between the two statements is only one of terms. Morgenstern thinks obviously of " passive assimilation " as total amalgamation, while we use the term to mean " undergoing changes which diminish the differences with the environment ". In this sense " active " and " passive " assimilation can hardly be disentangled. While assimilating the ways of their environment to themselves (" active " assimilation), the Jews assimilated at the same time themselves to the environment (" passive " assimilation). The establishment of the Science of Judaism, *e.g.*, by Leopold Zunz is such an act of " active " and at the same time " passive " assimilation. While putting the methods of German science and the ideas of romanticism at the service of Jewish research as an end in itself, he interpreted and, for that matter, changed simultaneously Judaism with a veiw to making it understandable and acceptable to German society.

6. A. J. Toynbee, *A Study of History*, ii, p. 248, declares the connection between penalisation and the intensity of the Jewish ethos to be an instance of a social law : " Thus, in Jewry, we find a gradual sequence of types—Ashkenazi, Sephardi, Dönme, crypto-Jew, and ci-devant Jewish Catholic—in which the Jewish ethos varies in intensity through all the degrees from maximum to vanishing point; and we observe that these variations in the intensity of the Jewish ethos correspond to variations in the severity of the penalisation to which Jewry has been subjected by

the Gentiles. The distinctive ethos of the penalized religious denomination becomes less and less sharply accentuated as the penalization is progressively remitted; and this social law is not valid only for the Jews. Its operation can be illustrated from the history of other penalized sects whose reactions we have examined above." Toynbee neglects the other factors on which the intensity of the Jewish ethos depends, e.g., the duration of the period of assimilation through which a certain Jewish community has passed, the immigration of Jewish groups with a more intense Jewish ethos, etc.

7. Without being able to go deeper into the problem of the racial homogeneity of the Jews, we should like to say this about the connection of Jewish race and Jewish group. The racial factor which cannot be simply stripped off, but can only be diminished by mixed marriages, is in itself not sufficient to constitute membership of the Jewish group. There are racially "full" Jews who have severed all relations to the Jewish community, and there are persons without a drop of Jewish blood who belong to it. The emphasis laid by anti-Semites on the racial criterion follows from their wish to make an unchangeable factor the basis of Jewish group existence.

8. Arthur Ruppin, *Soziologie der Juden*, ii, 175-6.§

9. The anomaly of the Jewish vocational distribution, however, indicates that the objective group characteristics were stronger than the subjective group consciousness. The Jews in Italy contributed, it is true, a somewhat lower percentage to commerce and traffic than the German Jews: 41·5 per cent of every 100 Jews in gainful occupations, in 1910, as against 69·4 per cent in Bavaria, in 1907, and 49·7 per cent in Germany, in 1907, according to Ruppin, *ibid.* i, 348. Nevertheless, the proportion of the Jews employed in commerce and traffic was still six times their proportion of the population—0·6 as against 0·1 per cent, Ruppin, *ibid.* i, 357. This anomaly was even increased by the fact that the surplus of people formerly occupied in commerce had obviously gone over to the professions and the bureaucracy, to which no less than 23 per cent of all gainfully occupied Jews belonged. Cf. Ruppin, *ibid.* i, 350.

10. Salo Wittmayer Baron, *A Social and Religious History of the Jews*, ii, 171; Ruppin, *op, cit.* i, 131.

11. Ruppin, *op. cit.* i, 131.

12. Ruppin, *op. cit.* i, 89.

13. Ruppin, *op. cit.* i, 157-8.

14. Cf. Louis Wirth, *The Ghetto*, p. 279.

15. Cf. F. Bernstein, *Der Antisemitismus als Gruppenerscheinung*; Arnold Zweig, *Caliban oder Politik und Leidenschaft*; Isacque Graeber and Steuart Henderson Britt, *Jews in a Gentile World*.

16. Bernstein, *op. cit.* p. 219; "Die zwischen den Gruppen herrschende Spannung und die zur Aeusserung gelangende Feindschaft ist keineswegs das Produkt von Eigenschaften oder Handlungen der Gegengruppe ". Zweig, *op. cit.* p. 30: " Das Wesen des Juden ist für das Zustandekommen des Antisemitismus ganz ausser acht zu lassen ".

17. Bernstein, *op. cit.* p. 145 and *passim*.

18. Sigmund Freud, *Group Psychology and the Analysis of the Ego*, pp. 55 *seq*.

19. W. Trotter, *Instincts of the Herd in Peace and War*, pp. 29 and 31.

20. Trotter, *op. cit.* p. 32.

21. Trotter, *op. cit.* p. 34.

22. Trotter, *op. cit.* p. 118.

23. Hugo Valentin, *Antisemitism*, p. 17.

24. Cf. Graham Wallas, *Human Nature and Politics*, p. 56; D. W. Harding, *The Impulse to Dominate*, p. 20; with special reference to the Jewish problem : Anonymous, " An Analysis of Jewish Culture ", in *Jews in a Gentile World*, pp. 246-7 and 248.

25. For the legitimacy of the demand for national homogeneity in modern democracy cf. Carl Schmitt, *Verfassungslehre*, pp. 231 *seq*.

26. Article, " Staat ", *Handwörterbuch der Staatswissenschaften*, vii, 725.§

27. Cf. article " Assimilation, Social ", by Robert E. Park in *Encyclopaedia of the Social Sciences*.

28. Cf. Baron, *op. cit.* ii, 224 *seq*.

29. Cf. Baron, *op. cit.* ii, 226-8.

30. Cf. J. O. Hertzler, " The Sociology of Anti-Semitism through History ", in *Jews in a Gentile World*, p. 81.

31. George Sacks, *The Jewish Question*, p. 38.

32. The theories of Bernstein and Zweig, *op. cit.*, have been accepted by Valentin and Ruppin, *op. cit.*

33. The importance which Georg Simmel attributes to this distinction is made clear in his footnote to p. 263 of his *Sociology* : " Alle Verhältnisse eines Menschen zu anderen sind in ihrem tiefsten Grund nach dieser Frage geschieden—wenn auch in unzähligen Uebergängen zwischen ihrem Ja und Nein— : ob ihre seelische Grundlage ein Trieb des Subjektes ist, der sich, als Trieb, auch ohne jede äussere Anregung entwickelt und erst seinerseits einen ihm adäquaten Gegenstand sucht—sei es, dass es ihn als adäquaten vorfindet, sei es, dass es ihn durch Phantasie und Bedürfnis bis zur Adäquatheit umgestaltet ; oder ob die seelische Grundlage in der Reaktion besteht die das Sein und Tun einer Persönlichkeit in uns hervorruft ; natürlich müssen auch zu ihr die Möglichkeiten in uns vorhanden sein, aber sie wären an sich latent geblieben und hätten sich nie von selbst zu Trieben gestaltet. In diesen Gegensatz stellen sich intellektuelle wie ästhetische, sympathische wie antipathische Verhältnisse zu Menschen ein und ziehen häufig nur aus diesem Fundamente ihre Entwicklungsformel, ihre Intensität und ihre Peripetie." (All the relations of one human being to another are fundamentally distinguishable according to the question—if in innumerable transitions from one alternative to the other—whether their psychological basis be an impulse of the subject, which develops without any external stimulus and seeks on his own for an adequate object—no matter whether it finds it as an adequate one or transforms it into an adequate one through fantasy and need ; or whether the psychological basis consists of the reaction aroused in us by the qualities and actions of a personality. Of course, the potentialities for this reaction must lie in us, but they would have remained latent and never, by themselves, grown into impulses. This is a distinction bearing on intellectual, aesthetic, sympathetic and antipathetic relations between people, and from this basis often spring their form of development, their intensity and their peripetia.§)

34. Freud, *Civilization and its Discontents*, p. 63 ; Freud, *Civilization, War and Death.* Selections from three works, pp. 9-12.

35. Freud, *Civilization, War and Death*, pp. 51 and 77-8.

36. Freud, *op. cit.* p. 78.

37. John Dollard and others, *Frustration and Aggression, passim.*

38. J. Suttie, *The Origin of Love and Hate*, p. 31 and *passim.*

39. Peter Nathan, *Psychology of Fascism*, pp. 38-9.

40. Freud, *Moses and Monotheism*, p. 146.

41. Cf. also J. F. Brown, " The Origin of the Anti-Semitic Attitude ", in *Jews in a Gentile World*, p. 138.

42. *Dr. Martin Luthers sämtliche Werke*, Erlanger Ausgabe, xxxii, 129; Jakob Friedrich Fries, review of Friedrich Rühs, " Ueber die Ansprüche der Juden an das deutsche Bürgerrecht " in *Heidelbergische Jahrbücher der Literatur*, No. 16, p. 251 ; Friedrich Rühs, *ibid. op. cit.*, p. 244; Eduard von Hartmann, *Das Judentum in Gegenwart und Zukunft*, pp. 61 *seq.*; Paul de Lagarde, *Deutsche Schriften*, p. 411; Eugen Dühring, *Die Judenfrage als Frage des Rassencharakters und seiner Schädlichkeiten für Existenz und Kultur der Völker*, p. 6 and *passim* ; Alfred Rosenberg, *Der Mythus des 20. Jahrhunderts*, p. 462; Adolf Hitler, *Mein Kampf, passim* ; (ed.) J. Singer, *Briefe berühmter Zeitgenossen über die Judenfrage, passim, e.g.*, pp. 132, 171, 187; Ernst Jörges, *Die weltgeschichtliche Bedeutung des Judentums und seine Zukunft*, p. 77.

43. Georg Simmel, Soziolgie, pp. 687-8.

44. Cf. also Harold D. Lasswell, *World Politics and Personal Insecurity*, p. 177 : " Also those who depart from the environment in which they have developed show varying degrees of personal disorganisation in the new environment. In the original situation the family, the church, school, fraternity, and neighbourhood were recurring stimuli for the preservation of the acquired inhibitions. In the new environment external supports to the super-ego are often missing ; indeed the older symbols . . . may not only be missing, but they may be treated with obvious disrespect by the new milieu." To avoid any misunderstanding it must be stressed that this study is not concerned with apologetics. Therefore the simple proof that the overwhelming majority of Jews do not essentially differ in the strength of their religious allegiance from their Gentile environment would be out of place. However thin the stratum of irreligious Jews may have been, public attention has been focused on them to an extent that makes it necessary to deal in detail with the reasons for this phenomenon.

45. Morris Ginsberg, *The Psychology of Society*, p. 111, draws attention to the common " dislike of change ", the " horror of innovation ", in which he suggests " there may be something elemental ".

46. Cf. J. F. Brown, " The Origin of the Anti-Semitic Attitude ", in *Jews in a Gentile World*, pp. 140-41.

47. *Op. cit.* vol. ii.

48. *Ibid.* p. 274.

49. *Ibid.* p. 271.

50. *Op. cit.* p. 686.§

51. James Parkes, *The Jew and His Neighbour*, Chapter III, " The Jews in Normal Surroundings ", pp. 45 *seq.*; Baron, *op. cit.* ii, pp. 13-14.

52. Cf. statistics in Jakob Lestschinsky, *Das wirtschaftliche Schicksal des deutschen Judentums, passim.*

53. Ruppin, *op. cit.* i, 327.

54. *Ibid.* i, pp. 326-7.

55. Cf. Gustav Schmoller, *Grundriss der allgemeinen Volkswirtschaftslehre*, i, pp. 333-4 and 356-7.

56. *Wirtschaft und Gesellschaft* (in *Grundriss der Sozialökonomik*, vol. iii), i, 269, 353; ii, 811; *Gesammelte Aufsätze zur Religionssoziologie*, iii : " Das antike Judentum", p. 378, and with special reference to the Pharisees, p. 407.

57. Louis Wirth, " Urbanism as a Way of Life ", in *The American Journal of Sociology*, vol. xliv, No. 1, p. 10.

58. Wirth, *op. cit.* p. 10.

59. Cf. Everett V. Stonequist, " The Marginal Character of the Jews ", in *Jews in a Gentile World*, pp. 296 *seq.*

60. Cf. Baron, *op. cit.* ii, 266-7.

61. Leonard Bloom, " The Jews of Buna ", in *Jews in a Gentile World*, pp. 195 and 197, throws an interesting sidelight on the difficulties which stand in the way of this tendency in America.

62. Useful statistics can be found in Lestschinsky, *op. cit.* Chapter IV, " Die Urbanisierung und Konzentrierung der Juden in Deutschland ", pp. 59 *seq.*

63. Alfred Rosenberg, *op. cit.* p. 82.§

64. Ruppin, *op. cit.* i, 329.

65. On the origin of clothes-making among Jews, cf. Baron, *op. cit.* ii, 14. Werner Sombart, *Die Juden und das Wirtschaftsleben*, p. 133, suggests that trading in old clothes developed into trading with new clothes, and this into manufacture of clothes.

66. Ruppin, *op. cit.* i, 460.§

67. Ruppin, *op. cit.* i, 461.

68. Ruppin, *op. cit.* i, 435.

69. Ruppin, *op. cit.* i, 352.

70. Ruppin, *op. cit.* i, 329.

71. Ruppin, *op. cit.* i, 330.

72. Sombart, *Die Juden und das Wirtschaftsleben*, p. 132.

73. Sombart, *ibid.*§

74. Cf. Anonymous, " An Analysis of Jewish Culture ", in *Jews in a Gentile World*, p. 251.

75. Erich Kahler, " Forms and Features of Anti-Judaism ", in *Social Research*, vol. vi.

76. Carl Mayer, " Anti-Judaism Reconsidered ", in *Social Research*, vii, 179-80.

77. Cf. also Adolf Leschnitzer, *Das Judentum im Weltbild Europas*, Teil I : " Das Judentum im Weltbild des Mittelalters ", Preface, pp. 4 *seq.*

78. Melville Jacobs, " Jewish Blood and Culture ", in *Jews in a Gentile World*, p. 54, emphasises the effects of equal economic, social, and educational opportunities for the assimilation even of the physical type.

79. Sigmund Freud, " The Uncanny ", in *Collected Papers*, iv, 401.

80. Joshua Trachtenberg, *The Devil and the Jews.*

81. Freud, *The Uncanny*, p. 402.

82. Great as have been the services of Mr. Trachtenberg in illuminating the superstitious elements in anti-Semitism, we cannot follow him to the conclusion that these superstitions are the most important cause of anti-Semitism. To us they seem rather as a still latent, but steadily diminishing predisposition for it which must depend on ever stronger stimuli for its actualisation.

83. *Am. Journ. Soc.*, May 1936-7, vol. xlii.

84. Karen Horney, *The Neurotic Personality of Our Time*; *v.* there pp. 20 *seq.* for an enumeration of those authors " who have recognised the importance of cultural factors as a determining influence in psychological conditions ".

85. Franz Alexander, " Psycho-Analysis and Social Disorganization ", in *Am. Journ. Soc.*, vol. xlii.

86. Erich Fromm, *The Fear of Freedom*, Appendix : " Character and Social Process ", p. 239.

87. We take over the term " social character " but reject the extension of the term which Dr. Fromm gives it later, pp. 242 and 245. This seems to imply the false assumption that the common traits of individuals affected by the same group situation are in the special circumstances of this group bound to be " necessary and desirable ". This, however, is not inevitably the case. The " social character ", *e.g.* of the Germans and, more specifically, of the German lower middle-class during the post-war period was typically neurotic, it showed signs of more than average exhaustion and hostility. It tended, therefore, to an attitude which prepared people for the acceptance of National Socialism. To call such an attitude " necessary and desirable " would not be admissible. Dr. Fromm's mistake seems to be that he attaches a positive value to the notion " social character ", identifying, as it were, " social character " with " healthy social character ". But it is just the temporary divergence of the " social character " from what in given circumstances is " necessary and desirable " that seems to indicate a collective psychical crisis.

88. For a critical discussion of these problems with bibliography cf. Morris Ginsberg, *The Psychology of Society*, Chapter IV : " The Theory of a Social or Group Mind ".

89. David Rodnick, " Group Frustration in Connecticut ", in *Am. Journ. Soc.*, September 1941, pp. 160-62, shows how keen competition immediately generates group hatred and different ways of its rationalisation. Cf. also : Louis Wirth, " Morale and Minority Groups ", *Am. Journ. Soc.*, vol. xlvii, No. 3, 1941, p. 423.

90. " ' State within the State '—that was the accusation which all adversaries of the Jews hurled into their faces ",§ Heinz Bender, *Der Kampf um die Judenemanzipation in Deutschland im Spiegel der Flugschriften 1815–1820*, p. 93.

91. Cf. Note 42 on p. 247.

92. Johann Gottlieb Fichte, *Beitrag zur Berichtigung der Urteile des Publikums über die französiche Revolution*, Zürich und Winterthur, 1844, pp. 134, 137.

93. Cf. Fries, *op. cit.*; Rühs, *op. cit.*; Fichte, *op. cit.* p. 132; Bender, *op. cit.* pp. 16-19.

94. Cf. allusions to the Jewish God as " hostile to humanity ",§ Fichte, *op. cit.* p. 133, to the Talmud; Fries, *op. cit.* p. 251, to the idea of the Chosen People; *v.* Note 42.

95. Werner Sombart, *Deutsche Volkswirtschaft im 19. Jahrhundert*, pp. 78-9.§

96. Walter Frank, *Hofprediger Adolf Stöcker und die christlichsoziale Bewegung*, p. 77.§

97. Frank, *op. cit.* p. 72.

II

THE EPOCH

98. " Capitalism, then, is by nature a form or method of economic change and not only never is but never can be stationary ", Joseph A. Schumpeter, *Capitalism, Socialism and Democracy*, p. 82.

99. The over-simplification of this description also will, we hope, be excused in consideration of the vastness of the subject-matter. We cannot deal with the slow decline of the medieval system of corporations, but think only of the gradual removal of pre-capitalist legal ties which took place during the period of manufacture and was completed during the industrial period. Classical examples are the abolition of the guilds by Turgot in France (1776), the final abolition of the Statute of Elizabeth, fixing the length of apprenticeship and providing for the fixing of wages by the magistrates (1813 and 1814) in England, and the establishment of free trade in Prussia in 1811.

100. How reluctantly people during early capitalism took to the methods of competition and technical progress is described by Sombart, *Der moderne Kapitalismus*, vol. ii, No. 1, pp. 36 *seq.*

101. " Continually we hope that we need not extend still farther, but we always

find that a delay in further extension would mean retrogression, and even to-day improvements and inventions follow each other so quickly that we are still as busy as ever ",§ Carnegie, *Autobiography*, quoted by Sombart, *Der Bourgeois*, pp. 450-51.

102. Werner Sombart, *Der moderne Kapitalismus*, vol. iii, No. 2, pp. 972 *seq.*

103. Werner Sombart, *Deutsche Volkswirtschaft im 19. Jahrhundert*, pp. 398-9, 400, 402.

104. Although Professor Oswald Bumke, *Kultur und Entartung*, 1922, p. 91, quoted by Morris Ginsberg, *Studies in Sociology*, p. 186, stated in 1922 that an increase in mental disease had not been proved, the possibility remains that this is due to the special difficulties of providing suitable evidence. There exists undoubtedly the widespread feeling that maladjustment and nervous disturbances have increased in modern times. Cf. C. E. Playne, *The Neuroses of the Nations*, especially pp. 33, 36 *seq.*, 42-3 ; Bertrand Russell, " The Intellectual in the Modern World ", in *Am. Journ. Soc.*, vol. 44, No. 2, p. 497 : " Hysteria, collective hysteria, is the great danger of the modern world " ; H. G. Baynes, *Germany Possessed*, p. 272 : " It is only too evident that our civilization is suffering from an abundance of ills. . . . The psychiatrists will point to the army of psychotics, neurotics, and psycho-neurotics, to the host of empty and unhappy marriages, to the number of lonely unmarried women, to those people who cannot eat, sleep, make love or perform the elementary bodily functions with any sense of inner security—these, and a multitude of other signs, all tend to show that civilized man is not at peace with his instinctive roots." Cf. also Note 137, quotation from Tillich.

105. Schumpeter, *op. cit.*

106. Schumpeter, *op. cit.* p. 145.

107. *Ibid.* p. 121.

108. *Ibid.* p. 63.

109. *Ibid.* p. 83 and Chapter VII.

110. Sombart, *Der moderne Kapitalismus*, vol. iii, No. 2, p. 1010.§

111. Sombart, *Der Bourgeois*, p. 462.§

112. *Ibid.* p. 449.

113. *Ibid.* p. 228.§

114. Sombart, *Deutsche Volkswirtschaft im 19. Jahrhundert*, pp. 80 *seq.*

115. Herbert Heaton, *Economic History of Europe*, p. 647.

116. Heaton, *op. cit.* pp. 649-50.

117. Milton Steinberg, *The Making of the Modern Jew*, p. 221.

118. The anti-Semite Heinz Bender, *op. cit.* p. 30, admits in his description of the period of counter-emancipation after the Napoleonic Wars : " In der vordersten Linie des Kampfes gegen die Juden standen die vier freien Städte ; Kaufmannschaft und Handwerker empfanden die Bedrohung durch jüdische Konkurrenz fast gleich stark " ; *v.* also Sombart, *Die Juden und das Wirtschaftsleben*, pp. 136 *seq.*

119. Cf. Sombart's distinction—*Die Juden und das Wirtschaftsleben*, pp. 140-41—between fraud and the clash of different " economic attitudes " (*Wirtschaftsgesinnungen*).

120. Sombart, *Die Juden und das Wirtschaftsleben*, *passim*.

121. Sombart, *Deutsche Volkswirtschaft im 19. Jahrhundert*, p. 117.

122. Cf. the judgment given by the anti-Semite Heinz Bender, *op. cit.* p. 55, upon a period as early as that between 1815 and 1820 : " Diese Juden standen zwar für das oberflächliche Urteil ziemlich nahe bei der deutschen gebildeten Gesellschaft ; sie trieben keinen Schacher, sie rochen nicht nach Knoblauch, sie trugen keinen wallenden Bart, sie verachteten das Jiddische so gut wie jeder Deutsche, sie lebten völlig nach westeuropäischem Stil, sie hielten sich für frei von den Erbsünden und Eigenarten ihres Volkes und für die geeigneten Träger der Emanzipation—und waren doch die echten Vertreter ihrer Rasse ".

123. Cf. Frederick L. Schumann, *Hitler and the Nazi Dictatorship. A Study in Social Pathology and the Politics of Fascism*, p. 314.

124. Karl Mannheim, *Diagnosis of Our Time*, p. 101.

125. Morris Ginsberg, *Moral Progress*.

126. " It may be the case that the distance between theory and practice increases instead of diminishing with the multiplications of opportunities for conflict and disharmony, and the weakening of the bonds of custom and authority in modern civilizations ", Morris Ginsberg, *Sociology*, p. 239.

127. L. T. Hobhouse, *World in Conflict*, pp. 33-4 and 36-7, drew attention to

this primary co-existence and its later dissolution; cf. also Franz Schnabel, *Deutsche Geschichte im 19. Jahrhundert*, iv, p. 378.

128. Cf. J. Huizinga, *Der Mensch und die Kultur*, p. 37, on the demoralising effect of the State posing as the measure of all things.

129. Ortega y Gasset, *The Rise of the Masses*, pp. 47-8, comments rightly on the peculiar mixture of a " sense of power " and a " sense of insecurity ".

130. Charles Horton Cooley, *Social Organization. A Study of the Larger Mind*. In spite of his outspoken optimism—cf., *e.g.*, pp. 100 and 354—the author rightly draws attention to the overstrain in modern society; cf. particularly Chapter X, " Superficiality and Strain ", pp. 98-103.

131. L. T. Hobhouse, *Democracy and Reaction*, p. 72.

132. Bertrand Russell, " The Intellectual in the Modern World", in *Am. Journ. Soc.*, vol. xliv, No. 2, p. 496.

133. J. Huizinga, *In the Shadow of To-Morrow. A Diagnosis of the Spiritual Distemper of Our Time*, pp. 54-6 and 59-60.

134. To quote only a few examples : L. T. Hobhouse, *Democracy and Reaction* (*N.B.* especially the remarks on the " Man in the Street ", pp. 71-2) ; L. T. Hobhouse, *The World in Conflict* (*N.B.* especially the remarks on the decline of European morality, pp. 8-11) ; Herbert Spencer, *Facts and Comments*, pp. 65 and 132-3 on " re-barbarization " ; Benedetto Croce, *History of Europe in the 19th Century*, pp. 311, 343, 344-5, on the spiritual situation of Europe before the first World War ; J. Huizinga, *In the Shadow of To-Morrow, passim* ; finally, a German account of the disappearance of ideals from public life and the dissolution of old community ties—Sombart, *Deutsche Volkswirtschaft im 19. Jahrhundert*, final remarks, pp. 371-474.

135. *Civilization, War and Death, passim*.

136. *Ibid.* pp. 51 and 77-8.

137. Paul J. Tillich, " Protestantism in the Present World Situation ", in *Am. Journ. Soc.*, xliii, 242-3 : " Protestantism is a highly intellectualized religion. . . . Protestant education in its reasonable and moralistic attitude, although it was capable of educating selected individuals, failed in the education of the masses. More and more individuals became unable to endure the tremendous responsibility of permanently having to decide in intellectual and moral issues. The weight of this responsibility became so heavy that they could not endure it ; and mental diseases have become epidemic in the United States as well as in Europe." It is interesting in this connection to juxtapose an American and a German view. Edward Scribner Ames, " Morale and Religion ", in *Am. Journ. Soc.*, vol. xlvii, No. 3, p. 391, gives an extremely optimistic description of a modern American religion " of practical reasonableness in accord with modern knowledge and better suited to foster a morale adequate to the needs of the times ". In contrast to this, Professor Ernst Tröltsch, *Spektatorbriefe*, p. 246, thus complains about the spiritual disintegration of the German post-war period. Germany, he argues, is being Americanised economically, technically, and socially. And this process is being carried out without the protection of that Christian and humanitarian outlook which, owing to the Puritan heritage and in spite of everything, still dominates America, checking anarchy and soothing consciences. " Our spiritual life ", Tröltsch continues,§ " lacks the synthesis of spirit, morality, business, and politics, which the Americans possess ". Tröltsch's historical explanation may be complemented by a psychological one. The secularised values of humanitarian idealism may well be sufficient for a healthy land with material prosperity and good individual prospects. In poverty-stricken post-war Germany, badly shaken by crises, they did not prove powerful enough to mobilise sufficient energy for the struggle against the lower human instincts.

138. The interdependence of overstrain and lowering of standards is also stated by Playne, *op. cit.* pp. 31, 33, 36, 44-5, 57-8.

139. Friedrich Meinecke, *Weltbürgertum und Nationalstaat. Studien zur Genesis des deutschen Nationalstaats*, first chapters, especially pp. 187 *seq.*

140. Cf. in this connection Benedetto Croce, *op. cit.* pp. 46 *seq.*, where the difference between the respective efforts demanded by either philosophy is properly expressed. Furthermore, Schnabel, *op. cit.* i, 235, and ii, 19-20; Fritz Strich, *Deutsche Klassik und Romantik oder Vollendung und Unendlichkeit. Ein Vergleich, passim*. Here the antagonism between classicism and romanticism as reflected by French feeling is especially interesting, p. 409 : " What after all has, so it is now being asked [in France], the German spirit brought to the world since it began its

251

world conquest? Chaos instead of order, darkness instead of brightness, anarchy instead of organisation, dream and illusion instead of truth and reality, historic relativism instead of well-founded security, vagrant music instead of plastic and solid shape, individual and national egoism for the idea of humanity, disruption for harmony, Asia for Greece." § Cf., furthermore, Treitschke, *Deutsche Geschichte im 19. Jahrhundert*, i, 308, as well as his remarks on the birth of the Historical Theory of Law from the romantic spirit, ii, 58 *seq.* Particularly pertinent is his remark about some " favourite notions of the Historical School " which oppose historical growth to deliberate creation—*ibid.* p. 63 : they " served thoughtless slothfulness as a welcome bed of ease " § (sie "dienten der gedankenlosen Ruheseligkeit zum willkommenen Lotterbette "). Friedrich Meinecke, *op. cit.* p. 149 calls the romantic conversions to Roman Catholicism " an act of mental exhaustion ".§ What the romantic converts sought in Catholicism was indeed an exoneration from responsibility and a retreat into the realm of those emotions which they had been forced to forgo under the sway of intellectualised Protestantism and humanitarianism.

141. Cf. Morris Ginsberg, *Studies in Sociology*, pp. 49 *seq.*, on the dangerous propensities of the Group Mind with which the Nation soon tended to be endowed by social philosophers.

142. " *Nationalism.*" A Report by a Study Group of Members of the Royal Institute of International Affairs.

143. Friedrich Meinecke, *Weltbürgertum und Nationalstaat.*

144. *Ibid.* p. 151.

145. *Ibid.* p. 207.§

146. *Ibid.* p. 265.

147. *Ibid.* p. 271.

148. *Ibid.* p. 292.§

149. *Ibid.* quoted in German, p. 307.§

150. Cf. similar statements in Schnabel, *op. cit.* They are not interconnected but occur separately in the following passages : i, 288-9 (Schiller), 290-91 (Kant), 295 and 298 (Fichte), 303 and 314 (general development) ; iii. 14, 21, 23, 26 (Hegel), 64-7 (Savigny, Beseler).

151. *Op. cit.* iii, 14 *seq.*, and especially p. 21.

152. *Democracy and Reaction*, pp. 83-7, 93-4.

153. *World in Conflict*, pp. 38 *seq.*

154. On the impression Bismarck made, particularly abroad, cf. Hobhouse, *Democracy and Reaction*, p. 81, and Croce, *19th Century*, chapter " Change in the Public Spirit of Europe (1870) ".

155. Herbert Spencer, *Facts and Comments*, p. 132 ; Morris Ginsberg, *Sociology*, p. 239.

156. *World in Conflict*, pp. 50-51.

157. *Op. cit.* p. 81.

157a. Sombart, *Deutsche Volkswirtschaft im 19. Jahrhundert*, p. 474.

158. Cf. the writer's article " Der Untergang des Judentums ", in *Der Morgen*, vol. viii, No. 1, pp. 68-9, where the degree of dependence of the cultural on the economic sphere is further discussed.

159. Cf. A. Menes, " Die Judenfrage im Lichte der Konjunkturentwicklung", in *Jüdische Wohlfahrtspflege und Sozialpolitik*, 1933, January–February, pp. 5-15.

160. Remarks on the moral potentialities of a prosperous society and the contrary are to be found in Schnabel, *op. cit.* ii, 94, iv, 378 ; Burckhardt, *Weltgeschichtliche Betrachtungen*, p. 66 ; Louis Wirth, " Morale and Minority Groups ", in *Am. Journ. Soc.*, xlvii, 432 ; Harold Laski, *Reflections on the Revolution of our Time*, pp. 152-3. On latent tendencies of contraction in capitalism, cf. Sombart, *19. Jahrhundert*, pp. 214, 221.

161. Cf. Hobhouse, *World in Conflict*, p. 30, and Playne, *op. cit.* pp. 28-9 on the moral implications of the Victorian style of life.

162. *Die Revolution des Nihilismus.*

163. Morris Ginsberg, *Sociology*, p. 241.

164. *Capitalism, Socialism, and Democracy*, p. 5.

165. *Ibid.* p. 6.

166. Adopting a definition by Professor Ginsberg—*Studies in Sociology*, p. 161— according to which class-consciousness consists of a feeling of equality in relation to the members of one's own class, of inferiority in relation to those above in the

hierarchy, and of superiority in relation to those below, the achievement of Marxism may be thus explained. It greatly strengthened the feeling of equality and transformed the feeling of absolute inferiority of a class at the bottom of the social ladder into one of absolute superiority, since this class was henceforth confident that it would supersede all the other existing classes.

167. Cf. August Bebel, *Sozialdemokratie und Antisemitismus*, p. 16.

168. Robert Michels, " Psychologie der antikapitalistischen Massen-Bewegungen ", in *Grundriss der Sozialökonomik*, vol. ix, No. 1, pp. 247 and 320, points out that the first supporters of Socialism came mostly from the lower middle-class. He explains this partly by the relatively better education of this class that " made it easier for them to grasp the ideas of socialism and qualified them to a higher extent for leadership in the movement than the totally uneducated factory workers, who came partly from the ranks of peasants and rural workers ".§

169. Eva Jungmann, *Spontaneität und Ideologie als Faktoren der modernen sozialen Bewegungen*, second part.

170. Cf. Michels, *op. cit.* pp. 287 *seq.* (education) ; p. 357 (discipline).

171. *Op. cit.* p. 7.

172. *Ibid.* pp. 14-15, 17.

173. *Ibid.* p. 19.

174. Sombart, *Der moderne Kapitalismus*, vol. iii, No. 1, p. 355.

175. Sombart, *19. Jahrhundert*, p. 27.

176. G. Neuhaus, " Die berufliche und soziale Gliederung im Zeitalter des Kapitalismus ", in *Grundriss der Sozialökonomik*, vol. ix, No. 1, p. 373.

177. Sombart, *19. Jahrhundert*, p. 395.

178. Goetz Briefs, " Das gewerbliche Proletariat ", in *Grundriss der Sozialökonomik*, vol. ix, No. 1, p. 188.

179. Sombart, *19. Jahrhundert*, p. 28.

180. " From 1895 to 1907 the number of employers in industry and mining decreased by 2·52 per cent, that of the workers increased by 44·28 per cent, that of the black-coated workers by 160·10 per cent. As compared with 1882, the number of employers decreased by 7·09 per cent, that of the workers increased by 109·78 per cent, that of the black-coated workers by 592·40 per cent. From 1882 to 1907, the proportion of black-coated workers in the population of the big cities increased from 6·5 per cent to 12·7 per cent, while at the same time the proportion of employers receded from 31·9 per cent to 18·8 per cent." From Emil Lederer and Jakob Marschak, " Der neue Mittelstand ", in *Grundriss der Sozialökonomik*, vol. ix, No. 1, pp. 127-8.§

181. The state of exhaustion should not be taken as indicating a mere bodily weariness resulting from strenuous work, which would, *e.g.*, not apply to part of the officials. It rather suggests a combination of both physical and mental strain to which urban conditions, tiring amusements, and the whole exertion of modern life contribute.

182. Goetz Briefs, *op. cit.* pp. 186 *seq.*

183. Sombart, *19. Jahrhundert*, p. 411.

184. The Wars of Liberation were, at the time when they broke out, waged predominantly by Prussia, later on by a coalition. At no time was the whole of Germany ranged on one side.

185. Morris Ginsberg, " Anti-Semitism ", in *Reason and Unreason in Society*, Chapter x, pp. 196 *seq.*

186. Cf. what has been said above—pp. 89 *seq.*—on Marxist Socialism. Cf., furthermore, V. M. Dean, " Attack on Democracy ", pp. 18-19, in *New Governments in Europe*, on the functioning of democracy in a prosperous and well-integrated society, also Schnabel, *op. cit.* ii, 137-8 ; the view that democracy is remote from the instincts is largely confirmed by Ortega y Gasset, *op. cit.* p. 83 : " The political doctrine which has represented the loftiest endeavour towards common life is liberal democracy. . . . Liberalism . . . is the supreme form of generosity. . . . It announces the determination to share existence with the enemy ; more than that, with an enemy which is weak. It was incredible that the human species should have arrived at so noble an attitude, so paradoxical, so refined, so acrobatic, so anti-natural. Hence it is not to be wondered at that this same humanity should soon appear anxious to get rid of it. It is a discipline too difficult and complex to take firm root on earth."

187. *19th Century*, pp. 321-2.

188. Graham Wallas, *Human Nature in Politics.*

189. Graham Wallas, *op. cit.* p. 5.
190. *Ibid.* p. 4.
191. *Ibid.* pp. 5, 174, 176-7.
192. A detailed appreciation of Wallas's book would be beyond the scope of this study. But this much should be said : it would be worth while to compare some of its remarks with corresponding passages of Hitler's *Mein Kampf.* A certain similarity cannot be denied. But while Wallas regards the imperfections of the shaping of the democratic will with serious anxiety, looking all the time for suitable remedies, Hitler sees in the same imperfections his great opportunity. Hitler is indeed the future cynic, the contemner of Man, whose horrible image Wallas sees emerge from the deficiencies of democracy, cf. pp. 173-4 : "After a time the politician may cease even to desire to reason with his constituents, and may come to regard them as purely irrational creatures of feeling and opinion, and himself as the purely rational 'overman' who controls them. It is at this point that a resolute and able statesman may become most efficient and most dangerous."
193. *Reflections on Violence.* Translated by T. E. Hulme.
194. Similarly disillusioned are the remarks of Sombart, *19. Jahrhundert*, pp. 471-2.
195. Cf. also his other work, *Les Illusions du progrès.*
196. *Les Illusions du progrès*, p. 335.
197. *Reflections on Violence*, pp. 270-76.
198. Cf. especially Sorel's praise of the anarchists who taught the workers "that they need not be ashamed of acts of violence", *Reflections*, etc., p. 41. His appreciation of an administration of law by the people as contrasted to ordinary jurisdiction (*Reflections*, p. 207) ominously foreshadows conditions in Nazi Germany.
199. *Les Illusions du progrès*, p. 335.
200. *Reflections*, p. 294.
201. *Ibid.* p. 298.
202. Eva Jungmann, *op. cit.* Part II.
203. Pietro Gorgolini says in his book *The Fascist Movement in Italian Life*, translated and edited by M. D. Petre, to which Mussolini wrote an introduction, calling it " the best publication on Fascism that has appeared in Italy since March, 1919, until to-day ", p. 34 : " His [Mussolini's] socialism could be defined as that of Sorel " ; p. 52 : " If we did not fear to be called heretics, or charged with exaggeration, we would simply declare that there is no great or substantial difference in ideas and programme between the Fascists and the Sorelian socialists ".
204. " Social duty no more exists than does international duty ", Sorel, *Reflections*, etc., p. 65 (in italics).
205. Democracy and Reaction, pp. 168-9.
206. In 1930 there was a poll of 82 per cent ; on 31st July 1932 of 84 per cent ; on 5th March 1933 of 88·7 per cent.
207. Cf. Morris Ginsberg, *Psychology of Society*, pp. 158 *seq.* ; Alfred Cobban, *Dictatorship. Its History and Theory*, pp. 239-40 ; V. M. Dean, *op. cit.* pp. 19-20 ; Buell, 2nd Preface, p. xvi, in *New Governments in Europe* ; Paul J. Tillich, " Protestantism in the Present World-Situation ", in *Am. Journ. Soc.*, xliii, 240 ; Erich Fromm, *Fear of Freedom*, p. 134.
208. Cf. Cobban, *op. cit.* pp. 231, 233, 236-7 ; Robert A. Brady, *The Spirit and Structure of German Fascism*, pp. 71, 74-5 ; Gasset, *op. cit.* pp. 120 *seq.*

III

THE SCENE

209. Schnabel, *op. cit.* i, 35-6.
210. *Ibid.* i, 82.
211. *Ibid.* i, 83-4.
212. Cf. Schnabel, i, 87, 104-5, ii, 16-17 ; Ernst Tröltsch, " Der Ansturm der westlichen Demokratie ", in *Die deutsche Freiheit*, p. 88.
213. This prepared the way for Hitler's deliberate falsification of the term, cf. below, pp. 219-20.

214. An illuminating comment on the way in which national questions, *i.e.* questions of foreign policy, counteracted home politics in Germany is to be found in Burckhardt, *Weltgeschichtliche Betrachtungen*, pp. 203-4 and 205.
215. Cf. Ernst Moritz Arndt's poem, "Was ist des Deutschen Vaterland?" and E. M. Arndt, *Geist der Zeit*, iv, 259.
216. Henri Pirenne, *Histoire de l'Europe des invasions au XVIème siècle*, p. 208, quoted by Buell, 2nd Preface, p. xvii, in *New Governments in Europe*.
217. William McDougall, *The Group Mind*, p. 128, attributes " the great myth of the racial unity and superiority of the German people " to the deliberate endeavour "to remedy by art the lack of natural boundaries and of a true national homogeneity ".
218. *Geschichte*, i, 90.
219. *World in Conflict*, p. 100.
220. " Wotan ", Chapter i, pp. 1 *seq.* in *Aufsätze zur Zeitgeschichte*.
221. *Die Erhebung Israels gegen die christlichen Güter*, p. 141.
222. *Europe and the German Question*, p. 446.
223. " Letter from Germany ", in *Stories, Essays, and Poems*, pp. 283-6.
224. Sombart, *19. Jahrhundert*, p. 443.
225. *Ibid.* p. 444.
226. Cf. also Croce, *19th Century*, pp. 125 *seq.*
227. *Op. cit.* ii, pp. 204-6.
228. *Ibid.* ii, p. 373.
229. Cf. Croce on the years between 1815 and 1830 : " This was truly the great European age of Germanism ", *19th Century*, p. 85.
230. The publisher Perthes, in referring to Hegel, pointed to " the dangers which will slowly but steadily move from professors and privy counsellors to school-teachers and clerks "; cf. Schnabel, *op. cit.* iv, p. 565.§
231. Equally significant is this remark of Treitschke's which deals with the great German literature since 1750, *v. Geschichte*, i, 90 § : ". . . this literary revolution has determined the character of German literature. It made this country again the focal country of heresy by developing the fundamental idea of the Reformation into the right of unrestricted enquiry (voraussetzungslos freie Forschung)."
232. This point is emphasised, *e.g.* by Schnabel, *op. cit.* iv, 563 *seq.*
233. *Ausgewählte Schriften*, p. 28.
234. *Geschichte*, i, 6-7.
235. Cf. also the following judgment on German irreligion written by Treitschke in 1861, *Ausgewählte Schriften*, vol. i, " Die Freiheit ", p. 26.§ (It is noteworthy that he does not oppose irreligion as such, but the lack of courage in professing irreligion). " He who has any idea to what a tremendous extent the younger generation has lost faith in the dogmas of Christian revelation, can only watch with deep concern with what thoughtlessness, with what laziness, nay, with what mendacity thousands pay lip-service to a faith which has become alien to their hearts." Edmond Vermeil, *Germany's Three Reichs*, p. 106, ascribes religious disintegration in Germany both to the confessional dualism and "confessional territorialism ". *Ibid.* p. 108, *v.* on " the immense advance of German culture after the middle of the eighteenth century ".
236. *Op. cit.* iv, 269 *seq.*
237. *Ibid.* iv, 575.
238. Schumpeter, *op. cit.* p. 6.
239. Treitschke, *Geschichte*, ii, 112-13 ; Schnabel, *op. cit.* ii, 34.
240. A detailed account of this is given by G. P. Gooch, *Germany and the French Revolution*.
241. *Ibid.* p. 354.
242. *Ibid.* pp. 295 *seq.* On the connection between the German political reality and Hegel's political theories, cf. also Vermeil, *op. cit.* p. 45.
243. *Die Berliner Romantik 1800 bis 1814*, and *Literaturgeschichte der deutschen Stämme und Landschaften*, i, 5 ; ii, 5 *seq.*
244. *Die Berliner Romantik*, p. 45.
245. *Literaturgeschichte*, iii, 1.§
246. *Ibid.* i, 6.§
247. *Ibid.* iii, 10.§ Treitschke, too—*Geschichte*, i, 309—sees the part played by the contrast between North and South Germany in romanticism.
248. On the shortcomings of early German nationalism, cf. Treitschke's judg-

ment on " Turnvater " Jahn, the last sentence of which sounds like a prophecy—
Geschichte, i, 306 : § " It showed an unhealthy state of affairs that the sons of a brilliant people revered a clamorous barbarian as their teacher ".

249. Schnabel, *op. cit.* iii, 52.

250. *Ibid.* iii, 52.

251. Treitschke, *Geschichte*, ii, 63 ; Schnabel. *op. cit.* iii, 59.

252. That also, apart from anti-Semitism, anti-capitalism was apt to foment the German discord can be clearly seen from a memorandum by George Erichson, " Manuskript aus Süddeutschland ", published in London, 1820. This pamphlet advocated the so-called Trias Policy, *i.e.* the unification of Southern Germany against Prussia on the one hand and Austria on the other. The pamphlet mentions, of course with disapproval, the " mobile tradesmen of the North " as against " the settled people of the highland ",§ by Treitschke, *Geschichte*, iii, 55.

253. Treitschke, *Geschichte*, ii, 63.

254. Cf. Morris Ginsberg's critical remarks on the Historical Law in *The Psychology of Society*, pp. 113-16.

255. Nadler, *Literaturgeschichte*, iii, 214, assumes even an especially close relation between Jews and romanticism.

256. *Antisemitismus und Anti-Germanismus*, pp. 35-6.§

257. *Mythus des 20. Jahrhunderts*, p. 22.§ Cf. also *ibid.* pp. 137 and 695-8.

258. Thorstein Veblen, *Imperial Germany and the Industrial Revolution*, p. 86 : " The case of Germany is unexampled among Western nations . . . as regards the abruptness, thoroughness, and amplitude of its appropriation of this technology and as regards the archaism of its cultural furniture at the date of this appropriation ". Sombart, *Kapitalismus*, p. 484, maintains that the 50 years between 1850 and 1900 brought about more profound changes in Germany than the whole of the preceding five centuries.

259. The industrialisation of Soviet Russia cannot serve as a basis of comparison as, owing to the nature of the regime, no spontaneous popular reactions could there be recorded. But it is these spontaneous reactions which, in the case of Germany, are our major concern.

260. Cf. Edward B. Reuter, *Race and Culture Contacts*, Introduction, pp. 13-14.

261. Cf. Thorstein Veblen, *op. cit.* p. 86, where this contradiction is attributed mainly to the taking over of a ready-made technology.

262. Schumpeter emphasises the intrinsic pacifism of capitalist economy, *op. cit.* pp. 127-9. Cf. also Veblen, *op. cit.* p. 253.

263. Georg Adler, *Geschichte der ersten sozialistischen Arbeiterbewegung in Deutschland*, pp. 160 *seq.*

264. *Ibid.* pp. 196 *seq.*

265. *Caliban oder Politik und Leidenschaft*, p. 32.§

266. Schnabel, *op. cit.* i, 98.

267. Cf. Schnabel, *op. cit.* i, 99 *seq.* ; Sombart, *19. Jahrhundert*, p. 468.

268. Schnabel, *op. cit.* ii, 57, 92.

269. Toynbee, *A Study of History*, ii, 58, regards the Prussian efficiency as an especially convincing example of the " stimulus of hard countries ".

270. Treitschke, *Geschichte*, iii, 199,§ remarks on the incorporation of the Catholic Rhine provinces : " Now arose . . . the incomparably more difficult task of accustoming also the focal countries of the Roman Catholic unity in faith and of the theocratic Weltanschauung to the common law of a State with religious equality. All enemies of Germany considered this undertaking as hopeless, and hoped confidently that Prussia would perish of the fatal gift (*Danaergeschenk*) of these Western provinces."

271. Schnabel, *op. cit.* i, 96.§

272. Cf. Schnabel, *op. cit.* ii, 271, 272 *seq.*, 303-6 ; Meinecke, *Weltbürgertum und Nationalstaat*, Part II : " Der preussische Nationalstaat und der deutsche Nationalstaat ".

273. Quoted by Meinecke, *op. cit.* p. 298.§

274. Cf. Meinecke, *op. cit.* pp. 487 *seq.* Schnabel, *op. cit.* ii, 132, attributes the consolidation of monarchical power in contrast to Western parliamentarianism to the personal weight of Bismarck, who prevailed " by the means that Prussian history had passed on to him ".§

275. *Geschichte*, i, 299-301.§

276. Cf. among others on this point Friedrich von Hügel, *The German Soul in*

its attitude towards Ethics and Christianity, the State and War, pp. 144 *seq.*; Playne, *op. cit.* p. 452.

277. R. J. Baker, "National Socialism and the Social Sciences", in *The Sociological Review*, xxxi, 96 and 99, discusses the consequences of the fact that acute class conflicts emerged at a time when Germany was still struggling towards national unity.

278. The difference between political conditions in Germany and Britain can be gauged by the following remarks of the British sociologist Dr. McDougall, *The Group Mind*, pp. 84-5 : " One other virtue of the group spirit must be mentioned. Although it tends to bring similar groups into keen rivalry and even into violent conflict, the antagonism between men who are moved to conflict by the group spirit is less bitter than that between individuals who are brought into conflict by personal motives. . . . The members of each group, recognising that their antagonists are also moved by the group spirit, by loyalty and devotion to the group, will sympathise with and respect their motives far more readily and fully than they would, if they ascribed to their opponents purely egoistic motives . . . in this way it (the group spirit) renders possible that continuance of friendly relations between members of bitterly opposed parties which has happily been the rule and at the same time the seeming anomaly of English public life." In Germany, the direct opposite was the case. The very allegiance to a political group different from one's own made a fellow-man one's personal enemy. Even close friendships were destroyed if political divergences divided the friends from each other. Michael Müller-Claudius remarks in *Deutsche Rassenangst*, p. 26 : " Nowhere on earth do political disagreements make such irreconcilable enemies as in Germany ".§ Treitschke, *Geschichte*, iii, 431,§ attributes this mutual intolerance between Germans to the " long centuries of German powerlessness ". Cf., furthermore, Cooley, *Social Organisation*, p. 302, on the peculiar German " class-bitterness " and Edward Alsworth Ross, *Foundations of Sociology*, p. 289, on the aggravating effect of hard times on group conflicts.

279. Mildred S. Wertheimer, *The Pan-German League, 1890-1914*, p. 21.

280. " The Pan-German League strives for . . . the co-ordination of the entire Deutschtum all over the globe " : Fritz Bley, *Die Weltstellung des Deutschtums*.§ Cf. also these passages from the official handbook of the Pan-German League for the year 1908, quoted and translated by M. S. Wertheimer, *op. cit.* p. 95 : ". . . to oppose everything which is un-German ", and : " It believes that the national development of the German people is not completed ". The programme of the League—*Handbook of 1914*, quoted and translated *ibid.*—says among other things : the League works for " the combating of all forces which check the German national development ".

281. A great deal of material taken from the German Press of 1912-13 is contained in Otfried Nippold, *Der deutsche Chauvinismus*. The material is the more convincing as it comprises much more than the official Pan-German literature. More evidence can be found in every publication of the Pan-German League.

282. Heinrich Class, the president of the Pan-German League from 1908, writes under the pseudonym Daniel Frymann in *Wenn ich Kaiser wär'* (If I were the Kaiser), p. 27 : § " The sanctity of peace in every speech from the throne, in all discussions on foreign politics within and without the parliament and in the Press, always those phrases on peace, until they become sickening to a healthy person ".

283. Class-Frymann, *op. cit.* pp. 5 *seq.*

284. Appeal of the Pan-German League printed on the cover of Fritz Bley, *op. cit.* : " The German race is a master-race ". *Alldeutsche Blätter, 1913*, p. 284, quoted by Veit Valentin, *Deutschlands Aussenpolitik von Bismarcks Abgang bis zum Ende des Weltkrieges*,§ p. 256 : ". . . a high-minded master-race that feels itself called to acquire world domination ".

285. Fritz Bley, *op. cit.* p. 24.§

286. Fritz Bley, *op. cit.* pp. 5 *seq.*

287. *Ibid.*§

288. Quoted by Rauschning, *Revolution des Nihilismus*, p. 172.§

289. Class-Frymann, *op. cit.* p. 27-8.

290. Cf. Wertheimer, *op. cit.* p. 73.

291. Cf. Wertheimer, *op. cit.* p. 70.

292. Cf. Hans Gerth, " The Nazi Party. Its Leadership and Composition ", in *Am. Journ. Soc.*, xlv, 525. Le Bon, *The Psychology of Socialism*, pp. 52-3, already mentions the rôle of teachers in movements of dissatisfied elements.

293. Fritz Bley, *op. cit.*: § " The position achieved in 1870–71 has imposed duties and tasks on the German people, the neglect of which would result in the ruin of our Volkstum ". Cf. also Lehr, *Zwecke und Ziele des Alldeutschen Verbandes*, p. 77, quoted by Wertheimer, *op. cit.* pp. 100-101.

294. *Op. cit.* p. 196.

295. According to Wertheimer, *op. cit.* p. 76, 32 per cent of the members in 1914 had the degree of Dr. Phil.

296. It will be sufficient to quote the statement of Benjamin Ginzburg, article " Anti-Semitism ", in *Encyclopaedia of the Social Sciences*, p. 121 : " The norm and archetype of modern anti-Semitism is to be found in Germany ", and *ibid.* : " In Germany anti-Semitism, in its peculiarly modern sense, has been developed as a philosophy and as a political movement ".

297. In making this statement we are not unmindful of the fact that, as a result of the central position of Germany, the Jewish problem there showed certain elements of tension which had disappeared in Western Europe, except in England after the mass immigration since the turn of the 19th century. But these elements of tension—such as comparatively large Jewish population, immigration first from the Jewish mass settlements in Posen, then from Poland, the relatively strong perseverance of Jewish religions and cultural interests—were largely compensated by the effect of Jewish-Gentile integration. That in spite of the steady normalisation of Jewish-Gentile relations, intellectual anti-Semitism continued to emphasise the contrast was mainly due to the national peculiarity which is being discussed here and to differences of political outlook.

298. Willi Buch, *Fünfzig Jahre antisemitische Bewegung*, p. 46, *e.g.*, complains that Professor Hasse, who led the League from 1900 to 1908, repudiated anti-Semitism.

299. Class-Frymann, *op. cit.* pp. 30 *seq.*, 116, 253 *seq.*

300. *Ibid.* p. 77.

301. *Ibid.*

302. Wertheimer, *op. cit.* pp. 99-100.

303. The Pan-German League was a corporative member of the Gobineau Association, built up along racial lines—Wertheimer, *op. cit.* p. 18.

304. For further examples for the close relations between Pan-Germanism and anti-Semitism *v.* Wertheimer, *op. cit.* pp. 136-7, 142-3.

305. *Geschichte*, iii, 703-4.

306. *Briefe berühmter christlicher Zeitgenossen über die Judenfrage*, ed. J. Singer, p. 163.

307. Ernst Jörges, *Die weltgeschichteliche Bedeutung des Judentums und seine Zukunft*, pp. 72-4.

308. Eugen Dühring, *Die Judenfrage als Frage des Rassencharakters und seiner Schädlichkeit für Existenz und Kultur der Völker*.

309. *Ibid.* pp. 107-8. It is worth mentioning that Dühring writes in connection with this matter that people tried to degrade him by imputing to him megalomania and persecution mania.

310. *Ibid.* p. 33.

311. *Ibid.* p. 7.

312. *Ibid.* Supplement, pp. 143 *seq.*, and *passim*.

313. *Ibid.* pp. 82 *seq.*

314. *Ibid.* p. 93.

315. *Ibid.* pp. 69-70.

316. *Ibid.* p. 11.

317. *Ibid.* p. 130.

318. *Ibid.* p. 71. This expression is obviously an allusion to the words attributed to the German Emperor Frederick III calling anti-Semitism " the shame of the century ".

319. *Ibid.* p. 113.

320. *Ibid.* p. 112.

321. Cf. Joseph Becker, *Paul de Lagarde*, pp. 37 *seq.*

322. *Ibid.* p. 24.

323. Quoted by Becker, *op. cit.* p. 30.§

324. Quoted by Becker, *ibid.* p. 31.§

325. Quoted by Becker, *ibid.*, p. 32.§

326. Quoted by Becker, *ibid.* p. 32.§

327. Paul de Lagarde, *Deutsche Schriften*, p. 413.§

328. Becker, *op. cit.* pp. 33 *seq.*

329. Paul de Lagarde, *Lipmann Zunz und seine Verehrer*, p. 161.

330. The Jews fail " to realise that a single soul only should live in a nation and that there should not exist Protestants by the side of Catholics, not to mention Jews by the side of both ". *Lipmann Zunz*, etc., p. 161.§

331. Houston Stewart Chamberlain, *Grundlagen des 19. Jahrhunderts*, Part I, p. 530.§

332. Houston Stewart Chamberlain, *The Foundations of the 19th Century*. Translated by John Lees, i, 531.

333. *Ibid.* German edition, i, 18.

334. *Ibid.* English edition, i, 576.

335. *Ibid.* English edition, i, 553.

336. *Ibid.* English edition, i, 328.

337. *Ibid.* German edition, i, 18.

338. *Ibid.* English edition, ii, 483.

339. It would lead too far to analyse the anti-Semitism of every German writer to see how far it was the outcome of specific German conditions. Yet with reference to Chamberlain, an utterance of his father-in-law, Richard Wagner, should be reported which is a particularly convincing example of anti-Semitic fear of catastrophe. Wagner, in a letter to King Ludwig II of Bavaria *—quoted by Curt von Westernhagen in *Nietzsche, Juden, Antijuden* §—protests against the King's "balanced judgment " on the Jews. He writes ". . . I consider the Jewish race the born enemy of pure humanity and of everything noble in it ; it is certain that especially we Germans shall perish from the Jews, and I am perhaps the last German who knows how to remain erect against Judaism which already rules everything ".

340. Wilhelm Stapel, *Antisemitismus und Anti-Germanismus, passim*.

341. *Ibid.* p. 76.§

342. *Ibid.* p. 30-31.§

343. *Ibid.* p. 71-2.§

344. *Ibid.* p. 108.§

345. *Ibid.* p. 105.§

346. Stapel also makes some utterly absurd statements ; he maintains, *e.g.* p. 59, that the posture of one who reads writings of a German-Jewish author becomes at once " peculiarly askew ",§ that the " nerve-messages flash into the forearms and hands and are strangely quick about it " ! § Equally far-fetched and objectionable is his criticism of the biographies of Goethe written by Jewish authors, p. 21.

347. Josef Nadler, *Literaturgeschichte der deutschen Stämme und Landschaften*.

348. Unfortunately Nadler revised his history of literature after the Nazi rise to power according to the National Socialist doctrine, in the Third Edition, of 1938. Our analysis is based on his earlier judgments on Judaism and Jews.

349. Cf. *ibid.* iv, 372 on Gabriel Riesser, Ludwig Simon-Trier, and Eduard Simson ; iv, 342 on Berthold Auerbach ; iv, 727 on Walther Heymann ; particularly characteristic is his judgment on the half-Jew Paul Heyse, iv, 459-60, and on Julius Moser, who came from a family that had been converted for 250 years and in which numerous mixed marriages had taken place, iv, 205 ; *v.* furthermore, remarks about joint literary work of Jews and non-Jews in Königsberg, iv, 183 ; and on Georg Herwegh, whom Nadler declares arbitrarily as of Jewish descent, iv, 243-4. The convert and later Protestant theologian Neander and the likewise converted composer Felix Mendelssohn Bartholdy are mentioned as examples of the " spiritual solution ",§ iv, 112-13.

350. Cf. the above-mentioned co-operation of Jews in the romantic movement, *ibid.* iii, 214 ; the journalistic talent of the Jews, iv, 156.

351. *V.* iv, 895-6. In this passage Nadler makes the mistake of assuming that Rainer Maria Rilke is of Jewish extraction. Incidentally, Nadler's instinct for the racial origin of the authors he discusses leaves much to be desired. This is particularly striking when those writers are concerned whose works Nadler considers literary masterpieces. The fourth and last volume of his history of literature, *e.g.*, ends with an apotheosis of Rudolf Borchardt, Rilke, and Hugo von Hofmannsthal. There Nadler says about the Jew Borchardt that his work " created a new spiritual situation among the Germans "—pp. 730-31 §—that it is " simply great Germanic tradition ", that its " inner configuration (Gefüge) " is " spiritually East German ", *ibid.*§ He uses similar words expressing the highest appreciation with regard to Hofmannsthal. He obviously does not know of the Jewish descent of both. Thus

---

* Of 22nd November 1881, published in *Bayrischer Festspielführer*, 1936, Bayreuth, pp. 105 *seq.*

he praises as the greatest living poets three men, two of whom are of Jewish origin which Nadler does not know, and one of whom he thinks to be a Jew although he is a non-Jew. It is less remarkable that Nadler equally fails to recognise the editor of the *Süddeutsche Monatshefte*, Nicolaus Cossmann, as of Jewish extraction—iv, 696. As to the converted son of Dorothea Mendelssohn's first marriage, the painter Philipp Veit, Nadler admits only reluctantly and belatedly his Jewish lineage—iv, 316. He mentions him repeatedly before, particularly iv, 71, as " adorned with the glory of the battles of Dresden, Kulm, and Leipzig, in which he had fought " § without, as is usually his custom, mentioning his Jewish parents.

352. *Ibid.* iv, 7.§
353. *Ibid.* iv, 10.§
354. *Ibid.* iv, 631-2.§
355. *Ibid.* iv, 19.§
356. *Ibid.* iv, 135.§
357. *Ibid.* iv, 137.§
358. *Ibid.* iv, 135.§
359. *Ibid.* iv, 169.§
360. *Ibid.* iv, 169, 190.§
361. *Ibid.* iv, 192.§
362. *Ibid.* iv, 218.
363. *Ibid.* iv, 306.§
364. *Ibid.* iv, 306.
365. *Ibid.* iv, 167.§ But for this achievement Jacoby receives unfortunately the attribute " born agitator " (*geborener Aufwiegler*), while the revolutionary part played by the non-Jew Büchner and his associates is highly praised, iv, 271.
366. *Ibid.* iv, 111.§
367. A noteworthy exception is Michael Müller-Claudius, the title of whose book, *Deutsche Rassenangst*, reveals the tenor of his protest.
367a. Felix A. Theilhaber, *Der Untergang der deutschen Juden.*

IV

THE CATASTROPHE

368. Cf. Graham Wallas, *Human Nature in Politics*, p. 106, on the relatively greater weight of opinions which are " nearer sense, nearer to our more ancient revolutionary past ".
369. Nationalism, ridding itself of more and more of its universal obligations and debased to an increasingly crude collective egotism, has been mentioned above as one of the most important examples of the lowering of standards during the 19th and 20th centuries. The same phenomenon has later been dealt with in its specifically German aspect. Since, in the degeneration of German nationalism after the first World War, elements of time and place can no longer be disentangled, the whole phenomenon will be discussed in the context of the trends primarily originating from the German scene, *v.* below, pp. 182 *seq.*
370. Cf. Hans Gerth, *op. cit.* pp. 529-30; Franz Neumann, *Behemoth*, p. 25; on the age of the Social Democratic members of the Reichstag compared with those of the Communist and National Socialist Parties *v.* Buell, *op. cit.* p. 168.
371. Franz Neumann, *op. cit.* pp. 330 *seq.*
372. Such an independent observer of his time as the philosopher Professor Ernst Tröltsch, speaks in his *Spektator-Briefe* repeatedly of a " class-struggle " waged by the formerly leading orders against the State of Weimar, *e.g.* on 19th December 1919, p. 91, and on 6th April 1920, p. 128. On 12th December 1921, pp. 242-3, he describes in what way German industry used the Press, which it had purchased to a considerable extent, for this struggle.
373. Cf. Ernst Tröltsch, *op. cit.*, on the change of the public attitude. On p. 14 Tröltsch remarks on the revolution of 1918 : § " Nobody thought as yet of the lie of the ' stab in the back ' or ' unconquered in the field '. Rather everyone felt he had been betrayed by the propaganda of the hitherto governing classes." However, on 23rd May 1919, p. 53, he writes : § " The whole legend asserted itself again that only the defeatists at home, the Jews and Social Democrats had broken the spine of the proud army ". And on 19th December 1919, Tröltsch writes, p. 92 : § " The great historical legend on which the whole Reaction is based, main-

taining that a victorious army was treacherously stabbed in the back by 'fellows without a fatherland', has thus become the dogma and the banner of the dissatisfied".

374. The general adoption of this view commenced with Hermann Rauschning's book, *Germany's Revolution of Destruction*. It is Rauschning's main thesis that National Socialism was founded on no ideology whatever, but was a fundamentally nihilist movement. A similar opinion is expressed in a particularly pertinent way by Hans H. Gerth in a review of Hans Kohn, "Revolutions and Dictatorships", in the *Am. Journ. Soc.*, November 1941, pp. 499-600. The same line is taken by Schumann, *op. cit.* p. 96. Positive attempts to discover the ideological genesis of Nazism are made by G. A. Borghese, "The Intellectual Origins of Fascism", in *Social Research*, vol. i, 1934, pp. 467 *seq.* and Alfred Cobban, *Dictatorship. Its History and Theory*, pp. 188 and 287-8. An especially valuable contribution to this discussion is also made by Carl Mayer in his article, "On the Intellectual Origin of Fascism", in *Social Research*, vol. ix, 1942. But despite all the qualifications he makes, he still takes the ideological foundations of Nazism too seriously.

375. Franz Neumann, *Behemoth*: "A National Socialist Economic Theory: The Myth of the Corporative State", pp. 187 *seq.*

376. Carl Schmitt: *Staat, Bewegung, Volk*; "Nationalsozialistisches Rechtsdenken", in *Deutsches Recht*, No. 10 of 25th May 1934, pp. 225-9; "Das Gesetz als Plan und Wille des Führers. A Lecture", in *Berliner Börsenzeitung*, No. 471, of 8th October 1935; "Die deutsche Rechtswissenschaft im Kampf gegen den jüdischen Geist", in *Deutsche Juristen-Zeitung*, No. 20 of 15th October 1936, pp. 1194-9.

377. The devastating effect of a debased Historical Law becomes, *e.g.*, clear from these remarks by Tirala, *Race, Mind and Soul*, p. 19: "Law is not the same among all men, but is as different as the peoples and races out of which it arises. Law is nothing else than the expression of a biological fact. . . . Equal rights and equal conceptions of the law exist just as little as do equal peoples and races."

378. *Op. cit.* p. 81.

379. *Op. cit.* pp. 297-8.

380. The emphasis laid on the distinction of the two phases before and after the seizure of power does not mean to suggest that distinctions might not be drawn between many other stages in the development of National Socialism, according to the criterion one chooses to apply. Since, in the context of this study, the criterion is the strength of German anti-Semitism, which can be assessed only by the spontaneous attitude of the German masses, the most important division lies at the point which changed this attitude from a spontaneous, though conditioned, one into one controlled by the Gestapo.

381. Freud, *Group Psychology and the Analysis of the Ego*, p. 105, with reference to festivals like the saturnalia, carnival, etc., which owe their cheerful character to the fact that they released the ego from renunciations and repressions usually imposed on it by the super-ego.

382. Freud, *Civilization, War and Death*, p. 12.

383. On the Nazi rejection of Reason, cf. Hitler, *Speeches*, p. 65; Rosenberg, *op. cit.* pp. 22, 137, 695-8; E. Krieck, *Wissenschaft, Weltanschauung, Hochschulreform*, pp. 38, 42, quoted by Baker, "National Socialism and the Social Sciences", in *Sociological Review*, xxxi, 108; Baldur von Schirach, *Die Bewegung, Zentralorgan des Nationalsozialistischen Deutschen Studentenbundes*, of 1st February 1938, p. 8, quoted by Charles E. Merriam, "The Assumptions of Aristocracy", in *Am. Journ. Soc.*, xlii, 867.

384. Cf. *Mein Kampf*, pp. 322, 323, 378, 379, 383; very significant is also the following passage by Rosenberg, *op. cit.* p. 627, which reads like an instruction for Nazi Party leaders: § "The Society of Jesus is the chosen instrument for forcing the frightened individual into its services by whipping up his imagination, and for blinding reason to those things which every valiant human being discovers at once. The whole machinery of the Roman Church is at work from the cradle to the grave to get a hold on the imagination and to exert its influence without any interruption. To this end the magic of the sacraments, to this end the infatuation of the senses, to this end also the demand for denominational education down to calligraphy."

385. In one of his early speeches, of 12th April 1922, *Speeches*, p. 20, Hitler said: "I would be no Christian . . . if I did not, as did our Lord 2000 years ago, turn against those by whom to-day this poor people is plundered and exploited".

More quotations dealing with the deification of Hitler in Schumann, *op. cit.* p. 265.
386. Cf. *op. cit.* pp. 114, 117.
387. *Revolution of Destruction, passim.*
388. Cf. Hitler on the uniting effect of a common enemy, *Mein Kampf*, p. 110;
v. also Georg Simmel, *Soziologie*, pp. 473-4, and Robert Michels, *op. cit.* p. 352.
389. *Mein Kampf*, pp. 104 *seq.*, 110, 160, 161, 522.
390. *Ibid.* p. 64.
391. *Ibid.* p. 240.
392. Maurice Samuel, *The Great Hatred.*
393. Sigmund Freud, *Moses and Monotheism*, pp. 147-8.
394. First type: Dühring and nearly all Nazis; second type: Lagarde, Chamberlain.
395. It is doubtful whether Hitler's words as reported by Rauschning in *Hitler Speaks* can be regarded as authentic or whether Rauschning inserted into them, as would be quite understandable from the lapse of time between the actual talks and the publication of the book, some of his own interpretations. But even so, Hitler's tirade against Christianity—*ibid.* pp. 55 *seq.* and p. 222, cf. also Rauschning's Preface to *The Ten Commandments*, New York, 1943—must be regarded as a brilliant presentment of the innermost essence of Nazism.
396. *Speeches*, p. 60, in relation to anti-Semitism : " We may be inhumane, but if we rescue Germany, we have achieved the greatest deed in the world ". *Ibid.* p. 76 : " It matters not whether these weapons of ours are humane ".
397. *Op. cit.* p. 169 : § " On the basis of the compulsory article of faith in the unlimited love and the equality of every human being before God on the one hand, and of the democratic doctrine of the ' Rights of Man ' on the other, which does not know of race and honour as rooted in nationhood, European society has ' developed ', as it were, into the guardian of everything inferior, sick, crippled, criminal, and rotten. ' Love ' plus ' humanity ' has become a doctrine disintegrating all vital commandments and ways of life of nation and State, and has thus rebelled against nature, which takes its vengeance to-day." Rosenberg, *op. cit.* p. 57,§ describes the Roman Emperor Marcus Aurelius as " weakened by Christianity " (*christlich geschwächt*), because " quite openly he made the protection of slaves, the emancipation of women, and the aid of the poor—we would call it unemployment assistance—into principles of government ". Similar statements, pp. 71, 147, 154, 155, 514, 560, 621.
398. This principle implied in Rosenberg's opinion the " end of the Roman world ", p. 58.§
399. Cf. *ibid.* pp. 21, 51, 84, 105, 143.
400. *Ibid.* p. 127.
401. *Ibid.* pp. 689-90.
402. *Ibid.* p. 40.
403. Some more significant views of leading Nazis on Christianity are these : Wilhelm Kusserow, *The Creed of the Nordic Race*, p. 9 : " The ultimate goal for the Christian religion is eternal peace. ' Nordic ' religion, in contrast, means belief in eternal struggle." Cf. also *ibid.* p. 16, Rödiger, *The Teaching of History. Its Purpose, Material, and Method*, p. 14 : " To avoid becoming Christians, many freedom-loving Nordic peasants in Norway set sail for Iceland. It is in keeping with the conception of race if . . . the children in the elementary schools hear of them and are stirred by their spirit."
404. Hitler, *Mein Kampf*, p. 294 : " The followers must not try to avoid being hated . . . but must welcome such hatred ".
404a. Morris Ginsberg, *Sociology*, p. 112.
405. *V.* Serge Chakotin, *The Rape of the Masses*, pp. 205-16.
406. The transformation of the word " Aryan " from a linguistic to a racial term is due to a misunderstanding which was prevalent in the days of the German scholar, Friedrich Max Müller, who worked during the second half of the 19th century in Oxford. Müller took great pains to stop the misuse. In 1888 he wrote, *Biographies of Words and the Home of the Aryan*, p. 120 : " I have declared again and again that if I say Aryas, I mean neither blood nor bones, nor hair, nor skull ; I mean simply those who speak an Aryan language. I assert nothing beyond their language when I call them Hindus, Greeks, Romans, Germans, Celts, and Slavs, and in that sense, and in that sense only, do I say that even the blackest Hindus represent an earlier stage of Aryan speech and thought than the fairest Scandinavians. To me an ethnologist who speaks of Aryan race, Aryan blood, Aryan

eyes and hair, is as great a sinner as a linguist who speaks of a dolichocephalic dictionary or a brachycephalic grammar. It is worse than a Babylonian confusion of tongues—it is downright theft."

407. *Mein Kampf*, p. 243.
408. *Op. cit.* p. 700.
409. *Ibid.* p. 639.
410. *Ibid.* p. 105.
411. *Ibid.* p. 11.
412. *History on a Racial Basis*, p. 8.
413. Rosenberg, *op. cit.* p. 70, makes Dante a Teuton; he points out, *ibid.* p. 76, footnote, that it is at least doubtful whether Jesus was a Jew. He makes, vol. i, chapter 1, Apollo a "Nordic god" in "Nordic Greece" (Hellas) and opposes him to Dionysos whom he calls "Asiatic-Semitic". This shows great ingratitude to Dionysos, to whose cult the Nazi unfettering of primitive impulses shows so much similarity; and Rosenberg is equally ungrateful to Machiavelli. He makes him out to be an Etruscan as contrasted to the "Nordic Latins", *ibid.* pp. 67-8 footnote. This statement is substantiated as follows: § "Machiavelli came from a predominantly Etruscan village". He adds: "A system of this kind which is based merely on human vileness and its acceptance as a creed has not sprung from a Nordic soul". Far more probable—although cited under the same reservation as stated on p. 262, Note 395—seems a report by Rauschning, *Gespräche mit Hitler*, p. 249,§ on the enthusiastic appreciation of Machiavelli by Hitler. Hitler is reported to have said that the perusal of Machiavelli's work exerted a "purifying and liberating [*befreiend*] effect" on him. On the dissolution of the parallelism between race and mind, cf. Rödiger, *op. cit.* p. 15: ". . . Luther, the man with an Eastern appearance and the soul of a Nordic hero". H. S. Chamberlain, *The Foundations of the 19th Century*, i, 502 *seq.*, already had taken great pains to "prove" that Luther had been of Germanic race.

414. Hitler, *Speeches*, pp. 54-5, mentions as those guilty of bringing about the first World War: Ballin, Bleichröder, Mendelssohn and Bethmann-Hollweg. The first three were Jews and Bethmann-Hollweg he calls a Jew, "the real article" (*waschecht*). Wilhelm Meister, Judas Schuldbuch, p. 14: § "Thus the German war became a Jews' war in every respect". Cf. also *ibid.* pp. 62, 70.

415. Fritz Merkenschlager, in *Götter, Helden und Günther*, raised an emphatic protest against this defamation.

416. *Op. cit.* p. 86.§
417. *Mein Kampf*, pp. 332-3.
418. *Speeches*, p. 16.
419. Hitler criticised the Imperial policy of Germanisation, because this was based on national, not on racial, principles. Cf. *Mein Kampf*, pp. 326-7: "What makes a people, or to be more correct, a race is not language but blood".
420. *Weltpolitische Betrachtungen*, pp. 162-3.§
421. *History Teaching*, etc., p. 15.
422. Morris Ginsberg, *Sociology*, p. 108.
423. Morris Ginsberg, *Studies in Sociology*, p. 141, lists "Exercise" among the "specific forms" which serve to satisfy "root interests" or "basic needs" of the human being.
424. *Revolution des Nihilismus*, p. 97.§
425. Karl Mannheim, *Diagnosis of Our Time*, p. 98, points also to this relationship.
426. Suttie, *op. cit.* p. 18.
427. An excellent exposition of the reasons why the Nazi gangs appealed so strongly to the youth is contained in article "De-Nazification" by Professor Gilbert Murray, reviewing the book on *Higher Education in Nazi Germany*, by Professor Wolf, in *Spectator* of 8th September 1944. But that Professor Murray also overrates the "heroic devotion" of these young people, notably in its moral implications, will be made clear by the paragraph and those following in the text. Cf. also Morris Ginsberg, *Moral Progress*, pp. 36-7; S. H. Steinberg, *A Short History of Germany*, p. 280.
428. It should be pointed out that the following remarks are in no way intended to belittle the heroism which has been shown by German soldiers in the second World War. We are not concerned with the attitude demonstrated during the actual battles, but exclusively with the part played by the appeal to heroism within the Nazi propaganda up to 1933.

429. *Mein Kampf*, p. 48; similar remarks, pp. 161, 395. Cf. also the repeated stressing of " emotionally devoted " (p. 380), " blindly obedient " (p. 381) masses, as well as of their " blind faith " (p. 383), *Speeches*, p. 69, etc.

430. *The Crowd. A Study of the Popular Mind*, pp. 40-41, 122.

431. *Massenpsychologie und Ich-Analyse*, p. 111.§

432. The present writer, who attended for the purpose of study, a Hitler meeting in the Berlin Sportpalast before the seizure of power, recalls the following exclamation by Hitler, marking one of his rhetorical climaxes : " Aren't you enthralled by me as I am by you ? " (" Bin ich nicht Euch so verfallen wie Ihr mir ? "). The erotic character not only of the words but also of the accompanying gestures was unmistakable. How decidedly the regression to a feminine and masochist attitude belongs to the whole make-up of the Fascist glorification of the Leader is also made clear by the following passage taken from a book on Fascism by the Italian Fascist Gorgolini, *op. cit.* pp. 37-8. The author maintains that Mussolini " knows to perfection the art of drawing people to himself and holding them ". He then describes his tricks as follows : " Mussolini makes people wait a long time . . . before admitting them to his presence, and when he appears, cold, haughty, and impressive . . . he looks his visitor fixedly in the eyes. . . . He treats everyone in a militarist manner, as though he were offering them an ultimatum. . . . He is authoritative and to some extent egocentric ; he knows the end for which he is making . . . he advances pitilessly until he attains it. . . . We may not love such men, but we cannot help admiring them. The cries of those who have been trampled under their feet may sound painfully in our ears and pain our feelings, but such are the methods of men who go far and accomplish great things."

433. Hitler, *Mein Kampf*, pp. 136, 137 ; *Speeches*, p. 15.

434. Hitler, *Mein Kampf*, p. 137.

435. *The New Spirit of Military Education*, p. 19.

436. *Ibid.* p. 20. Cf. also Kusserow, *The Creed of the Nordic Man*, p. 12 : " The idea of death has no horror for Nordic Man ".

437. *Op. cit.* p. 43.

438. Cf. also *ibid.* pp. 14 and 44 on mass heroism.

439. Cf. the criticism by Cooley, in *Social Organisation*, Chapter XIV.

440. *V.* Neumann, *Behemoth*, p. 188. Cf. also Hitler's ambiguous statements on agrarian reform, *Speeches*, pp. 64-5. Moreover, an official Party Manifesto on the improvement of agriculture in the Nazi State, *Speeches*, pp. 767-74, lays the responsibility for the unfavourable situation of agriculture entirely at the door of the Jews.

441. What became of this fight after the department stores had been taken over by " Aryans " is made clear in an article by Herbert Block, " Industrial Concentration ", in *Social Research*, vol. x, No. 2, pp. 195-6. Instead of passing into communal property, the department stores were simply forbidden to have hairdressing departments! Everything else remained as it had been before. Block quotes the following sentence from a book by Ulrich Müller, entitled *Die Entwicklung des Handwerks in den letzten Jahren unter besonderer Berücksichtigung der Nationalsozialistischen Handwerkerpolitik und Handwerkergesetzgebung*, Berlin, 1938, p. 104 : " The National Socialist government shifted the struggle against the department stores to the spiritual level ".

442. " Economic Foundations of the German Totalitarian State ", in *Am. Journ. Soc.* vol. xlvi, 1940-41, pp. 471, 477.

443. Cf. the title of the book by Erich Fromm, quoted above.

444. Cf. also the entirely incomprehensible definition of the word " freedom " by Rosenberg, *op. cit.* p. 529.

445. Cf. Hitler, *Mein Kampf*, p. 88 : " Our German democracy . . ." Hitler in a speech in Kiel, made on 6th November 1933, " I want to show by this election to other governments that real democracy is with us. . . ." Goebbels in a speech to representatives of the international Press, made in Geneva on 28th September 1933 : " If it is the meaning of true democracy to guide the peoples and to show them the way towards work and peace, then, I believe, this democracy has been realised in Germany, and indeed against the parties which represented only its caricature ".

446. *Speeches*, p. 77.

447. In this connection should also be mentioned Hitler's appeal to Reason and Thinking in his speech at Harvest Thanksgiving at Bückeburg, of 3rd October 1937, *Speeches*, p. 205, as well as his confession of loyalty to the idea of international

understanding, *N.B.* before the seizure of power, *ibid.* p. 77. In the same connection may also be mentioned Rosenberg's polemic against the State-idol, *op, cit.* p. 528, and against the arrogance of bureaucrats, *ibid.* p. 525. The Nazis made themselves unhesitatingly mouthpieces of any popular resentment, without giving the slightest heed to the fact that their own regime would provide much more food for the same resentment than any previous government.

448. Cf. Hitler's speech to the Sudeten Germans of 2nd December 1938, *Speeches*, pp. 88-90, 92.

449. Cf. particularly Hitler, *Mein Kampf*, p. 64 : " The more I came to know the individual leaders . . . of Social Democracy, my love for my own people increased correspondingly. . . . The more I came to know the Jew, the easier it was to excuse the workers."

450. Hitler, *Speeches*, pp. 26-7.

451. Cf. Hitler, *Mein Kampf*, pp. 265 *seq.*; *Speeches*, i, 7 : " ' Christian capitalism ' is already as good as destroyed, the international Jewish Stock Exchange capital gains in proportion as the other loses ground ". Rosenberg, *op. cit.* p. 17 : § " To extirpate from German life Marxist materialism and its support by finance-capital as a Syrian-Jewish alien product, is the great mission of the new movement of German workers ".

452. *Speeches*, pp. 777-829.

453. *Mein Kampf*, pp. 459 *seq.*

454. That Hitler planned this frontal assault already very early is proved, *e.g.*, by this passage in *Mein Kampf*, p. 378 : " For a Weltanschauung is intolerant and cannot permit another to exist side by side with it. . . . And the same holds true of religions. Christianity was not content with erecting an altar of its own. It had first to destroy the pagan altars. It was only in virtue of this passionate intolerance that an apodictic faith could grow up." This passage also throws light on what might have been regarded as a bow to Christianity, *e.g.*, *op. cit.* p. 225. Yet even there he says : until " a substitute is available ".

455. *Mein Kampf*, p. 104.

456. *Ibid.* p. 461 : " I have to guard against the possibility of some immature brain arising in the patriotic movement which thinks it can do what even a Bismarck failed to do ".

457. In this light, centralism is also seen by Louis Wirth, in " Localism, Regionalism, and Centralism ", in *Am. Journ. Soc.*, xlii, 501 ; Trotter, *op. cit.* pp. 122, 124 ; Simmel, *Soziale Differenzierung*, p. 101.

458. *Mein Kampf*, p. 455.

459. *Ibid.* p. 462.

460. *Ibid.* p. 469 : " We must oppose such centralization because . . . it helps to reinforce . . . the present Jewish democratic Reich. . . ."

461. " I beg you not to abuse the Prussians while at the same time you grovel before the Jews, but show yourself stiff-necked against the folk of Berlin. And if you do that, then you will have on your side in the whole of Germany, millions and millions of Germans. . . ." *Speeches*, i, 38-9 ; similarly *ibid.* p. 78.

462. A good illustration of Hitler's ambiguity in this question can be found when two of his speeches are compared. In his speeches of 2nd February and 12th March 1933, he commented on particularism, in the first favourably, in the second unfavourably, the contradiction being so marked that both the editor of the speeches, Professor Baynes, and also, as Professor Baynes points out, S. H. Roberts in his book *The House that Hitler Built*, London, 1939, p. 67, expressed their astonishment. (*Speeches*, pp. 266, 268-70.) But the explanation is simple. These two speeches were separated by the last elections for the Reichstag, which were still to some extent free elections. These took place on 5th March 1933. Before this event, Hitler would not openly admit this anti-particularist outlook. Immediately after it, on the 31st March and the 7th April, the Laws for the Co-ordination of the German States with the Reich (*Gleichschaltungsgesetze*) were promulgated. On the 1st September 1933 Hitler said, during the Nuremberg Party Rally : " The National Socialist Movement is not the preserver of the German States of the past, but their liquidator ", *Speeches*, p. 274.

463. Hitler, *Mein Kampf*, p. 507 : " Whenever we read of attacks against Germany taking place in any part of the world, the Jew is always the instigator ".

464. *Ibid.* p. 508.

465. *Ibid.* pp. 509-10. On the English question also : *ibid.* pp. 519 *seq.*; *Speeches*, p. 47 ; Rosenberg, *op. cit.* p. 656.

466. Hitler, *Mein Kampf*, p. 510.
467. Hitler, *Speeches*, p. 46.
468. Hitler, *Mein Kampf*, p. 508; *Speeches*, p. 47.
469. Hitler, *Speeches*, p. 48.
470. Hitler, *Mein Kampf*, pp. 520 *seq.*; Rosenberg, *op. cit.* p. 656.
471. Very characteristic is the following example of the way in which Hitler tried to conceal the principles of his propaganda; in *Mein Kampf*, p. 388, he says: " In all truth it can be said that we did not court public favour, but made an onslaught on the follies of our people ". As proof he mentions that he had dissuaded the people from their view that the German-Russian peace treaty of Brest-Litovsk of 1917 had been an act of violence. That may well have been so. But, in point of fact, he opposed public opinion in a matter in which the people were glad to be persuaded that they had not been guilty of wrong-doing. They were happy to be absolved from their feelings of guilt in this special respect. Hitler would have been far less successful if he had considered it advantageous to influence them the other way round.

472. According to a Memorandum of the Reich Ministry of the Interior, V. 1641 B., of 30th March 1922, pp. 8-9, the number of Eastern Jews residing in Germany increased by about 55,000 during and after the first World War. The number of the Jews living in the formerly German provinces, ceded to Poland, Danzig, Lithuania, etc., who settled within the frontiers of post-war Germany, is estimated by Jakob Lestschinsky, *op. cit.* p. 58, at about 10,000.

473. Jakob Lestschinsky, *op. cit. passim*, with special reference to Chapter VII, pp. 85 *seq.*, and Chapter IX, pp. 112 *seq.*

474. Cf. *Friedhofsschändungen in Deutschland, 1923–1932. Dokumente der politischen und kulturellen Verwilderung unserer Zeit.*

475. Samuel Lowy, *Man and His Fellow-Men*, pp. 105-6. The author, a psycho-analyst from Prague, reports that anti-Semitism played a strikingly·small part in the " free association " even of his professedly anti-Semitic patients. While allowing for all kinds of possible explanations of this phenomenon, he cautiously suggests that at the root of the so-called anti-Semitism there is nothing but hatred, which, if given free vent, as is the case during analytical treatment, need not pretend to be caused by Jewish objects. This observation, as well as the conclusion drawn from it, provides an interesting confirmation of our own distinction between " objective " and " subjective " anti-Semitism.

476. " Spontaneous, popular anti-Semitism is still weak in Germany. This assertion cannot be proved directly, but it is significant that, despite the incessant propaganda to which the German people have been subjected for many years, there is no record of a single spontaneous anti-Jewish attack committed by persons not belonging to the Nazi Party. The writer's personal conviction, paradoxical as it may seem, is that the German people are the least anti-Semitic of all " (Franz Neumann, *Behemoth*, pp. 103-4). Further evidence of the unpopularity of anti-Semitic measures is provided by the following observers: Consul-General Bell, British Consul-General in Cologne, in *Papers concerning the Treatment of German Nationals in Germany, 1938–39*, pp. 17-19; E. Amy Buller, *Darkness over Germany*, pp. 100, 111, 113, 181; Sopade, *Deutschland-Berichte der Sozialdemokratischen Partei Deutschlands, passim*; Max Seydewitz, *Civil Life in War-Time Germany*, p. 95. Nazi admissions of the unpopularity of anti-Semitism: " We have experienced how difficult it is to mobilise the powers of defence of all strata of the population against the Jews. We have, above all, spent year after year trying to convince certain business circles that business and finance cannot only do without Jews, but will fare better without them. The volumes of the ' Schwarzes Korps ' are a chronicle of this martyrdom of untiring and inexorable monitors " (*Das Schwarze Korps*, No. 46, 17th November 1938).§ " This talk about the decent Jews is like a contagious disease that is hard to stamp out. Again and again one·meets some blockhead who will repeat this dangerous nonsense like a parrot. Also there is no end of people who simply cannot forgo private intercourse with them." *Westdeutscher Beobachter*, Köln, 19th January 1938).§ " Reich and Party went unperturbed the road which they had deemed necessary, starting with the boycott against the Jews. The understanding of the German people lagged behind the course of events. They often did not comprehend what ends were served by these measures. Even the active partisans who were responsible for the enactment of the anti-Jewish policy according to the Party programme, have seldom been able to give a rational ground for it. Apart from those for whom our aims are a matter

of course, there remains the host of those people who feel embarrassed when they hear the word Jew. It was they whom the expert meant who wrote that in wide circles of the intelligentsia anti-Jewish discussions continue to be very unpopular " (Klaus Schickert, " Israel ", in *Wille und Macht*, September–October 1943, Berlin).§ Cf. furthermore: Dr. E. H. Schulz and Dr. R. Frercks, *Warum Arierparagraph? Ein Beitrag zur Judenfrage*, particularly p. 7; F. M. Dose, *Sind 500,000 Juden ein deutsches Problem? passim*; *Basler National-Zeitung* of 1st July 1935 and 1st August 1935; *Der Stürmer*, No. 30/1935 and No. 29/1926 (containing photos of Christians attending Jewish funerals); *Schwarzes Korps*, No. 46 of 17th November 1938; *Chemnitzer Tageszeitung*, 10th March 1938; *N.S. Parteikorrespondenz* (Official Nazi Party News Letter), 23rd August 1938; *Westfälische Landeszeitung*, Dortmund, 30th December 1938; *Stuttgarter N.S.-Kurier*, No. 274, 4th October 1941; *The Yellow Spot*, quotations in Chapter 12.

477. *Op. cit.* iv. 128-9.

BIBLIOGRAPHY

ADLER, GEORG, *Geschichte der ersten sozialistischen Arbeiterbewegung in Deutschland.* Breslau, 1885.

ALEXANDER, FRANZ, " Psychoanalysis and Social Disorganization ", in *The American Journal of Sociology*, vol. xlii. Chicago, 1936–37.

American Journal of Sociology, The, Chicago, abbrev. *Am. Journ. Soc.*

ARNDT, ERNST MORITZ, *Geist der Zeit*. Revised by R. Lorenz, Magdeburg (no year).

BAKER, R. J., " National Socialism and the Social Sciences ", in *Sociological Review*, vol. xxxi. London, 1939.

BARON, SALO WITTMAYER, *A Social and Religious History of the Jews.* New York, 1937.

BAYNES, H. G., *Germany Possessed*. London, 1941.

BAYNES, NORMAN H., *The Speeches of Adolf Hitler, April 1922–August 1939*. Translated and edited. (Quoted : Speeches.) London, New York, Toronto, 1942.

BEBEL, AUGUST, *Sozialdemokratie und Antisemitismus*. Berlin, 1906.

BECKER, JOSEPH, *Paul de Lagarde*. Lübeck, 1935.

BECKERATH, HERBERT VON, *In Defence of the West*. Durham, North Carolina, 1942.

BELL, *v. Papers*, etc.

BENDER, HEINZ, *Der Kampf um die Judenemanzipation in Deutschland im Spiegel der Flugschriften, 1815–1820*. Jena, 1939.

BERNSTEIN, F., *Der Antisemitismus als Gruppenerscheinung. Versuch einer Soziologie des Judenhasses.* Berlin, 1926.

BLEY, FRITZ, *Die Weltstellung des Deutschtums*. Munich, 1897.

BLITZ, SAMUEL, *Nationalism—a Cause of Anti-Semitism*. New York, 1928.

BLOCK, HERBERT, " Industrial Concentration Versus Small Business. The Trend of Nazi Policy ", in *Social Research*, vol. x, No. 2. New York, 1943.

BLUEHER, HANS, *Die Erhebung Israels gegen die christlichen Güter.* Hamburg, Berlin, 1931.

BLUMER, HERBERT, " Social Disorganization and Individual Disorganization ", in *Am. Journ. Soc.*, vol. xlii. 1936–37.

BONN, M. J., " The Political Situation in Germany ", in *Political Quarterly*, vol. iv. London, 1933.

BORGHESE, G. A., " The Intellectual Origins of Fascism ", in *Social Research*, vol. i. New York, 1934.

BRADY, ROBERT A., *The Spirit and Structure of German Fascism.* London, 1937.

BREYSIG, KURT, *Die soziale Entwicklung der führenden Völker Europas in der neueren und neuesten Zeit.* Leipzig (no year).

BRIEFS, GOETZ, *Das gewerbliche Proletariat. Grundriss der Sozialöko-nomik*, vol. ix, No. 1. Tübingen, 1926.

BRINKMANN, CARL, article, "Alien" in *Encyclopaedia of the Social Sciences*. London, 1930.

BUCH, WILLI, *Fünfzig Jahre antisemitische Bewegung*. Munich, 1937.

BULLER, E. AMY, *Darkness over Germany*. London, New York, Toronto, 1934.

BURCKHARDT, JAKOB, *Weltgeschichtliche Betrachtungen*. Edited by Jakob Oeri. 4th ed. Stuttgart, 1921.

BUTLER, ROHAN D'O., *The Roots of National Socialism, 1783-1933*. London, 1941.

CHAKOTIN, SERGE, *The Rape of the Masses*. Transl. by E. W. Dickes. London, 1940.

CHAMBERLAIN, HOUSTON STEWART, *Die Grundlagen des 19. Jahr-hunderts*. 2nd ed. Munich, 1900.

The Foundations of the 19th Century. Transl. by John Lees. London, New York, 1909.

COBBAN, ALFRED, *Dictatorship. Its History and Theory*. London, 1939.

Constructive Democracy. A Symposium. London, 1938.

COOLEY, CHARLES HORTON, *Social Organization. A Study of the Larger Mind*. New York, 1929.

CROCE, BENEDETTO, *History as the Story of Liberty*. Transl. by Sylvia Sprigge. London, 1941.

History of Europe in the 19th Century. Transl. by Henry Furst. London, 1934.

Democracy in Transition, by a Group of Social Scientists in the Ohio State University. New York, 1937.

Denkschrift des Reichsministers des Innern, V. 1641.B. über die Ein- und Auswanderung nach bezw. aus Deutschland in den Jahren 1910 bis 1920. Denkschriften des Deutschen Reichstages, 1922. No. 8. Berlin.

Dictatorship in the Modern World.. Edited by Guy Stanton Ford. 2nd ed. Minnesota, London, Oxford, 1939.

DOLLARD, JOHN, etc., *Frustration and Aggression*. Edited by Karl Mannheim. London, 1944.

DOSE, F. M., *Sind 500,000 Juden ein deutsches Problem?* Köln, Kalk, 1935.

DUEHRING, EUGEN, *Die Judenfrage als Frage des Rassencharakters und seiner Schädlichkeiten für Existenz und Kultur der Völker*. 6th ed. Leipzig, 1930.

FALK, WERNER, "The Sociological Interpretation of Political Ideas", in *Sociological Review*, vol. xxvi. London, 1934.

FICHTE, JOHANN GOTTLIEB, *Beitrag zur Berichtigung der Urteile des Publikums über die französische Revolution*. Reprint of the edition of 1793. Zürich and Winterthur, 1844.

FOERSTER, FRIEDRICH WILHELM, *Europe and the German Question*. London, 1941.

FRANK, WALTER, *Hofprediger Adolf Stöcker und die christlich-soziale Bewegung.* 2nd ed. Hamburg, 1935.

FRANKENSTEIN, ERNST, *Justice for my People. The Jewish Case.* London, 1943.

FREUD, SIGMUND, *Civilization and its Discontents.* Auth. transl. by Joan Riviere. London, 1930.

Civilization, War and Death. Selections from three works. Edited by John Rickmann. London, 1939.

Group Psychology and the Analysis of the Ego. Auth. transl. by James Strachey. London, Vienna, 1922.

Massenpsychologie und Ich-Analyse. Wien, Zürich, 1921.

Moses and Monotheism. Transl. by Katherine Jones. London, 1939.

" The Uncanny ", in *Collected Papers,* vol. iv. Auth. transl. under the supervision of Joan Riviere. London, 1925.

Friedhofsschändungen in Deutschland 1923 bis 1932. Dokumente der politischen und kulturellen Verwilderung unserer Zeit. Edited by Centralverein deutscher Staatsbürger jüdischen Glaubens. 5th ed. Berlin, 1932.

FRIEDMANN, W., *World Revolution and the Future of the West.* London, 1942.

FRIES, JAKOB FRIEDRICH, " Besprechung eines Buches von Friedrich Rühs : Ueber die Ansprüche der Juden an das deutsche Bürgerrecht ", in *Heidelbergische Jahrbücher der Literatur,* No. 16. Heidelberg, 1816.

FRYMANN, DANIEL (Heinrich Class), *Wenn ich Kaiser wär'.* 5th ed. 1914.

FROMM, ERICH, *The Fear of Freedom.* London, 1942.

FULTON, J. S., and MORRIS, C. R., *In Defence of Democracy.* London, 1935.

GASSET, JOSE ORTEGA Y, *The Revolt of the Masses.* Auth. transl. London, 1932.

GERTH, HANS, " The Nazi Party, its Leadership and Composition ", in *Am. Journ. Soc.,* vol. xlv, 1939-40.

" Review of Hans Kohn, Revolutions and Dictatorships ", in *Am. Journ. Soc.,* vol. xlvi. 1941.

GINSBERG, MORRIS, *Reason and Unreason in Society. Essays in Sociology and Social Philosophy.* London, New York, Toronto, 1947.

Moral Progress. Glasgow, 1944.

Sociology. 2nd impr. London, 1937.

Studies in Sociology. London, 1932.

The Psychology of Society. 6th ed. London, 1944.

GINZBURG, BENJAMIN, article " Antisemitism ", in *Encyclopaedia of the Social Sciences.* London, 1930.

GOBINEAU, ARTHUR DE, *The Inequality of the Human Races.* Transl. by Adrian Collins. London, 1915.

GOOCH, G. P., *Germany and the French Revolution.* London.

GORGOLINI, PIETRO, *The Fascist Movement in Italian Life*. Transl. and edited by M. O. Petre. London, 1923.

GRAEBER, ISACQUE, and BRITT, STEUART HENDERSON, *Jews in a Gentile World*. New York, 1942.

HARDING, D. W., *The Impulse to Dominate*. London, 1941.

HARTMANN, EDUARD VON, *Das Judentum in Gegenwart und Zukunft*. 2nd ed. Berlin, 1885.

HEATON, HERBERT, *Economic History of Europe*. New York, London, 1936.

HEIDEN, KONRAD, *Hitler*. London, 1936.

HERFORD, C. H., *The Post-War Mind of Germany and Other European Studies*. Oxford, 1927.

HERMA, HANS, " Goebbels' Conception of Propaganda ", in *Social Research*, vol. x. New York, 1943.

HERTZ, FRIEDRICH, " National Spirit and National Peculiarity ", in *Sociological Review*, vol. xxvi. London, 1934.

" The Nature of Nationalism ", in *Social Forces*, vol. xix, No. 3. 1941.

HITLER, ADOLF, *Mein Kampf*. Transl. by James Murphy. London, 1939.

HOBHOUSE, L. T., *Democracy and Reaction*. London, 1904.

The World in Conflict. London, 1915.

HORKENBACH, CUNO, *Das Deutsche Reich von 1918 bis heute*. Berlin, 1935.

HORNEY, KAREN, *The Neurotic Personality of our Time*. London, 1937.

HOWARD, EARL DEAN, *The Cause and Extent of the Recent Industrial Progress of Germany*. London, 1907.

HUEGEL, BARON FRIEDRICH VON, *The German Soul in its Attitude towards Ethics and Christianity, the State and War*. London, 1916.

HUIZINGA, J., *Der Mensch und die Kultur*. Stockholm, 1938.

In the Shadow of To-Morrow. A Diagnosis of the Spiritual Distemper of our Time. Transl. by J. H. Huizinga. London, Toronto, 1936.

Jews in a Gentile World. The Problem of Anti-Semitism. A Symposium. New York, 1942. Cf. also Gräber, etc.

JOERGES, ERNST, *Die weltgeschichtliche Bedeutung des Judentums und seine Zukunft*. Berlin, 1926.

JOHNSON, FANNY, *The German Mind as Reflected in their Literature from 1870 to 1914*. London, Sydney, 1922.

JONES, ERNEST, " Evolution and Revolution ", in *International Journal of Psycho-Analysis*, vol. xxii. London, 1941.

JUNG, C. G., *Aufsätze zur Zeitgeschichte*. Zürich, 1946.

JUNG, EDGAR J., *Die Herrschaft der Minderwertigen. Ihr Zerfall und ihre Ablösung durch ein neues Reich*. 3rd ed. Berlin, 1930.

JUNGMANN, EVA, *Spontaneität und Ideologie als Faktoren der modernen sozialen Bewegung*. Diss., Heidelberg, 1924.

KAHLER, ERICH, " Forms and Features of Anti-Judaism ", in *Social Research*, vol. vi. New York, 1939.

KLOEBER, W. VON, *From the World War to National Revolution, 1914–1933*. Friends of Europe-Publications, London.

KUSSEROW, WILHELM, *The Creed of the Nordic Race*. Friends of Europe-Publications, London.

LAGARDE, PAUL DE, *Deutsche Schriften*. Göttingen, 1886. " Lipmann Zunz und seine Verehrer ", in *Mitteilungen*. 2nd vol. Göttingen, 1887.

LASKI, HAROLD J., *Reflections on the Revolution of our Time*. London, 1943.

LASSWELL, HAROLD D., " The Psychology of Hitlerism ", in *The Political Quarterly*, vol. iv. London, 1933. *Psychopathology and Politics*. Chicago, 1930. *World Politics and Personal Insecurity*. New York, London, 1935.

LAWRENCE, D. H., " Letter from Germany ", in *Stories, Essays, and Poems*. London, 1939.

LE BON, GUSTAVE, *The Crowd. A Study of the Popular Mind*. London, 1896. *The Psychology of Socialism*. London, 1899.

LEDERER, EMIL, and MARSCHAK, JAKOB, " Der neue Mittelstand ", in *Grundriss der Sozialökonomik*, vol. ix, No. 1. Tübingen, 1926.

LEERS, JOHANNES VON, *History on a Racial Basis*. Friends of Europe-Publications, London.

LESCHNITZER, ADOLF, *Das Judentum im Weltbild Europas*. First part, " Das Judentum im Weltbild des Mittelalters ". Berlin, 1935.

LESTSCHINSKY, JAKOB, *Das wirtschaftliche Schicksal des deutschen Judentums. Aufstieg, Wandlung, Krise, Ausblick. Schriften der Zentralwohlfahrtsstelle der deutschen Juden und der Hauptstelle für jüdische Wanderfürsorge*, No. vii. Berlin, 1932.

LEWIN, KURT, " Psycho-Sociological Problems of a Minority Group ", in *Character and Personality. An International Psychological Quarterly*, vol. iii. Durham, London, Berlin, 1934–35. " Some Social-Psychological Differences between the United States and Germany ", in *Character and Personality*, vol. iv. 1935–36.

LEWISOHN, LUDWIG, *Israel*. London, 1926. *The Answer*. New York, 1939.

LINDSAY, A. D., *The Essentials of Democracy*. London, 1929. *I Believe in Democracy*. London, New York, Toronto, 1940.

LIPPMANN, WALTER, *The Good Society*. London, 1937.

LOWY, SAMUEL, *Man and his Fellow-Men*. London, 1944.

LUDENDORFF, ERICH, *Kriegführung und Politik*. 2nd ed. Berlin, 1922.

LUTHER, DR. MARTIN, *Sämtliche Werke*. Erlangen, 1842.

McDOUGALL, WILLIAM, *The Group Mind*. Cambridge, 1939.

MANNHEIM, KARL, *Diagnosis of our Time*. London, 1943. *Mensch und Gesellschaft im Zeitalter des Umbaus*. Leiden, 1935.

MAYER, CARL, "Anti-Judaism Reconsidered", in *Social Research*, vol. vii. New York, 1940.
"On the Intellectual Origin of National Socialism", in *Social Research*, vol. ix. New York, 1942.
MEINECKE, FRIEDRICH ; TROELTSCH, ERNST ; SERING, MAX, etc. *Die deutsche Freiheit.* Five lectures. Gotha, 1917.
MEINECKE, FRIEDRICH, *Weltbürgertum und Nationalstaat. Studien zur Genesis des deutschen Nationalstaats.* Munich, Berlin, 1908.
MEISSNER, ERICH, *Germany in Peril.* London, New York, Toronto, 1942.
MEISTER, WILHELM, *Judas Schuldbuch. Eine deutsche Abrechnung.* 3rd and 4th ed. Munich, 1919.
MENES, A., "Die Judenfrage im Lichte der Konjunktur-Entwicklung", in *Jüdische Wohlfahrtspflege und Sozialpolitik.* Berlin, 1933.
MERKENSCHLAGER, FRITZ, *Götter, Helden und Günther.* Nuremberg.
MERRIAM, CHARLES E., "The Assumptions of Aristocracy", in *Am. Journ. Soc.*, vol. xliii. 1937–38.
The New Democracy and the New Despotism. New York, London, 1939.
MESS, HENRY A., *Social Structure.* London, 1942.
MICHELS, ROBERT, "Psychologie der antikapitalistischen Massenbewegungen", in *Grundriss der Sozialökonomik*, vol. ix, No. 1. Tübingen, 1926.
MORGENSTERN, JULIAN, "Assimilation, Isolation or Reform?" in *Contemporary Jewish Record*, April 1942. New York.
MUELLER, F. M., *Biographies of Words and the Home of Aryas.* London, 1888.
MUELLER-CLAUDIUS, MICHAEL, *Deutsche Rassenangst.* Berlin, 1927.
MURRAY, GILBERT, "De-Nazification", in *The Spectator*, 8th September 1944. London.
MURRY, JOHN MIDDLETON, *The Defence of Democracy.* London, 1939.
NADLER, JOSEF, *Die Berliner Romantik 1800–1814.* Berlin, 1921.
Literaturgeschichte der deutschen Stämme und Landschaften. 4 vols. 3rd ed. Regensburg, 1929–32.
NATHAN, PETER, *The Psychology of Fascism.* London, 1943.
Nationalism. A Report by a Study Group of Members of the Royal Institute of International Affairs. London, New York, Toronto, 1939.
NEUHAUS, G., "Die berufliche und soziale Gliederung im Zeitalter des Kapitalismus", in *Grundriss der Sozialökonomik*, vol. ix, No. 1. Tübingen, 1926.
NEUMANN, FRANZ, *Behemoth.* London, 1942.
"The Decay of German Democracy", in *Political Quarterly*, vol. iv, 1933. London.
New Governments in Europe. The Trend toward Dictatorship. A Publi-

cation of the Foreign Policy Association Inc. Rev. Preface by Raymond Leslie Buell. Ronald Press Cy., New York, 1937.

NIPPOLD, OTFRIED, *Der deutsche Chauvinismus*. Reprint of the edition of 1913. Bern, 1917.

NITTI, FRANCESCO, *Bolshevism, Fascism and Democracy*. Transl. by Margaret M. Green. London, 1921.

OTTEN, KARL. *A Combine of Aggression. Masses, Élite and Dictatorship in Germany*. Transl. by Eden Paul and F. M. Field. London, 1942.

PALYI, MELCHIOR, " Economic Foundations of the German Totalitarian State ", in *Am. Journ. Soc.*, vol. xlvi. 1940–41.

Papers concerning the Treatment of German Nationals in Germany, 1938–39. London, 1939.

PARK, ROBERT E., article, " Social Assimilation ", in *Encyclopaedia of the Social Sciences*. London, 1930.

PARKES, JAMES, *The Jew and his Neighbour. A Study of the Causes of Antisemitism.* 2nd ed. London, 1938.

PLAYNE, C. E., *The Neuroses of the Nations*. London, 1925.

POLANYI, M., " Jewish Problems ", in *The Political Quarterly*, vol. xiv. London, 1943.

RAUSCHNING, HERMANN, *Gespräche mit Hitler*. 2nd ed. New York, 1940.

Hitler Speaks. A Series of Political Conversations with Adolf Hitler on his Real Aims. London, 1939.

Die Revolution des Nihilismus. 2nd ed. Zürich, New York, 1938. *Germany's Revolution of Destruction.* Transl. by E. N. Dickes. London, Toronto, 1939.

REICHMANN-JUNGMANN, EVA, " Der Untergang des Judentums ", in *Der Morgen*, vol. viii, No. 1. Berlin, 1932.

REIK, THEODOR, " Aggression from Anxiety ", in *International Journal of Psychoanalysis*, vol. xxii. London, 1941.

REUTER, EDWARD B., *Race and Culture Contacts*. New York, London, 1934.

RIEZLER, KURT, " On the Psychology of the Modern Revolution ", in *Social Research*, vol. x. New York, 1943.

ROBINSON, ARMIN L., (ed.), *The Ten Commandments*. New York, 1943.

RODNICK, DAVID, " Group Frustrations in Connecticut ", in *Am. Journ. Soc.*, vol. xlvii. 1941.

ROEDIGER, WILHELM, *The Teaching of History. Its Purpose, Materiai and Method.* Friends of Europe-Publications, London.

ROSENBERG, ALFRED, *Der Mythus des 20. Jahrhunderts*. 29th-30th ed. Munich, 1934.

ROSS, EDWARD ALSWORTH, *Foundations of Sociology*. New York, 1905.

RUPPIN, ARTHUR, *Soziologie der Juden*. Berlin, 1930–31.

RUSSELL, BERTRAND, " The Intellectual in the Modern World ", in *Am. Journ. Soc.*, vol. xliv, No. 2. 1939.

SACKS, GEORGE, *The Intelligent Man's Guide to Jew-Baiting*. London, 1935.

The Jewish Question. London, 1938.

SAMUEL, MAURICE, *The Great Hatred*. London, 1943.

SCHERR, JOHANNES, *Deutsche Kultur- und Sittengeschichte*. 8th ed. Leipzig, 1882.

SCHMALHAUSEN, SAMUEL D., *The New Road to Progress*. London, 1935.

SCHMIDT, GERHARD. *The Foreigners. Unprinted MS.*

SCHMITT, CARL, " Das Gesetz als Plan und Wille des Führers ", a lecture, in *Berliner Börsenzeitung*, No. 471, of 8th October 1935.

" Die deutsche Rechtswissenschaft im Kampf gegen den jüdischen Geist ", in *Deutsche Juristenzeitung*, No. 20, of 15th October 1936. Berlin.

" Nationalsozialistisches Rechtsdenken ", in *Deutsches Recht*, No. 10, of 25th May 1934. Berlin.

Staat, Bewegung, Volk. Hamburg, 1934.

Verfassungslehre. Munich and Leipzig, 1928.

SCHMOLLER, GUSTAV, *Grundriss der allgemeinen Volkswirtschaftslehre.* Leipzig, 1900.

SCHNABEL, FRANZ, *Deutsche Geschichte im 19. Jahrhundert.* 4 vols. Freiburg, i.B., 1929–37.

SCHNEIDER, HERBERT W., *Making of the Fascist State.* New York, 1928.

SCHULZ, DR. E: H., and FRERCKS, DR. R., *Warum Arierparagraph? Ein Beitrag zur Judenfrage.* Berlin, 1934.

SCHUMANN, FREDERICK L., *Hitler and the Nazi Dictatorship. A Study in Social Pathology and the Politics of Fascism.* 3rd ed. London, 1936.

SCHUMPETER, JOSEPH A., *Capitalism, Socialism and Democracy.* London, 1943.

SCRIBNER, AMES EDWARD, " Morale and Religion ", in *Am. Journ. Soc.*, vol. xlvii. 1941.

SEYDEWITZ, MAX, *Civil Life in War-Time Germany.* New York, 1945.

SIMMEL, GEORG, *Soziologie.* Leipzig, 1908.

" Ueber soziale Differenzierung ", in *Staats- und sozialwissenschaftliche Forschungen.* Edited by Gustav Schmoller. Leipzig, 1890.

SINGER, J., (ed.), *Briefe berühmter christlicher Zeitgenossen über die Judenfrage.* Wien, 1885.

SLIGHT, DAVID, " Disorganization in the Individual and in Society ", in *Am. Journ. Soc.*, vol. xlii. 1936–37.

SOMBART, WERNER, *Der Bourgeois. Zur Geistgeschichte des modernen Wirtschaftsmenschen.* Leipzig, 1913.

Die deutsche Volkswirtschaft im 19. Jahrhundert und im Anfang des 20. Jahrhunderts (quoted : *19. Jahrhundert*). 5th ed. Berlin, 1921.

Die Juden und das Wirtschaftsleben, 10., 11. Tausend. Munich, Leipzig, 1920.

Der moderne Kapitalismus. Leipzig, 1902.

SOPADE, *Deutschland-Berichte der Sozialdemokratischen Partei Deutschlands.* Prague, Paris, 1934–40.

SOREL, GEORGES, *Les Illusions du progrès.* 3rd ed. Paris, 1921.

Reflections on Violence. Transl. by T. E. Hulme. London, 1916.

SPEIER, HANS, " Nazi Propaganda and its Decline ", in *Social Research*, vol. x. New York, 1943.

SPENCER, HERBERT, *Facts and Comments.* London, 1902.

STAPEL, GUSTAV, *Antisemitismus und Anti-Germanismus.* Hamburg, 1928.

STEINBERG, MILTON, *The Making of the Modern Jew.* London, 1934.

STEINBERG, S. H., *A Short History of Germany.* Cambridge, 1944.

STOLPER, GUSTAV, *German Economy, 1870–1940. Issues and Trends.* London, 1940.

STRICH, FRITZ, *Deutsche Klassik und Romantik oder Vollendung und Unendlichkeit. Ein Vergleich.* 3rd ed. Munich, 1928.

SUTTIE, JAN D., *The Origins of Love and Hate.* London, 1935.

THEILHABER, FELIX A., *Der Untergang der deutschen Juden.* Berlin, 1927.

THOMA, RICHARD, article " Staat ", in *Handwörterbuch der Staatswissenschaften*, vol. vii. 4th ed. Jena, 1926.

TILLICH, PAUL J., " Protestantism in the Present World Situation ", in *Am. Journ. Soc.*, vol. xliii. 1937–38.

TIRALA, L. G., *Race, Mind and Soul.* Friends of Europe-Publications. London.

TOYNBEE, ARNOLD J., *A Study of History.* 2nd ed. London, 1935.

TRACHTENBERG, JOSHUA, *The Devil and the Jews. The Mediaeval Conception of the Jew and its Relation to Modern Anti-Semitism.* New Haven, London, 1943.

TREITSCHKE, HEINRICH VON, *Ausgewählte Schriften.* Leipzig, 1911.

Deutsche Geschichte im 19. Jahrhundert. Five vols. Leipzig, 1879–1894.

TROELTSCH, ERNST, *Spektator-Briefe. Aufsätze über die deutsche Revolution und die Weltpolitik, 1918–1922.* Tübingen, 1924.

TROTTER, W., *Instincts of the Herd in Peace and War.* London, 1916.

VALENTIN, HUGO, *Antisemitism.* Transl. by A. G. Chater. London, 1936.

VALENTIN, VEIT, *Deutschlands Aussenpolitik von Bismarcks Abgang bis zum Ende des Weltkriegs.* Berlin, 1921.

VEBLEN, THORSTEIN, *Imperial Germany and the Industrial Revolution.* London, 1939.

" The Intellectual Pre-Eminence of Jews in Modern Europe ", in *Political Science Quarterly*, vol. xxxiv. New York, 1919.

VERGIN, FEDOR, *Subconscious Europe*. Transl. by Raglan Somerset. London, 1932.

VERMEIL, EDMOND, *Germany's Three Reichs. Their History and Culture*. Transl. by E. W. Dickes. London, 1944.

VRIES DE HEEKELINGEN, H. DE, " Introduction to the Study of Fascism ", in *A Survey of Fascism. The Year Book of the International Centre of Fascist Studies*, vol. i. London, 1928.

WALLAS, GRAHAM, *Human Nature in Politics*. 3rd ed. London, 1938.

WEBER, MAX, *Gesammelte Aufsätze zur Religionssoziologie*. Third vol. : *Das antike Judentum*. Tübingen, 1923.

" Wirtschaft und Gesellschaft ", in *Grundriss der Sozialökonomik*, iii. 2 vols. Tübingen, 1925.

WERTHEIMER, MILDRED S., *The Pan-German League, 1890–1914*. New York, 1924.

WESTERNHAGEN, CURT VON, *Nietzsche, Juden, Antijuden*. Weimar.

WIRTH, LOUIS, *The Ghetto*. Chicago, 1928.

" Localism, Regionalism, and Centralization ", in *Am. Journ. Soc.*, vol. xlii. 1936–37.

" Morale and Minority Groups ", in *Am. Journ. Soc.*, vol. xlvii. 1941.

" Urbanism as a Way of Life ", in *Am. Journ. Soc.*, vol. xliv, No. 1. 1938.

Yellow Spot, The. London, 1936.

ZIEGLER, PROF. DR., *The New Spirit of Military Education*. Friends of Europe-Publications, London.

ZIEGLER, THEOBALD, *Die geistigen und sozialen Strömungen des 19. Jahrhunderts*. Berlin, 1899.

ZWEIG, ARNOLD, *Caliban oder Politik und Leidenschaft*. Potsdam, 1927.

INDEX OF SUBJECTS

INDEX OF NAMES